How Then Shall We Answer?

How Then Shall We Answer?

Joe Boot

New Wine Press

New Wine Ministries
PO Box 17
Chichester
West Sussex
United Kingdom
PO19 2AW

ISBN 978-1-903725-81-8 (paperback edition)
ISBN 978-1-905991-21-1 (hardback edition)

Typeset by CRB Associates, Reepham, Norfolk
Cover design by CCD, www.ccdgroup.co.uk
Printed in the United States of America

Dedicated to my loving wife Jenny,
the faithful mother of our three children,
Naomi, Hannah and Isaac,
whose selfless support over the past nine years
has made it all possible.

Contents

Foreword

This book represents Joe Boot's *summa apologetica* – a summary of apologetics, consistent with the Augustinian and Van Tillian tradition, infused with insights from Blaise Pascal, another noted Augustinian apologist. Bold, imaginative and instructive, it is written for a general audience rather than for a specialized one. His prose is remarkable not only for his wisdom in the field of apologetics but also for the distinctive way he does it. With various imageries and anecdotes, he provides a clear, engaging articulation of a fresh set of perspectives on several topics. Full of biblical and theological insights, and written with an evangelistic heart, this book serves to nourish the faithful, stimulate good arguments for the seeker and build a strong rational basis for the causative relation between faith and reason, the former being the presupposition of the latter.

Augustine's motto of *fides quaerens intellectum* (faith seeking understanding) supplies Joe with a methodological starting point by which he constructs his arguments. He conceives of the process of faith seeking understanding as one in which faith endeavors to see for itself why the propositions which it affirms are true. This does not mean faith does so without the assistance of divine grace. Thus he could not have written this book unless he already believed, for faith precedes understanding.

He is of the position that reason does not usurp the primacy of faith, but assists in providing a rational foundation for the way things are. That which God has revealed to us, such as his existence and attributes, the uniqueness of Jesus Christ, can be shown by reason to be rational and believable. Nevertheless rationality, an innate power within us, unaided by divine revelation, could not develop discernment concerning divine things. Man, far from seeking the true God through the application of his rational power, is bent on declension from God and the blessedness that God would freely bestow. Left to itself, human reason cannot arrive at wisdom. Thus faith in Christ is our source of authority, and must necessarily precede rational understanding. This is borne out in Isaiah 7:9, which Augustine quotes favorably: "Unless you believe, you shall not understand."

With Augustine, Joe's aim is not to introduce new doctrine by reason; rather it is to show the reasonableness of the faith by reason. This too is borne out in Joe's model of anthropology, which coincides with the reformers' (Luther and Calvin), that man has no free will in spiritual matters because he is systemically opposed to the source of divine freedom – God. Only by the intervention of grace could he spiritually perceive and rationally choose the Good, Wisdom, Light, and Truth, which is God. Thus Grace becomes the necessary presupposition, or the first principle of the origin and goal, of Joe's apologetic enterprise. What more can we ask than to extol the efficacious grace in all our human activities?

In the postmodern world dominated by the spirit of anti-intellectualism, and in modern churches where more credence is given to ritualistic performance and subjective experience than to doctrinal teaching and rigorous theological reflection, Joe's book becomes a timely corrective to such preoccupations. Dr John Mackay, the former president of Princeton Theological Seminary, once remarked aptly: "Commitment without reflection is fanaticism in action. But reflection without commitment is the paralysis of all action." Joe's book is certainly a living proof of a tight combination of intelligent reflection and passionate commitment. With rigor and relevance, he constitutes a seminal apologetic that enables readers to grasp the signs of divine transcendence, and to apprehend, or rather to be apprehended by the beauty of Christ. The avowed anti-intellectualism can be combated by the words of Charles Simeon: "For the attainment of divine knowledge we are directed to combine a dependence on God's Spirit with our own researches. Let us, then, not presume to separate what God has thus united." And this is precisely what Joe has done in the production of his *summa apologetica*. Both putting to use his mind to understand and his self-humbling before God are signs of his hunger for divine beauty and holiness, whose hunger God will eagerly fulfill, just as He promises (Proverbs 2:1–6).

As one of Joe's mentors, I commend him for his laborious work, and praise God for the endowed gift of articulating his faith in a way that gives apologetics its rightful place, accentuating it as the "well-being", though not the "being", of the church.

Dennis Ngien PhD
Research Professor of Theology at Tyndale Seminary
Founder of Center for Mentorship and
Theological Reflection, Toronto, Canada

Introduction

For over ten years I have worked as a vocational Christian evangelist and apologist. For eight of these years, I have traveled extensively in Europe, from a home base in England and also in North America, based in Canada. My calling involves articulating and defending the Christian faith in a wide diversity of contexts – some more friendly than others! On some occasions, I am encouraging, training, and equipping others to share and defend their faith. On other occasions, I am directly involved in the apologetic task myself, through open forums, public debates, mission events of many kinds, and media discussions and interviews. And, although this lifestyle is accompanied by some profound challenges that urge me onto my knees before God, it brings some rare privileges. One such privilege is the opportunity to speak with people from all over the world.

This book arose organically as I received repeated requests at various events for a copy of the address. In the last five years, I noticed that certain lectures generated requests so often it occurred to me that I might do the cause of evangelism and apologetics a modest service if I brought these together into a single volume and equip others. This is the first book I have written primarily for the Christian believer. Of the subjects I have covered, sermons on several occasions if you like, half were delivered to Christian audiences and half to non-believers. My intention is to both *instruct* and to *model* a defense of the faith. My hope is that this book will be of use to both Christian and skeptic who want answers to questions about Christianity.

The work is in two parts. The first part, Explorations and Expositions, brings together addresses and papers written to inspire and instruct. They seek to develop a Christian mindset in the believer and a biblical understanding of the world that demonstrates how our faith deals with the great questions of life. The talks were first prepared for presentations at a wide variety of training events from Lahore, Pakistan to Dubai in the Middle East, to Washington DC to Toronto. In this first part of the book I seek to define and elucidate the meaning and task of Christian apologetics, giving practical advice concerning the messenger, the message, and the method. In the second part, Persuasions – Crafting Our Defense, I draw together lectures and addresses delivered again in a wide variety of settings, from formal parliamentary-style debates at Universities, mission style guest-events, televised addresses for the average viewer, and lectures at the Oxford Centre for Christian Apologetics at Wycliffe Hall, Oxford. In each case, they are prepared and delivered with the non-Christian in mind. Usually they were first presented to a crowd of skeptics and seekers. My aim is to reinforce what is learned in Part One and to model in Part Two how I approached a variety of the objections we face in contemporary culture in varying situations, such as debate, special occasion sermon and group teaching. In Part Two, I give examples of how I have used Christian rhetoric, the art of persuasion, in an effort to communicate truth effectively.

Because I rarely speak from a complete script, many of the lectures that people have requested were nowhere near ready for publication. I have therefore expended considerable effort in expanding, editing, and revising the texts of most of the papers with the patient help of my associate apologist and research assistant, Rachel Tulloch. She has helped to make some of my work flow, nevertheless, any errors and mistakes are mine alone. Sometimes I have combined two addresses on one topic that were delivered in separate parts, these are easily identified because they are the longer chapters. Writing and speaking, as any preacher knows, are different skills. It is a difficult challenge to take lectures and sermons prepared over several years for an audience and make them flow effectively for the written page! Pathos, perspicuity and power through the pen are different from persuasiveness from the pulpit and since my primary gift is in oratory, I readily acknowledge my limitations in this regard. For better or worse, the lectures retain the flavor of an edited address as opposed to a paper prepared for a book or journal.

To provide the reader some understanding of the context in which each lecture was delivered, I have identified the location and context for which it was first prepared, but my memory has had to retrieve this information at times long after the event. I have also attached discussion questions at the end of each chapter to help readers consider the material, either individually or in a study group. I have tried to track down all the sources I used in footnotes but if I have inadvertently omitted any, will be pleased to rectify this in later editions.

Finally, my dependence upon and admiration for St Augustine, the master theologian of the early Church in the fourth and fifth centuries, will be more than apparent throughout. I make no apology for this, despite the climate of hostility toward the teaching of Augustine in some academic circles. It has been said that all of western thought can be summed up as footnotes to Augustine, because of his penetrating and far-reaching thought and influence. The reason that I cling to the Augustinian tradition in apologetics, reflected in the diverse work of philosophers and apologists Blaise Pascal, Alvin Plantinga and Cornelius Van Til and others, will become clear in reading this book. My desire is that you may be inspired to read Augustine's *Confessions*, Pascal's *Pensées* or Van Til's *Christian Apologetics*, these key works of acknowledged masters of apologetics. If you find this book is a stepping stone to consulting these great guides, my task will have been more than accomplished.

May God equip you for the privileged task of giving a defense to anyone who may ask a reason for the hope that is in you (1 Peter 3:15), and trust you will, in reverence for God, together with me try to "persuade others" (2 Corinthians 5:11) to follow.

PART ONE

Expositions and Explorations

CHAPTER 1

Thirsty Souls and Living Water

The missio Dei *and His compassion for the alienated*

[*This address was delivered at an apologetics training seminar in Lahore, Pakistan.*]

> "As time went by and Isaac grew and was weaned, Abraham gave a big party to celebrate the happy occasion. But Sarah saw Ishmael – the son of Abraham and her Egyptian servant Hagar – making fun of Isaac. So she turned to Abraham and demanded, 'Get rid of that servant and her son. He is not going to share the family inheritance with my son, Isaac. I won't have it!' This upset Abraham very much because Ishmael was his son. But God told Abraham, 'Do not be upset over the boy and your servant wife. Do just as Sarah says, for Isaac is the son through whom your descendants will be counted. But I will make a nation of the descendants of Hagar's son because he also is your son.' So Abraham got up early the next morning, prepared food for the journey, and strapped a container of water to Hagar's shoulders. He sent her away with their son, and she walked out into the wilderness of Beersheba, wandering aimlessly. When the water was gone, she left the boy in the shade of a bush. Then she went and sat down by herself about a hundred yards away. 'I don't want to watch the boy die,' she said, as she burst into tears. Then God heard the boy's cries, and the angel of God called to Hagar from the sky, 'Hagar, what's wrong? Do not be afraid! God has heard the boy's cries from the place where you laid him. Go to him and comfort him, for I will make a great nation from his descendants.' Then God opened Hagar's eyes, and she saw a well. She immediately filled her water container and gave the boy a drink. And God was with the boy as he grew up in the wilderness of Paran."
>
> (Genesis 21:8–20)

Family matters

This passage in Genesis describes a situation of considerable family tension. Abraham is a great servant and friend of God. Furthermore, God has promised him that through his descendants all the nations of the world would be blessed (Genesis 12:3). However, time passes, and Abraham still has no son. At his wife Sarah's suggestion, he sleeps with his wife's Egyptian maid, Hagar, and soon has a son called Ishmael. But Ishmael is not the son through whom God will fulfill His promise. Instead, in keeping with His remarkable promise that had caused the aging Sarah to laugh in disbelief, God gives them a son from aged Sarah's womb called Isaac; the one who will establish the line through which God would enact the great drama of salvation.

However, the tension from the couple's previous decision to "help the promise along" remains. Increasingly irritated by the reminder of her unbelief and its consequences, the presence of her maid and stepson Ishmael reminds Sarah that the inheritance will be split between her blood son and the stepson. So, Sarah begins to treat Hagar harshly. In turn, Ishmael and his mother mock the younger brother Isaac at his weaning party. This offends Sarah and she responds in an extreme way, demanding that the slave woman and her son be banished and disinherited. Deeply upset by the demand, Abraham initially looks as though he will not comply, but eventually does what Sarah has asked after being assured by God that it will turn out for good. Hagar is sent away with Ishmael into the desert with food and water, wandering aimlessly, alienated, rejected, and eventually finding herself in a place of total despair and desperation. The remarkable account of God's grace that follows speaks vitally important truths about the Church's task in the world today as we seek to reach those lost in the desert of despair.

The desert of despair

When Hagar and Ishmael mocked Isaac, Ishmael was just an ignorant boy, led on by his mother in her anger about being harshly treated. Perhaps there was also an element of sibling rivalry here, since Sarah obviously favored Isaac. Regardless of the reasons, scorning God or the things of God always has a price. By mocking Isaac, they were mocking the promises of God and God will not be mocked. Ignorance does not always mean innocence. When people reject the things of God, knowingly or in ignorance, Scripture shows us that there is always a price. Part of that price is estrangement – alienation from the promises of salvation.

For example, when parents reject the revelation of God and the promises given in Christ, they lead their children by their example, and their children pay the price. We are evidently living in such a generation now. When there is widespread mocking of God and disobedience to the gospel, the inevitable result is the fruit of aimlessness and despair. This is the vivid picture painted for us in this account. Why does this happen? Because when we are in rebellion against God we become slaves of sin. Sin infects our hearts, our reason, and our consciences. Fear, guilt, anxiety and confusion then stalk us; we are alienated from God.

The apostle Paul makes this very interpretation in Galatians 4:24–31 where he compares the two women, Hagar and Sarah, to the two covenants. One is the woman of slavery and the other of freedom. Paul also says that we who are children of the free woman are persecuted by the children of the other woman, just as Ishmael persecuted Isaac! Sadly, today, God's people still experience great suffering and persecution at the hands of those who oppose their faith.

To understand this account properly, it is important to see the magnitude of this situation. In grief, Abraham reluctantly sends Hagar and Ishmael away with a skin of water and bread. Hagar, a child clinging to one arm and the water skin slung over the other, with nowhere to go, wanders off aimlessly into the wilderness. The water is soon used up. Despairing, she resigns herself to a slow death. She puts the boy down under a bush and goes to sit a hundred yards away, as she cannot bear to watch him die. Anyone would despair in such a situation! In context, her actions were perfectly understandable, even tragically appropriate. In a desert of despair like that, what else could anyone do? The heartbreak is manifested when she weeps aloud.

The Christian message forces us to face reality. This narrative provides us with an analogy of the human condition apart from Christ. Just as alienation from the covenant family left Hagar and Ishmael in a desperate situation, so those who reject and scorn the revelation of God in creation and redemption experience despair and hopelessness. Whether people have consciously reached this realization or not, they are destitute. As Paul puts it, "In those days you were living apart from Christ. You were excluded from God's people, Israel, and you did not know the promises God had made to them. You lived in this world without God and without hope" (Ephesians 2:12). It is vital for Christians to remember this in a time when religious pluralism seeks to dissolve this ultimate axiom of Scripture by compromising the uniqueness of Christ.

The Bible distinguishes between two ultimate conditions, two cities, two spirits, two loves, two princes and two destinies of men and women, in this world and the next. This division is called the biblical antithesis.

The Scriptures are incomprehensible without this ultimate divide. Before we become bitter about criticism directed against God's Church or rant and rave at the world in resentment, we would be wise to remember this story. Regardless of the bravado of many in our society, this destitution is the ultimate underlying spiritual reality. Our Lord Himself clearly says to those who have refused His message and rejected His divinity:

> "I assure you that everyone who sins is a slave of sin. A slave is not a permanent member of the family, but a son is part of the family forever. So if the Son sets you free, you will indeed be free . . . Why can't you understand what I am saying? It is because you are unable to do so! For you are the children of your father the Devil and you love to do the evil things he does. He was a murderer from the beginning and has always hated the truth. There is no truth in him. When he lies, it is consistent with his character; for he is a liar and the father of lies." (John 8:34–36, 43–44)

The spiritual king of the earthly city, the city of sin and selfishness, whose citizens are slaves and not sons, is the devil. Those who pattern their lives after his rebellion are his spiritual offspring according to our Lord. But Jesus, the one promised long ago, makes free sons of promise. So, the first task of the Christian apologist is to recognize the actual human condition revealed by Christ and to have compassion upon those alienated from Him.

In context

In our contemporary situation, there is a growing loneliness. This generation has been instructed in the philosophies of meaninglessness, purposelessness, and godlessness. Our culture celebrates sin. This reality should grieve us, stir us, and motivate us, but most of all it should move us with compassion. When people are without God, despair can seem rational and suicide can appear reasonable. Blaise Pascal gives this vivid description of what the world might be like from an unbeliever's perspective:

> "Imagine a number of prisoners on death row, some of whom are killed each day in sight of the others. The remaining ones see their condition in that of their fellows, and looking at each other with grief and despair await their turn. This is a picture of the human condition."[1]

This is indeed a horrific image, but it reveals spiritual reality. People's experience of death row takes many forms: broken lives, ruined relationships, guilt, loneliness, fear, and hopelessness. Many of us who are now believers were once living in such alienation from God ourselves. C. S. Lewis wrote that despair can simply be the result of "[t]he routine of adversity, the gradual decay of youthful loves and youthful hopes."[2] This, he says, is a quiet despair that is hardly felt as pain. It does not require a monumental tragedy to bring about this sense of grief, purposelessness, and futility.

What I am describing can be called the "context principle" – the idea that the reasonableness of any action, emotion, or thought is largely determined by the context in which it takes place. For example, we employ this principle when we dress up for a banquet in a suit and tie rather than wearing swimming shorts and a pair of slippers. Similarly, the emotion of despair makes sense or fits in the context of life without God.

We are conscious of the patterns around us that are the *cultural context* of our actions, things like manners, customs, laws, expectations in relationships and job situations. However, few people take the time to consider the *ultimate context* of life, to which Pascal was powerfully drawing our attention. What is our ultimate context? Do we live in a meaningful world created by a God to whom we are accountable, granting all our actions ultimate significance or do we not? Some skeptics have acknowledged the diminishing significance of human beings as implicit in the denial of the God of creation. Physics professor Lawrence M. Krauss writes:

> "I believe that our universe is not unique. As science has evolved, our place within the universe has continued to diminish in significance: first it was felt that earth was the center of the universe, then that the sun was the center, and so on. We now realize that we are near the edge of a galaxy that is itself located nowhere special in a large, potentially infinite universe full of other galaxies ... I find it satisfying to speculate that not only are we not in a particularly special place in our universe, but that our universe itself may be insignificant itself on a larger cosmic scale. The idea represents perhaps the ultimate Copernican revolution."[3]

There are a number of highly questionable assertions belonging to the realm of religious faith that are made in this passage. Nonetheless, there is an important lesson in Professor Lawrence's argument. If you accept his framework that there are multiple universes and no intelligent author of our universe, you might grant his conclusion – that the cosmos is relatively insignificant and we (human beings) are even more so. But, it is his whole paradigm, not just his conclusion that is wrong. Reasoning without revelation leads to a mindset that will accept almost anything except God. This ultimate context has been received uncritically by many in our culture and we are reaping the social consequences. People do what is right in their own eyes. Just as Hagar lifted up her voice and wept for her son under the tree, so our nations weep. One only needs to listen in order to hear it. One only need talk to the next-door-neighbor, read the newspapers, listen to the radio, or turn on the television in order to apprehend it. Beneath the bravado of human pride, despair can be seen and heard. Christians now face the challenge of developing a theologically grounded post-secular response in this alienated world. What a wonderful opportunity we have!

A well in the wilderness

Although despair is powerful, it does not have the last word according to God. The God of eternity, who made heaven and earth and holds all things together by the word of His power, "heard the boy's cries" (verse 17). That statement alone is almost enough to convey the great mercy and compassion with which God responds in this story. Furthermore, this great mercy of God has continued throughout human history and I cannot help but be moved by these words when I read them. Thank the Lord that He does not leave us in our desperate condition! We do not cry to a god of cold, passionless, rationalist philosophy. Ours is the personal God of the Bible. He is transcendent yet immanent, and bottles the tears of our sorrows and knows the number of hairs on our heads. He even notices when a sparrow falls from the sky. God hears, God sees, and God knows. He hears those who are cut off and alienated from the covenant family. He does not want any to perish, but everyone to come to repentance (2 Peter 3:9). In a world marked by the ravages of sin, there is no child whose cry God does not hear, no person beyond the embrace of His presence, no place so distant He does not perceive our helplessness.

God not only hears the boy's cries, but He acts! He sends an angel to speak to Hagar in her desert of despair: "Do not be afraid! God has heard the boy's cries from the place where you laid him. Go to him and comfort him for I will make a great nation from his descendants" (Genesis 21:17–18). He brings comfort and offers something incredible – He offers a well in the wilderness of estrangement, alienation, and despair: "God opened Hagar's eyes and she saw a well" (verse 19). These words are full of theological significance. God opened her eyes to see what He had provided. The well was there, but she did not see it. She was blind to it until God opened her eyes. Here, through a concealing and then a revealing of God's provision, a slave woman and her son received the personal attention of the almighty God in a drink of water! That is the God of Scripture. Not a vague, unmoved principle, but a relational God concerned even with our basic physical needs.

This story is a foreshadowing of the gospel itself. The prophet Isaiah tells us, "With joy you will draw water from the wells of salvation" (Isaiah 12:3 ESV). Water and wells are frequent metaphors in Scripture for the thirst-quenching gift of salvation. *Christ is God's well to meet the thirst of the human soul.* It is here, and here alone, that men and women can find rivers of living water, where the thirst for happiness, peace and satisfaction is quenched.

Well encounters

This encounter with Hagar is not the only time that Christ meets an alienated gentile woman by a well. In John 4:7–26, Jesus has an incredible conversation with a Samaritan woman by a famous well of one of Abrahams' descendants:

> " 'If you only knew the gift God has for you and who I am, you would ask me, and I would give you living water' . . . 'Are you greater than our ancestor Jacob who gave us this well?' . . . 'People soon become thirsty again after drinking this water. But the water I give them takes away thirst altogether. It becomes a perpetual spring within them, giving them eternal life' . . . 'Please, sir,' the woman said, 'give me some of that water!' "

> " 'God is spirit. So those who worship him must worship in spirit and in truth.' . . . The woman said, 'I know the Messiah will come – the one who is called Christ. When he comes, he will explain everything to us.' Then Jesus told her, 'I am the Messiah.' "

Although these may be familiar words to many, they take on rich, new significance in the light of God's conversation with Hagar in the desert. The Samaritan woman was obviously thinking of ordinary water, the same water that Hagar drank from the well. But Christ was pointing to the spiritual reality that He Himself is the giver of the water of life – the gift of the Holy Spirit. In both of these accounts, God is speaking to people alienated from the covenant. Through the gift of God, we have become part of the greater promise for all nations. This promise is available to all, the well of eternal life, through Abraham's offspring, our Lord Jesus Christ.

The problem for the Samaritan woman, just as for Hagar, was not the existence and availability of water, but whether her eyes could see it or not.

"If you only knew ... who I am, you would ask me and I would give you living water", Jesus said.

In our day, as in every age, people are desperate for living water, though many do not realize the cause of their parched souls. The world runs to quench its terrible thirst everywhere except in God, the very one to whom this thirst points, and the only one in whom it can be satisfied! Pascal once commented that "sinners lick the dust". While trying to satisfy their deep thirst, people will even lick the dust of sin rather than see and receive living water from Christ, which fully satisfies. As John Calvin wrote, "The smallest drop of the Spirit resembles an ever flowing fountain, which never dries up."[4]

Water works

The beginning of the great apologetic task is to assure people that there is a God to be found who is worth finding and to point them to where He can be encountered, in Jesus Christ. The minds and hearts of this generation need more than abstract arguments for the existence of God. Rather, with an understanding of God as relational Trinity, we need to focus on the great points of contact that the gospel has with the human predicament that is so painfully on display in the parched hearts all around us. It is through Christ revealed in the Scriptures that people encounter the personal God of creation and redemption. This God, who meets us in our alienation and despair, who draws us through our awareness of brokenness and guilt, and who speaks to us in creation, is a relational God of infinite compassion.

Belief in the existence of a god of some kind is not rare but very common. In Canada, where I live, nearly 90% of people tell the census-taker they are Christian, but less than 20% go to church.[5] This reveals a common misunderstanding. We know that to believe in God in a general way does not make you a Christian. It is the God of the Bible, Christ Himself, whom this generation desperately needs to encounter. He is the well in the wilderness of humanistic philosophy, of materialism, of religious pluralism, and relativism. Jesus is still the answer. The only question remaining is whether people's eyes will be opened to see the well – for only this water truly works in quenching our human thirst.

Miracle or mirage

We must always remember that God is the initiator and the primary agent in the opening of blind eyes. We should remain humble in our approach or we will lose the battle even though we may win arguments. Skeptics are not new on the scene. Skepticism, honest doubt, and cynicism are as old as civilization. It was not an invention of the enlightenment, nor of the ancient Greeks. Skepticism is as old as the Fall of humanity. Indeed, a certain amount of skepticism seems almost appropriate to the human predicament. There is enough light to see indicators of God everywhere. God has assured us that those who truly seek Him will find Him, so there is no excuse for rejecting Him. Yet, there is also a great deal of obscurity and distortion of truth because our minds are limited as humans, and because our hearts are so often hard toward God. The Christian faith does not claim to clear up all obscurities and mysteries, but shows us why there is obscurity and mystery through the explanatory power of the biblical narrative. In this way, the claims of Christ challenge the skeptic's view that obscurity is ultimate.

An inquirer once asked Sadhu Sundar Singh, one of India's famous converts to Christianity, why no one can demonstrate the reality of God to the satisfaction of all, so people can know the truth with certainty. The Sadhu writes,

> "Some claim that God is unknowable, but this is utter nonsense. Such an assertion can only be made on limited knowledge of God. If God is completely beyond our knowing, how can we know that he is unknowable? . . . Our spirits live and grow in our human bodies much like a chick develops

> inside an egg. If it were possible for the chick to be told that a great world waits beyond its shell, that this world is filled with fruits and flowers, rivers and great mountains, and that its own mother is there waiting for it to be set free and to experience this splendor, the chick could still neither comprehend nor believe it. Even if one explained that its feathers and wings and eyes were developing so that it could fly and see, still it would not be able to believe it, nor would any proof be possible, until it broke through its shell. In the same way there are many people who cannot comprehend the spiritual life or the existence of God because they cannot see beyond the confines of their own bodily sense."[6]

Although there are elements of dualism and mysticism here, the general direction of this thought is insightful. Paul tells us that the carnal mind does not accept the things of God's Spirit, because they are spiritual and spiritually discerned (1 Corinthians 2:14–16). Taking up this thought, Sundar Singh writes regarding spiritual truth,

> "If our hearts are filled with the presence of God, then our minds will also find enlightenment. Our physical eyes are useless, unless the light of day illuminates the world around us. Similarly, our minds and the eyes of our understanding are useless without the spiritual light of truth. The wisdom and understanding of the mind can easily be turned to clever instruments of evil if they are not subjected to the light of spiritual truth."[7]

There is a real sense in which evil – people's lusts, passions and selfish desires – get in the way of knowledge of God. We desperately need God's illumination of truth. Many human beliefs are actually exposed as moral decisions. The problem is not only with the mind, but with the will.

In our account, Hagar needed to have her eyes opened to see the well. The skeptic, being drawn by grace, needs her eyes opened to see reality clearly. She must be broken free from the shell of the worldly mind. As Christians, we are called to play an important role in this process. Paul writes to the Corinthians, "Knowing, then, the fear of the Lord, we persuade people" (2 Corinthians 5:11 HCSB). It is to this task of persuasion which we must devote prayerful effort. For many, no amount of evidence will be enough unless something radical happens in their attitude and will. In apologetics, it becomes evident that those who believe it is their intellect preventing them from coming to faith in Christ are misguided. The noted religious skeptic Voltaire (1694–1778), laughs at the offense of the cross, unwilling to kneel before his Maker. Sarcastically, he accuses God of immorality and contradiction. He writes,

> "God Himself came down to earth from heaven and died to redeem mankind and extirpate sin forever from the face of the earth; yet He left the greater part of mankind prey to error, to crime, and to the devil. This, to our weak intellects, appears a fatal contradiction. But it is not for us to question Providence; our duty is to humble ourselves in the dust before it."[8]

Even the ministry of Jesus was surrounded by seemingly bullet-proof skepticism. On one occasion, a voice even came out of heaven – a sign many hardened skeptics today claim would be enough to convince them. But, even then, "some said it thundered" (John 12:29). Because their interpretation of the event rested upon a belief structure that was opposed to Christ, they dismissed what they heard as "thunder". On other occasions, people decided that Christ's miracles were accomplished through demonic power. Furthermore, in Jesus' account of the rich man and Lazarus, Abraham says of Lazarus' brothers, "If they do not believe Moses, they will not believe even if someone were to rise from the dead." (Luke 16:31) This is Jesus' own teaching on the matter! The ultimate, physical proof was given by God in Jesus' resurrection from death, which was testified to by hundreds of eye witnesses, but many still rejected Him even though they knew the facts. This tells us something very important – seeing the truth is no guarantee of accepting the truth! Admitting something is true is not the same thing as committing yourself to it. Demonstration, whether philosophical or miraculous, does not guarantee commitment! Ten lepers were healed, but only one came back to say thank you (Luke 17:11–19). As the prophet reminds us, "The heart is deceitful above all things and desperately wicked; who can know it?" (Jeremiah 17:9 NKJV).

Climate change

The apostle John records how Christ wept over Jerusalem and lamented how He had longed to gather the people as a hen gathers her chicks, but they "would not" (Matthew 23:37). Being a Jew was no guarantee of *seeing the well* even though the Jews were the bearers of the glorious promises of God to the world. As Paul points out in Galatians 4:25, Jerusalem's children live in slavery. The way that Jesus describes his mission in John 9:39 is interesting, "I have come to give sight to the blind and to show those who think they can see that they are blind." Christ is not only the *creative* Word and the *saving* Word, but He is also the Word that enlightens and makes *knowledge* possible.

Given that many people are blind to the gospel even when faced with a mountain of evidence, what then is our role in evangelism and apologetics? What part do we play in helping people to see the *"well of water which springs up to eternal life"*? As far as possible, through humble persuasion, our goal ought to be to create an intellectual and imaginative climate favorable to faith. As an example, when I get home from work, I would rather see and speak to my daughters than to infer their presence from the toys strewn all over the floor. True knowledge of my little girls must be relational since they are persons. Even if I can legitimately infer their presence, this does not in itself enable me to know them. Similarly, people who struggle with finding God and have had no experience of Him need more than arguments. This makes perfect sense. How many of us are Christians only because we infer that it is the best explanation for human existence? It may be "a" reason, but it is not the final reason! Our faith goes much deeper than that. We know *whom* we have believed, as well as propositions *that* we have believed!

Nonetheless, when we begin to talk to skeptics, it is very important to show that the Christian faith is not *contrary* to reason; rather it is the *pre-condition* of an intelligible use of reason. Since the Christian faith is internally coherent, and is supported by excellent historical and textual evidence, we can demonstrate that it is not reason that makes the ultimate decision about these questions for the skeptic, but other underlying influences and motives.

When people acknowledge that it is not sheer brain power or a knock-down argument that decides the issue, they are often more open to explore the message of Christ. Characteristically, this involves a change of attitude. Jesus was always looking for this and we need to look for it too. God resists the proud, but gives grace to the humble (1 Peter 5:5). He is interested in the motives of the heart. We are seeking, with God's help, to move people into a position where a loving knowledge of God can arise in God's time. In order for this to happen, conceit, dishonesty, arrogance, and intellectual pride must be challenged, both in ourselves and in those with whom we are interacting. Christ requires poverty of spirit. We need to be properly prepared in our moral disposition before we can come to know and love Him. Jesus is clear about the adjustment that is required, "Unless you become as a little child you cannot enter the kingdom of heaven" (Matthew 18:3 REF). The imaginative and intellectual climate favorable to faith is a childlike one, humble, open, seeking, willing, trusting, and honest.

We can help the skeptic to see how certain human inclinations and desires point them towards the true God, how creation, moral conscience, and rationality are signals of God's presence. When they begin to see how the biblical epic is compelling and has the unique resources to account for the experiences of our lives, we can, with the Spirit's aid, create a climate in which the skeptic is prepared to seek God. When people sincerely seek after God they are finally in a position to meet Him. A paradigm shift needs to happen to create the position whereby a personal knowledge of God can arise. The subject must be in a situation where the object in question can be encountered. A deaf man cannot hear the sound of the ocean as he walks a coastal path, but that does not mean the sea is silent to all. It is his ears that need healing. As the writer of Hebrews says, "Anyone who comes to God must believe that he exists and that he rewards those who sincerely seek him" (Hebrews 11:6). We need to encourage people to take that step of faith and to discover that what they are walking on is solid and real. We must point thirsty souls toward the well of living water and assure them it is not a mirage! They can enter the oasis of God's living presence and see for themselves!

If, to return to my previous analogy, I want to see my daughters, I should go where they live, follow their trail, and listen for their little voices. This way I am putting myself in the most conducive circumstance to encounter them. Likewise, seekers and skeptics should be encouraged to spend time around Christians, read the Bible, pray to God, put aside attitudes that offend the Holy Spirit and listen to preaching from God's Word. If someone begins to do this with an honest heart, God the Holy Spirit will meet with that person and turn his or her heart of stone into a heart of flesh. The apologist must encourage people to seek God while He may be found and discover Him in the person of Christ where God promises to meet us. For without the mystery of the incarnation of Christ, God made flesh, there can be no knowledge of God.

Alienation to reconciliation

Alister McGrath, in his book on apologetics, *Bridge Building*, tells of a scholar and skeptic at Oxford University who came to faith partly through the gentle guidance of C. S. Lewis. His name was Sheldon Vanauken. He could sense the self-authenticating ring of truth in the Christian message, yet he struggled with doubt and fear. He evocatively describes his wavering thoughts and the indecision so typical of the "seeking doubter" in the following passage:

> "There is a gap between the probable and the proved. How was I to cross it? If I was to stake my whole life on the risen Christ, I wanted proof. I wanted certainty. I wanted to see Him eat a bit of fish. I wanted letters of fire across the sky. I got none of these. And I continued to hang about on the edge of the gap ... It was a question of whether I was to accept Him or reject. My God, there was a gap behind me as well! Perhaps the leap to acceptance was a horrifying gamble – but what of the leap to rejection? There might be no certainty that Christ was God – but, by God, there was no certainty that He was not. This was not to be borne. I could not reject Jesus. There was only one thing to do once I had seen the gap behind me. I turned away from it, and flung myself over the gap toward Jesus."[9]

From the human perspective, faith is a decision. There is no contradiction here with God's sovereignty and gracious calling. In Pascal's wager, a reasonable faith steps out, daring to see that Jesus holds our weight. And when we take Christ's hand like a child, He reaches out to us and embraces us until we know that we know that we know: "My Lord and my God!"[10] The wind blows where it wishes and so it is with those born of the Spirit (John 3:8). The nature of true faith must then cast itself onto Christ. Hagar needed no empirical proof that the water could quench her thirst. Ishmael needed no final syllogism to be convinced to take the water from his mother's hand; they simply drank and gave us a picture of the gospel of grace. Those once alienated from the covenant have free access to the water of life.

So, we are called to announce that the Kingdom provision of God is here; God in Christ *is* reconciling the world to Himself. Even those who have scoffed at the sacred and those who were alienated from the promises are invited to come to the well and drink, without money and without cost. Thank God, Christ came to fulfill the promise to Abraham that through him all the nations of the world would be blessed. All who come to God in faith are the true children of Abraham. Paul reminds us that it is not the one who is marked outwardly who is a true son of Abraham, but those who come to God by faith. Paul writes in Romans 9:23–26,

> "He also has the right to pour out the riches of his glory upon those he prepared to be the objects of his mercy – even upon us, whom he selected, both from the Jews and from the Gentiles. Concerning the Gentiles, God says in the prophecy of Hosea,
>
> 'Those who were not my people,
> I will now call my people.
> And I will love those
> whom I did not love before.'
>
> And,
>
> 'Once they were told,
> "You are not my people."
> But now he will say,
> "You are children of the living God."'"

As Christians, we must be ever mindful of our parched and thirsty world, with millions alienated from the covenant, without hope, living in quiet despair. Yet in that very desert, a well has been provided! We are privileged to be part of God's work in opening blind eyes to see the well. We are to be co-workers with the Holy Spirit. He has put this treasure in *you* and *me*. We are the bearers of this good news. Let us call our world, specifically in our own sphere of influence, to lift up their eyes to see the well and pray that God would call out a great people for Himself from among us.

Discussion questions

1. How does the way we *view* those we speak to affect the way in which we *communicate* to them?
2. How do you think we can best adjust our view of others to be more like the way God views them?
3. What types of people are alienated or marginalized that Christians need to reach out to?
4. What are the attitudes displayed by Christians that are most likely to draw people to their message?
5. What are the attitudes displayed by Christians that most often alienate people from their message?
6. What actions can we encourage people to take in order to seek God and place themselves in a position where they are open to encounter Him?
7. List some points of contact whereby the felt human predicament is addressed by the gospel of Jesus Christ. In other words, what things about the Christian message relate to the common human experience of those around us?
8. How do you think we can best balance the use of reason and the appeal to human experience in apologetics?
9. What other biblical examples, like that of Hagar, help us understand this?

Notes

1. Blaise Pascal, *Mind on Fire*, from *The Works of Blaise Pascal*, ed. James M. Houston (Bethany House Publishers, 1997), p. 125.

2. C. S. Lewis, *The Screwtape Letters* (Fount Paperbacks, 1982), p. 120.
3. Krauss M. Lawrence, cited in *What We Believe but Cannot Prove*, edited by John Brockman (Harper Perennial, London, 2006), pp. 214–215.
4. John Calvin, *Calvin's Wisdom*, anthology by Graham Miller (The Banner of Truth Trust, 1992), p. 148.
5. Douglas John Hall, *Hope for the World*, edited by Walter Brueggemann (John Knox Press, Westminster, 2001), p. 37.
6. Sundar Singh, *Wisdom of the Sadhu* (Plough Publishing House, 2000), pp. 55–56.
7. *Wisdom of the Sadhu*, p. 94.
8. Voltaire, cited by William Lane Craig, *The Historical Argument for the Resurrection of Jesus During the Deist Controversy, Text and Studies in Religion*, Vol. 23 (Edwin Mellen, Lewiston, New York, 1985), p. 89.
9. Alister McGrath, *Bridge Building* (Inter-Varsity Press, Downers Grove, 1992), p. 89.
10. John 20:28.

CHAPTER 2

The Gospel Net in a Sea of Faiths

Proclaiming and defending the faith in the modern world

[*This lecture was first delivered at an RZIM banquet in the City of Toronto, Canada.*]

> "As light and darkness, piety and impiety, justice and iniquity, sin and right-doing, health and feebleness, life and death, are contraries, so too are truth and falsehood." (St Augustine)

> "When Jesus heard that John had been arrested, he left Judea and returned to Galilee. But instead of going to Nazareth, he went to Capernaum, beside the Sea of Galilee, in the region of Zebulun and Naphtali. This fulfilled Isaiah's prophecy:
>
> 'In the land of Zebulun and of Naphtali,
> beside the sea, beyond the Jordan River –
> in Galilee where so many Gentiles live –
> the people who sat in darkness
> have seen a great light.
> And for those who lived in the land where death cast its shadow,
> a light has shined.'
>
> From then on, Jesus began to preach, 'Turn from your sins and turn to God, because the kingdom of heaven is near.' One day as Jesus was walking along the shore beside the Sea of Galilee, he saw two brothers – Simon, also called Peter, and Andrew – fishing with a net, for they were commercial fishermen. Jesus called out to them, 'Come, be my disciples, and I will show you how to fish for people!' And they left their nets at once and went with him. A little

> farther up the shore he saw two other brothers, James and John, sitting in a boat with their father, Zebedee, mending their nets. And he called them to come, too. They immediately followed him, leaving the boat and their father behind. Jesus traveled throughout Galilee teaching in the synagogues, preaching everywhere the Good News about the Kingdom."
>
> (Matthew 4:12–23)

The relentless Christ

When the blockbuster movie *The Passion of the Christ* was released in 2004, it once again thrust the life and death of Christ into popular and commercial public consciousness. Numerous reputable periodicals and national newspapers ran articles about the film. Not surprisingly, the divisions that usually occur when the figure of Christ enters public discourse emerged. The story about Christ was mocked or condemned by some while praised and adored by others. Whatever we make of this particular film artistically, we simply cannot shake free of Jesus Christ. He is relentless in his confrontation of humanity. Furthermore, we see again how His message is always divisive. As Jesus Himself taught, we are either for Him or against Him (Matthew 12:30), and He came not to bring artificial peace but, metaphorically, a sword of division that would divide even immediate family (Matthew 10:34).

There is no neutrality or fence-sitting when it comes to the identity of Christ. Everyone must choose how to respond to the claims of Jesus and how you respond depends on your attitude towards the Scriptures. This is because it is in the Scriptures that we learn who Jesus is. Because many in our society reject God's Word, they are incredulous toward the historical testimony about Him. Similarly, Jesus said to the Pharisees that if they had believed Moses they would have believed Him (cf. John 5:46). Because the world rejects God's Word in Scripture, it rejects the Word made flesh. Sometimes this rejection is obvious and accompanied with insults and hatred, but it is more often disguised in the costume of academic freedom and respectability. For example, this is expressed in the so-called "scholarship" that tries to construct an "historical Jesus" that will be more palatable than the one found in the New Testament.

Phillippe Antonello wrote an article regarding the well-known "quest for the historical Jesus":

> "Too often the quest descends to this, reconstructing an historical Jesus based on no more than what appeals to the writer . . . When even the most prominent of the scholars remains locked in this closed loop, doing theology rather than history – and with a faith that rivals the fundamentalism they reject – it may be that their labor will never yield any more than the plain fact that is known now. Jesus lived, taught, was crucified. And rose again, millions of people worldwide would add. The rest, no matter how often the life of Jesus is recreated in books or films – is silence and faith."[1]

First, this article highlights that Jesus is so permanent a figure, even for those who reject Him, that anything new being said or done concerning Him causes a media frenzy, as seen in the recent flurry of publications since Dan Brown's utterly bogus *The Da Vinci Code* appeared. As publishers saw the dollars to be made out of Jesus, numerous books on conspiracy theories, pagan religious origins for Christianity, Jesus' supposed marriage to Mary Magdalene and their offspring, not to mention so called rival gospels, have cluttered the shelves to entertain readers with little regard for credible history. Although many in our culture have attempted the implicitly impossible – to rise above religious commitments in public life – people are still captivated and divided by Christ and express their views publicly.

Secondly, the article rightly notes that attempts to undermine the testimony of the Bible concerning Jesus are circular. They are not based on sound reasoning or compelling proof, but rather they are based entirely on people's religious pre-commitments regarding the nature of God, the world, and human beings. It is usually those who already do not believe that miracles are possible that conclude that the miracles in the gospels are not historical.

Why is all of this important? Because Christ Jesus, by the Holy Spirit, is still speaking to our confused culture today as clearly and with as much controversy as He did in Palestine 2,000 years ago. The fundamental issues are still the same. The same "gospel net" that Jesus cast during the first century must be cast again today.

The sea of faith and the waves of despair

Fulfilling the prophecy of Isaiah 9:1–2, Jesus went to Capernaum, a town on the shore of lake Galilee. It was referred to as "Galilee of the Gentiles", because Gentiles and Jews lived in close proximity there and also because faith in the God of Israel was found alongside paganism. In this part of Northern Palestine, the Israelites first forsook God by adopting Canaanite religious practices and were oppressed by invading rulers.

There is also the description "beyond the Jordan" referring to Galilee "by way of the sea." The sea is a very important image in Scripture. For us, images of beaches and summer vacation spring to mind; but not for those who originally read the prophecy. For them, it had negative overtones of invasion, confusion, turmoil, and darkness. The prophet is portraying not merely a local religious phenomenon, but the state of the human race as a whole. Jesus comes into the midst of human ignorance, superstition, and moral corruption. With so many nationalities living in the region of Galilee, it was a multicultural society. Pluralism was the prevailing religious background. It was in many respects like our own context – a sea of faith and confusion, where superstition, ignorance, and indifference were found alongside violent fanaticism.

About sixty years before Jesus was born, the Romans had conquered His homeland. They were the last in a long line of pagan nations to do so. Into this situation that was incredibly disheartening for the Jewish people, God breaks in. Matthew quotes Isaiah: "The people who sat in darkness have seen a great light, and for those who live in the land where death casts its shadow, a light has shined" (Matthew 4:15, quoting Isaiah 9:1). To those in the spiritual shadow of death, a light has dawned! The morning star is rising! As Paul put it in Ephesians 5:14: "Awake, you who sleep, arise from the dead, and Christ will give you light" (NASB).

What was the message that the living light brought to the darkness? It was a call to awaken from carelessness. Jesus did not say, "Tolerate everything; for after all, God just wants you to be happy." No, He said:

> "Repent, for the Kingdom of heaven is at hand." (Matthew 4:17 NASB)

Christ's message was divisive because He claimed to reveal more than just another religious teaching or ethical system; He was revealing the nature of the true God in His own person. His message was Himself! Truth was no longer a mere abstraction of the philosophers like the Greeks believed, nor the privileging of one nation like the Jews understood, nor a mere allegiance to the glory of political power or military strength like the Romans pursued. Rather, truth was embodied in the person of Christ. He proclaimed,

> "*I am* . . . the truth." (John 14:6, emphasis added)

Although many religious teachers have claimed that they have found some spiritual truth or been enlightened by the truth or can point toward truth, Jesus' message begins and ends with the assertion that He *is* the truth, who has always been – "before Abraham was, I am."[2]

In a land of confusion, despair, and sin, when the world and its philosophy did not know God, God sent His Son. The waves of despair were overcome by the One who spoke to the storm, "Peace, be still."[3] So the gospel net was cast by our Lord: "Repent and believe the gospel."[4]

The call to fish for people

Matthew tells us how Jesus called some of the early disciples as they were busy fishing. Jesus calls them and their response is immediate (Matthew 4:18–20). It is significant that Christ selects those who were not formally educated in the great academies of the day, not those who the cultural elite would have approved for a leading role. He comes to find them as they are performing ordinary tasks – in this instance, casting their nets for a catch. Many of us feel that we are ill-equipped to reach those in our sphere of influence with the good news. Perhaps we feel they are too educated, too smart, too skeptical or too antagonistic. But this was no doubt also true of many living in the time of these ordinary fishermen who were called to take the gospel to peasants and princes, to priests and philosophers. We should take courage from their example.

The fishing image that Jesus uses when He calls His disciples is significant. His call involved two things. The men were to *"follow"* Him and to *"fish for people"*. The same call is issued to God's people today. You cannot accept one part of the call without accepting the other. Following Christ intrinsically involves the call to fish for people drowning in the waves of despair. They are lost, without hope and without God in the world (Ephesians 2:12). As John Calvin wrote,

> "Christ's allusion to fishing is apt in dealing with the preaching of the Gospel, for men drift and float about the world, as in a vast and troubled sea, and they are brought in by the Gospel."[5]

Being a follower of Christ means being a fisher of men and women, yet many of us believe or sometimes use the excuse that proclaiming and defending the gospel is "not for us". However, Jesus' call is to all of His followers. As if to reinforce this, Jesus says a few verses later,

> "You are the light of the world. A city that is set on a hill cannot be hidden. Nor do they light a lamp and put it under a basket, but on a lamp stand, and it gives light to all who are in the house. Let your light so shine before men, that they may see your good works and glorify your Father in heaven."
> (Matthew 5:14–16 NKJV)

By God's grace, we have been pulled from that sea of confusion and despair and brought into His family. Someone – a friend, a parent, or a stranger – cared enough about this call to cast the net around us and draw us in. How can we not do the same for others? Jesus said,

> "Anyone who hears these words of Mine and acts on them, may be compared to a wise man who built his house upon the rock ... Everyone who hears these words of Mine and does not act on them, will be like a foolish man who built his house upon the sand." (Matthew 7:24–26 NASB)

The foundation, the rock, which Christ speaks of, is His word. Only His word can withstand the raging torrent of arguments and pretensions that "set themselves against the knowledge of God" (see 2 Corinthians 10:4–6). What we build will crumble to ruin if we build on any other foundation. We not only need to defend the Bible and its message, but to recognize that the Bible itself is the very foundation of that defense. The Scriptures are not a collection of hopelessly outdated writings that need to be propped up by my apologetic arguments, as if my authority were greater than that of God's Word. Giving a defense does not require a PhD in philosophy, as though Aristotle laid the foundation that Christ builds on. Studying philosophy can be helpful, but it is Scripture that provides the principles and framework for my defense.

Peter, the apostle, is one of those fishermen whom Jesus called who responded by putting Christ's words into practice. He later writes the great charter for Christian apologetics,

> "Set apart the Messiah as Lord in your hearts, and always be ready to give a defense to anyone who asks you for a reason for the hope that is in you."
>
> (1 Peter 3:15 HCSB)

The word "defense" here is the Greek word *apologia*, the same word Paul uses in Acts 22:1 and it means to offer a vindication or defense of the Christian message.

First, Peter tells us to "Sanctify the Lord God in [y]our hearts". Before we can go fishing for people, we must first set apart Christ as Lord in every area of our lives, even intellectually. He must be Lord over all of our thinking. All of our arguments and reasoning must begin with the presupposition that Christ is Lord and that our human reason and our scientific and historical inquiry are dependent upon Him.

Secondly, he cautions us to "always be prepared", that is, be adequately equipped and alert. Often, we fail to take seriously our responsibility to do apologetics. If we neglect this responsibility by leaving the task of giving a defense up to the pastors and experts, then our communities and our nations will suffer as a result. Peter's commission is to the whole Church, not the elite few. The word "prepared" in this verse means literally "get fit". Giving a defense may not come naturally or easily for many of us, but if we are diligent and faithful, our evangelism will become exciting and effective. Our own faith and confidence in God will grow and we will feel more confident to share His good news with others.

The habitat and habits of the catch

I have been told that the best fishing is at night, because many species of fish hide during the day. This explains why, on one occasion, Peter was frustrated that he had caught nothing even after fishing all night. In the human fishing Jesus calls us to, we find a similar principle at work. John tells us that people love darkness rather than light because their deeds are evil (John 3:19). In other words, men and women hide from God. Deep down, they recognize that they are creatures of God, and that this whole world speaks about Him, because they are made in God's image. Nonetheless, they suppress this reality by hiding from and ignoring the claims of God. Paul clarifies this in Ephesians 4:17–20:

> "With the Lord's authority let me say this: Live no longer as the ungodly do, for they are hopelessly confused. Their closed minds are full of darkness; they are far away from the life of God because they have shut their minds and hardened their hearts against him. They don't care anymore about right and wrong, and they have given themselves over to immoral ways. Their lives are filled with all kinds of impurity and greed. But that isn't what you were taught when you learned about Christ."

Thus, when we present and defend the truth of the gospel, we are appealing to a truth that is known, but has been suppressed (Romans 1:19). This is not only an intellectual exercise. This is a moral confrontation! We want to bring people into the light by the enlightening work of the Holy Spirit. Although responding to the different worldviews that cloud people's minds can be complex, biblical apologetics is essentially simple in its analysis of the human condition. Human beings are not gods and are not a law unto themselves. God is the ultimate source of all knowledge and truth. He is the independent reference point for human life, while we are created and dependent. However, in every area of life, people do not acknowledge this and are, therefore, idolaters. Sin has blinded their minds and skewed their knowledge since they are alienated from God. To put it illustratively, people either pray the prayer of submission that Jesus taught us to pray or they pray the prayer of rebellion:

> "Our brethren who art on earth,
> Hallowed be our name.
> Our kingdom come, our will be done
> On earth, for there is no heaven.
> We must get this day our daily bread;
> We neither forgive nor are forgiven.
> We fear not temptation,
> For we deliver ourselves from evil.
> For ours is the kingdom and the power
> And there is no glory and no forever.
> Amen." (Lyman Abbot)

Although the "habitat and habits" of non-Christian thought vary considerably, we can summarize the difference between the Christian and non-Christian perspectives. First, regardless of the particularities of any one worldview, there are some implicit philosophical positions that are common to unbiblical worldviews. They deny that there is an ultimate distinction between the Creator and creatures, and they either believe that humans are god or that God is like human beings. They assert their autonomy and independence from any god that may exist, making humanity the measure of all things and the ultimate reference point for truth.

Despite the rhetoric, non-Christian thought is never neutral. For example, some philosophies hold that nothing is true unless it can be proved by independent thought. However, in believing only what we "think" human beings can rationally demonstrate for themselves, we commit ourselves to faith in our own authority. Paul calls this authority "the principles of this world" (Colossians 2:8).

The problem the non-believer consequently faces is that every *reason* that she offers to *support* her independence from God rests upon the *prior unjustified assumption* of independence. Because to proceed with rational arguments for independence from God assumes that one has an intelligible set of concepts for life, thought, rationality, logic, reasoning and knowledge without any recourse to God. This unwarranted assumption is taken as a "given" that needs *no defense*. But this assumption does need a defense, yet one cannot be offered. The philosophical position of the non-believer can be compared to someone adrift without landmarks in the ocean, on a raft of "reason." He looks up at the stars, which are a real externally valid point of reference, but instead decides to navigate using himself as the point of reference. Since the point of reference now moves with the raft, he can never know where he is, where he is going, or where he has come from – he can have no knowledge of his position. This is the dilemma of human beings in rebellion against God. They are caught between total uncertainty and asserting their total certainty – in defiance of God. They are both rational and irrational at the same time. They are caught in this mental web when thinking about God, themselves, or the world around them.

The Christian position, however, is different. Paul writes in 1 Corinthians 2:12,

> "Now we have received, not the spirit of the world, but the Spirit who is from God, that we might know the things that have been freely given to us by God." (NASB)

The Christian view of reality rests upon God and His revelation. Supremely, it rests upon Christ who is the Word – God revealed in the Son of Man. Because God knows the universe exhaustively, He alone can teach people the truth. He alone knows everything there is to know about everything. Solomon writes, "The LORD gives wisdom; from His mouth come knowledge and understanding ... For wisdom will enter your heart, and knowledge will be pleasant to your soul" (Proverbs 2:6, 10 NASB). God's revelation touches all areas of human life and provides the basic outline by which we build our philosophy of reality.

The Christian world is a rational one since it depends upon the knowledge, plan, and sovereignty of God. Uncertainty and doubt is still present at times, for we are fallible creatures, dependent on our God who knows all but does not reveal all nor offer answers to all our questions. Furthermore, our certainty is based on His revelation, not on ourselves. We can be confident and certain of our Christian witness because God's testimony in His Son is true. Those enlightened by the Spirit see this by the Spirit.

The tears of compromise and mending our nets

Matthew 4:21–22 tells us of Jesus' encounter with two other brothers:

> "A little farther up the shore he saw two brothers, James and John, sitting in a boat with their father, Zebedee, mending their nets. And he called them to come, too. They immediately followed him, leaving the boat and their father behind."

Two of the disciples Jesus called, James and John, were *mending their nets* with their father because they too were fishermen. Fishermen fish for fish and Christians are called to fish for people. In order to fish effectively, we need nets that are sound and not torn or the fish will escape or miss the net altogether. Therefore we must be vigilant about the condition of our net.

Our net is the gospel. Sadly, many times, we compromise the Scriptures and therefore weaken or completely lose the revelation of the gospel that is found there. The net becomes torn when we ignore unpopular aspects of God's Word, often in the name of "relevance" or "sensitivity," or when we force the Bible to conform to "scientific" or "philosophical" frameworks that are foreign to Scripture. We need to be *instructed by* God's Word, not *sit in judgment* over it. When we give our own culture, our own wisdom or our own assumptions more authority than that of Scripture, ultimately we will undermine people's confidence in the gospel that is communicated through Scripture, and our net tears as a result.

This is a challenge to us as God's Church in our day. There are only two choices in life and there are only two ways to live: by the hidden things of shame or by the unadulterated word (2 Corinthians 4:2–3). Ever since our first parents did so, we have been distorting God's revelation. In the Greek language, to "adulterate the word" means *"to deceitfully mix with human tradition."* Throughout history, men and women have deceitfully distorted the Word of God by mixing it with the "word" of humans. We have traded the authority of God for human authority. We have transferred infallibility from God to ourselves. We have put our trust in human myths and theories, scientific or otherwise, rather than in the words of God. Yet, Jesus defeated Satan himself by saying,

> "It is written, man shall not live by bread alone but by every word that proceeds from the mouth of God." (Matthew 4:4 NKJV)

Facts and fables

In 2 Corinthians 4:6, Paul reminds us that Christ has, "shone in our hearts to give the light of the knowledge of the glory of God in the face of Jesus Christ" (NKJV). Yet, the temptation to adulterate the Word is always with us. One of the twentieth century's most famous neo-orthodox theologians, Karl Barth, wrote that,

> "... [the biblical writers'] Natural Science, conception of the world, and also to a great extent their morality cannot be binding for us. They told all sorts of sagas and legends and at least made a free use of all kinds of mythological material. In many things they said – and in some important propositions they contradicted each other."[6]

In contrast to this, Peter writes,

> "For we did not follow cleverly devised tales when we made known to you the power and coming of our Lord Jesus Christ ..." (2 Peter 1:16 NASB)

And,

> "So we have the prophetic word made more sure ... But know this first of all, that no prophecy of Scripture is a matter of one's own interpretation for no prophecy was ever made by an act of human will, but men moved by the Holy Spirit spoke from God." (2 Peter 1:19–21 NASB)

The apostle Paul equally condemns speculation that stems from the authority of "expert opinion" that opposes Scripture saying "... nor to pay attention to myths and endless genealogies, which give rise to mere speculation rather than furthering the administration of God which is by faith" (1 Timothy 1:4 NASB).

Notice that it is *faith* in God and His Word that is our criterion for truth, not the speculations and distortions of people. Paul's concern is that the "saving purpose" of God is by faith in Christ. The writer of Hebrews tells us even about the creation of the world itself:

> "By faith we understand that the worlds were prepared by the word of God, so that what is seen was not made out of things which are visible."
>
> (Hebrews 11:3 NASB)

If we are vigilant about the condition of our net, we will be aware of the distinction between the *formal* and *material* authority of Scripture. *Formal authority* refers to how the Bible conceives of its own authority and how we express that in a system or structure. *Material authority* refers to how that authority operates in practice, churches, and society. The risk of focusing on formal authority alone is that we might focus so much on our definitions of Scripture that we forget to be shaped by its truths in the world in which we live every day.

Even Christians sometimes see the Bible as a book whose authority has been constructed by the mind of humans. At times, the temptation is to use a foreign philosophical idea or a scientific hypothesis as an "external" guiding principle for interpretation. We have pre-established ideas that we then wish to impose on Scripture. Then we use those same ideas to proclaim the Bible's reliability by the fact that it measures up to this same human theory or tradition, whether scientific or otherwise – thus retaining a much prized "academic respectability." Classic examples of this today would include modern strained attempts to "accommodate" big-bang cosmology or neo-Darwinian evolutionary theory into Genesis 1–3 via various types of mythologizing or literary "frameworks," or efforts to impose neo-Marxist social and economic theory into the teaching of Christ or James in the New Testament.

Instead, the Scriptures actually come to us as a crown authority would speak to her subjects. The Bible makes unquestionable claims upon us, not because it measures up to an abstract standard human beings have erected, but because it is the Word of God from the mouth of the great

"I AM." Scripture speaks to us with the highest authority imaginable as a revelation to all men and women.

According to the apostle Paul, we can only be successful fishers when we do not adulterate the Word of God. In 2 Timothy 4:3–4, he reinforces the same point:

> "For the time will come when they will not endure sound doctrine; but wanting to have their ears tickled, they will accumulate for themselves teachers in accordance to their own desires; and will turn away their ears from the truth, and will turn aside to myths." (NASB)

Two things stand out here. First, the real motivation in a deceitful use of the Word of God is to bring the word into line with our own desires, not a sincere desire to reach the seeker! Second, Paul tells us that in such times people turn aside to myth. The Greek word here is *muthos*, meaning "to instruct." It is from *muthos* that we derive the modern term "mythology," which means "a fable," or a story that may communicate some lofty notion but did not actually happen historically. In the New Testament, *muthos* is a *lying fable*, a pretense, or a falsehood. In fact, myth is that which is *fabricated by the mindset, not the real and actually true*. Myths may use logic and reasoning or come with great sophistication. However, their source is the imagination of human beings. Consequently, we have a responsibility as bearers of the gospel to deliver the good news as it is given in Christ and His Word. John Calvin forcefully highlights the pitfall of failure to be faithful:

> "As soon as men depart, even in the smallest degree from God's word, they cannot preach anything but falsehoods, vanities, impostures, errors, and deceits . . . The preaching of the gospel, which is committed to [the church], is the spiritual scepter of Christ, by which he displays his power."[7]

If we depart from the gospel, we become full of error and vanity. History shows that the great times of revival in the Church and awakening in the world were times of reformation and devotion to Christ and His Word as authoritative. The eighteenth-century revivals under John Wesley and George Whitefield in England and Jonathan Edwards in America serve as excellent historical examples of this truth. Consequently, the gospel that was preached during these times was clear and powerful. However, much of the decline and disillusionment in the Church in our day is due to the deplorable condition of our gospel net.

As Augustine said of the Scriptures, "If you believe what you like in the Bible and reject what you like, it is not the Bible you believe but yourself."

This question of authority is extremely important because in our fallen condition we tend to resent all authority except our own. We must decide whether we are to believe what God has spoken in His Word or whether we are to be "pick and mix" Christians. If we decide the latter, any lasting results in our evangelistic efforts are only a result of God working "in spite of us," by a miracle of grace, not in view of our faithfulness.

Jesus Himself did not accuse nor reprimand the Pharisees because they spent too much time in the Torah (the books of Moses, the first five books of the Bible). Instead, when they came to Him with their trick questions, He responded, "You are mistaken, not knowing the Scriptures nor the power of God" (Matthew 22:29 NKJV). This is not only true of non-believers, but it is also true of compromised believers whose nets are hopelessly torn. We must first mend our nets by renewing trust in God and faithfulness to His Word and then developing a comprehensive faith through a firm grasp of the biblical faith and worldview. We need to learn the plot of the Bible and present our message as Scripture does: paradise lost through to paradise regained. We also need to *apply* the authority of this paradigm in every area of life. There is no discipline or area of life where we do not need to be shaped by the Christian worldview, expressed in the law of God and the gospel of Christ.

Furthermore, in mending our nets in our time, we need to recover the biblical emphasis on the message of God's justice, righteousness and holiness. Paul says that the law of God is like a schoolmaster whose task is to bring us to Christ (Galatians 3:24). He says elsewhere, "through the law we become conscious of sin" (Romans 3:20 NIV). The knowledge of sin and righteous judgment will transform our contemporary perception of the God of Scripture as a "sugar daddy" in heaven who is only there to give me what I want, into the consuming fire and judge of all the earth who is righteous, holy, awesome, yet merciful and forgiving, abounding in love. Equally, we need to recover the challenge of repentance and total transformation rather than settling for a gospel that is like receiving a free film voucher or ticket to the theater. We will never be able to call people to repentance effectively unless the Church begins to practice virtue in life, speech, and public discipline – we must live the justice of the great commandments as well as faithfully preaching them.

Caught and captivated by Christ

Although we often have honest motives, desiring to draw people with a gospel that is appealing to them, our erroneous methods and misguided message have had some disastrous consequences. Some estimate that as many as 70% of North American youth from Christian homes now lose their faith before they leave public school. We must wake up and mend our nets! We are a peculiar people: a royal priesthood, a holy nation, a people belonging to God (1 Peter 2:9). Although our message may at first appear strange or outmoded in our society, it is that message which defines us – the Church of the living God, the city of God down the ages – and we cannot sacrifice it. The true gospel has always confronted godless culture, not conformed to it. The pilgrim has always been a sojourner in a foreign land. Taking the call of Christ seriously to follow Him absolutely and immediately means fishing for people with a net that is strong. Then we can cast the gospel net into the sea of faith around us with confidence that the supreme fisher of people will say "Friend, cast your net on the other side" and give us a catch that is so large we will have trouble accommodating all the people!

To fish for people with the gospel net means not only to be vigilant about the message (the net) but also about the messenger (the fisher). Like those early fishers of people, so wholly captivated by the beauty of Christ that they immediately left everything to follow Him, let us keep our eyes upon Jesus first and foremost and follow hard after Him even as we seek to persuade others to be His disciples. As St Augustine wrote, "When I set before the eyes of my heart, such as they be, the . . . beauty of him out of whose mouth nothing false proceedeth . . . I am so inflamed with love of that surpassing comeliness, that I despise all human considerations which would recall me thence."

Only if we ourselves are captivated by Christ and this glorious gospel will we cling to Him and faithfully call others to do the same.

Discussion questions

1. In what ways do you think we have most damaged our "net" in order to fit in with our culture?
2. (a) In what ways do you think we are free to adapt to our surroundings in order to fish for people?
   (b) In what ways do you think adapting would compromise the integrity of our net?
3. What are some of the philosophies and cultural opinions that have the largest impact on the "habitat" of those in our culture we are trying to reach?
4. How can we most effectively use the Scriptures in our apologetic with those who are unfamiliar with them?
5. How do you think the many commercialized controversies about Jesus have affected public opinion about Christian claims?

Notes

1. Phillippe Antonello, *MacLeans Magazine*, 8th March, 2004.
2. John 8:58 NASB.
3. Mark 4:39 NASB.
4. Mark 1:15 NASB.
5. John Calvin, *Calvin's New Testament Commentaries: A Harmony of the Gospels, Matthew, Mark and Luke* (Grand Rapids: Eerdmans, 1994), p. 158.
6. Karl Barth, *God Here and Now* (New York and Evanston, 1964), p. 48.
7. John Calvin, *Calvin's Wisdom*, anthology arranged by Graham Miller (The Banner of Truth Trust, 1992), pp. 252, 257.

CHAPTER 3

Presuppositions and Conversations

[*The lecture was first delivered at a Sola Scriptura apologetics conference in Toronto, Canada.*]

> "As for Philip, an angel of the Lord said to him, 'Go south down the desert road that runs from Jerusalem to Gaza.' So he did, and he met the treasurer of Ethiopia, a eunuch of great authority under the queen of Ethiopia. The eunuch had gone to Jerusalem to worship, and he was now returning. Seated in his carriage, he was reading aloud from the book of the Prophet Isaiah.
>
> The Holy Spirit said to Philip, 'Go over and walk along beside the carriage.'
>
> Philip ran over and heard the man reading from the prophet Isaiah; so he asked, 'Do you understand what you are reading?'
>
> The man replied, 'How can I, when there is no one to instruct me?' And he begged Philip to come up into the carriage and sit with him. The passage of Scripture he had been reading was this:
>
> 'He was led as a sheep to the slaughter.
> And as a lamb is silent before the shearers,
> he did not open his mouth.
> He was humiliated and received no justice.
> Who can speak of his descendants?
> For his life was taken from the earth.'
>
> The eunuch asked Philip, 'Was Isaiah talking about himself or someone else?' So Philip began with this same Scripture and then used many others to tell him the Good News about Jesus." (Acts 8:26–35)

Defining apologetics

Many people today consider apologetics to be a purely academic discipline, only practiced by a few intellectuals, bearing little relevance to everyday life and the faith of ordinary people. However, this is a serious misunderstanding. The task of giving a reasoned defense is a mandate given to the whole Church, not to an elite few.

> "But set apart the Messiah as Lord in your hearts, and always be ready to give a defense to anyone who asks you for a reason for the hope that is in you. However, do this with gentleness and respect, keeping your conscience clear, so that when you are accused, those who denounce your Christian life will be put to shame." (1 Peter 3:15–16 HCSB)

Not everyone can follow complex philosophical arguments, nor articulate the faith like C. S. Lewis, but thankfully this is not a requirement for talking about our faith in Christ. Some people are especially gifted at articulating the faith in ways that are intellectually sophisticated. As we might expect, not all of us are as capable of this or inclined this way. Nonetheless, we *are* each called to prepare ourselves to give an answer to those in our sphere of influence. To the best of our ability, we are commissioned to give a reason for the hope that is "in us." The apostle Jude reminds us:

> "Dearly loved friends, I had been eagerly planning to write to you about the salvation we all share. But now I find that I must write about something else, urging you to defend the truth of the Good News. God gave this unchanging truth once for all time to his holy people."
> (Jude 3)

Surrendering to Christ's lordship completely – including our intellectual lives – we "ready ourselves" (literally "get fit") to give a defense to those who voice objections or to those who are seeking reasons to believe. This task, Scripture insists, is given to us all.

The function of Scripture

The Scriptures are foundational for our apologetics. Taken as a whole, they are clearly a missional document. They communicate God's activity in history, especially His plan of reconciliation and redemption since the fall of humanity into sin. The Scriptures tell us who we are, what this world is, why the world is as it is and what God has done to restore the world. It presents us, in other words, with *a paradigm* with which we are to understand all of life. The intent of Scripture is not simply to give us information about this world and about ourselves, but to call us to repentance and completely reorient every aspect of life and thought towards God.

The *missiological* orientation of Scripture means that Scripture is also an apologetic document. Through the mouths of the prophets, priests, kings, apostles, and the Son of God Himself, we hear the voice of God. This voice reasons with us (Genesis 4:3–12), calls us (Revelation 22:17), tries to persuade us (Isaiah 1:18–20), cross-examines us (Job 40:1–24), appeals to us (Deuteronomy 30:19–20) and warns us (Revelation 22:12–15, 18–20), just as we are to do with others in the task of apologetics. Of course, God does not support His authoritative claims by appeal to human thinking and expertise as we so often do. Rather, He speaks on His own authority as the triune Creator God. Consequently, there are no rationalistic arguments from bare facts of nature for God's existence or appeals to human authorities and experts in the pages of the Bible. Seventeenth-century Christian apologist, scientist, and thinker Blaise Pascal writes:

> "It is a remarkable fact that no writer *within the canon* has ever used nature to *prove* the existence of God. They all try to help people believe in him. Neither David, nor Solomon, nor others ever said: 'There is no such thing as a vacuum, therefore God exists.' They must have been smarter than the smartest of their successors, all of whom have used proofs from nature. This is most significant."[1]

However, there are many other kinds of arguments, persuasions, justifications and admonishments to belief in Scripture. For example, in

Romans 1, the apostle Paul simply *asserts* that the testimony of God in the created order, including the human consciousness, is sufficiently evident that men and women are left without excuse for not believing in God. This argument is not taking supposed "neutral facts" of nature to argue for the *probability* of theism. Rather, Paul is saying that the "giveness" of the world and human consciousness makes God an inescapable reality – we are directly aware of God's being and character by virtue of creation, though many "hold down" this knowledge in unrighteousness. No further proof is necessary. The writer of Hebrews exhorts us that the necessity of faith (embracing the revelation of God) precedes true knowledge and understanding:

> "Anyone who wants to come to him must believe that there is a God and that he rewards those who sincerely seek him." (Hebrews 11:6)

Jesus also reminds us,

> "Keep on asking and you will be given what you ask for. Keep on looking, and you will find. Keep on knocking, and the door will be opened. For everyone who asks, receives. Everyone who seeks, finds. And the door is opened to everyone who knocks." (Matthew 7:7–8)

The apostle Paul, when reasoning with the philosophers in Athens in Acts 17, takes their conception of an unknown God and builds his argument on that foundation. He emphasizes that the true God is the One in whom we "live and move and have our being." He quotes their own poets to show that it is *this God* of whom we already have a conception in our minds and hearts. As he progresses with his argument, he exposes the resulting absurdity of their idolatry and religious ceremonies:

> "You have been worshiping him without knowing who he is, and now I wish to tell you about him. He is the God who made the world and everything in it. Since he is Lord of heaven and earth, he doesn't live in man-made temples, and human hands can't serve his needs – for he has no needs. He himself gives life and breath to everything, and he satisfies every need there is ... For in him we live and move and exist. As one of your own poets says,

> 'We are his offspring.' And since this is true, we shouldn't think of God as an idol designed by craftsmen from gold or silver or stone."
>
> (Acts 17:23–25, 28–29)

The necessity for conversation

Sometimes in our evangelistic efforts, Christians engage more in *monologue* than in *dialogue*. If apologetics is to be fruitful, *conversation* is crucial. As seen in Paul's ministry (Acts 17:16–17), meaningful interaction is usually necessary for a successful presentation and defense of the gospel. In human experience, few things give us more pleasure than a good, interesting conversation. When we communicate meaningfully, we are imitating our Creator, who made us in His image: "In the beginning . . . God said" (Genesis 1:1, 3), and "In the beginning *the Word* already existed" (John 1:1, emphasis added). It is this same God who "conversed" with our fathers and mothers in the faith as we would converse with a friend. We see this in the remarkable dialogue between God and Abraham concerning the destruction of Sodom:

> "The LORD remained with Abraham for a while. Abraham approached him and said, 'Will you destroy both innocent and guilty alike . . . should not the Judge of all the earth do what is right?' And the LORD replied, 'If I find fifty innocent people in Sodom, I will spare the entire city for their sake' . . . 'Suppose only ten are found there?' And the LORD said, 'Then, for the sake of the ten, I will not destroy it.' The LORD went on his way when he had finished his conversation with Abraham."
>
> (Extracts from Genesis 18:22–33)

Since apologetics can sometimes be intimidating, it is helpful to see apologetics as fundamentally a great *conversation*! It is a conversation between human beings in the context of the cosmic conversation – that between God and the creation He loves. Ours is not a distant, passionless God, who simply issues commands from on high, without concern for the thoughts, feelings, and freedom He has given his people. Remarkably, ours is the living God who genuinely interacts with His creatures, engaging them in two-way conversation. We see this all through the Old Testament among the great saints, from Adam and Eve through David and the prophets. In the New Testament, we read of the master conversationalist, Jesus Christ. Just think of some of His remarkable conversations, such as the night-time discussion with Nicodemus the Jewish teacher, His dialogue with Roman centurions, the Samaritan woman, and with the procurator of Judea, Pontius Pilate.

Questions, conversations and presuppositions

Why is conversation so important in apologetics? We know it is very easy for misunderstandings to arise in our interactions with others. Just think about politics! There are various reasons for misunderstandings – cultural, ethical, intellectual, spiritual, and emotional – but we all know what it is like to experience them. How often have you misunderstood somebody's intention or meaning and then had the misunderstanding cleared up in a later conversation? Sometimes in our apologetic efforts, we are prone to be too hasty. We expect people to understand our meaning and the content of the gospel based on a few sentences we preach. At the same time, we are busy answering a question they are not even asking, because we have not been careful enough to listen to their questions or to consider what lies beneath them.

Conversations take many different forms according to context. There is no particular script we need to memorize in order to have an apologetic conversation. Rather, it is a creative opportunity for interaction. This is *not* because all views are equally valid, but because through conversation we are able to hear what the person is really saying. As we listen to each other, we can begin to see which views are sound and which are not. The ancient Greek saying, "Speak that I may see thee," is a helpful insight here.

Conversations help expose our motives, assumptions, presuppositions, and biases. Indeed, they help us see and begin to articulate what we believe and why, sometimes for the first time. From experience, I know that it is often easier to break through barriers of disinterest through conversation than through lecturing. Jesus did this all of the time. He asked over 100 questions of others in the New Testament. Unlike us, Jesus did not need information from people to overcome His ignorance. When He asked questions, He was helping people to face themselves and recognize their own assumptions and underlying motives.

There are many examples of this. On one occasion, recorded in Matthew 22:15–22, He was asked a complex question about whether taxes should be paid to Caesar or not. This question might appear quite innocent, until the context is considered. The Jewish people were under the rule of a foreign power – Rome. The Roman imperial authority taxed the people, which the Jews greatly resented. Tax collectors, who appear often in the New Testament, were despised by their fellow Jews. At the same time, not to pay your taxes was a serious offense against the emperor and to encourage others not to pay tribute was treason. This was one charge leveled at Jesus by the Jewish authorities at His trial before the Roman governor. Jesus knew that the questioners were simply trying to trap Him, so rather than falling into their ambush, He exposed their evil motives: "You hypocrites!" he said. "Whom are you trying to fool with your trick questions? Here, show me the Roman coin used for the tax" (Matthew 22:18–19). If at this point He had said, "Yes, pay up", He would have been accused of being "pro-Roman" and a traitor to the people of Israel, supporting their subjugation and so could not possibly be the "Christ" of Israel, the Deliverer. On the other hand, if He had said, "No, do not pay the tax", they would have had legitimate ground for accusing Him of sedition before the Roman authorities. Consequently, Jesus requested a Roman coin and asks a famous question of His own,

> " 'Whose picture and title are stamped on it?'
>
> 'Caesar's,' they replied.
>
> 'Well, then,' he said, 'give to Caesar what belongs to him. But everything that belongs to God must be given to God.' " (Matthew 22:19–21)

The following verse records that, "His reply amazed them, and they went away."

Apologist Ravi Zacharias says that if they had been wise they would have asked the next obvious question, "What belongs to God?" He says our Lord's answer might have come, "Whose image is on you?"

Jesus amazed the questioners with the wisdom of His response, by asking the right question and exposing hidden motives and bias. In a similar incident, in front of a large crowd, He is asked about the authority upon which He is saying and doing the things He does by the Jewish priests and legal experts (Matthew 21:23ff.).

"Who gave you such authority?" they retort. Again, sensing the questioners' motives were wrong, Jesus answers the question with a question. "I'll tell you who gave me the authority to do these things if you answer one question ... Did John's baptism come from heaven or was it merely human?" This brilliant rhetorical strategy turned the tables completely. They had set a trap for Jesus. If He had answered in a straightforward manner, simply saying that He had cleansed the temple in *God's authority*, they would have accused Him of blasphemy by claiming equality with the Almighty. They could then have tried to kill Him by rousing the crowd into an angry mob to stone Him (something they tried to do on many occasions). Alternatively, if He had said, "I did it on My own authority", they would simply have asked why anyone should bother listening to or obeying His word if it were merely human. The reason Jesus' response is so brilliant is clearly revealed in the account itself, as the Jewish leaders talk over His question amongst themselves:

> "'If we say it [John's Baptism] was from heaven, he will ask why we didn't believe him. But if we say it was merely human, we'll be mobbed, because the people think he was a prophet.' So [to escape their dilemma] they finally replied, 'We don't know.'" (Matthew 21:25–27)

Jesus' response in answer to this brings a smile to my face every time I read it: "Then I won't answer your question either."

Their biases and motives had been exposed by an insightful question. Even though we will never have the insight Jesus had, we can learn to ask good questions in our own apologetic conversations. Our questions both reveal things to us and they can also reveal things to the person with whom we are speaking, just as Jesus' questions did. We must learn to ask the right questions with wisdom at the right time.

The question that lies beneath the question

The best conversations will probe the real issues that lie beneath the faith assertions or questions of others. What we should be listening for is the question that lies beneath the question since, more often that not, a deeper, more fundamental question underpins popular objections. When the real question has been fully understood, the assumptions and presuppositions of the questioner become clearer. Since all questions arise out of the worldview of the questioner, questions will often reveal the *point of conflict* between the questioner's worldview and the worldview they are being presented with. At this point, the conversation often reaches a turning point. There is no neutrality with respect to God, so a response of some kind to this alternative worldview is inevitable. Those who conversed with Jesus in the Gospels usually responded in one of three ways. Either they accepted His word joyfully and followed Him (Matthew 4:18–23), went away dejected, as the rich man did in Mark 10:17–30, or they reacted with great hostility, even to the point of trying to kill Him (Matthew 12:14).

Scripture teaches that sinners are hostile to God and they suppress the truth in unrighteousness (Romans 1:18–21). Conversations can either progress meaningfully or they can go down endless rabbit trails leading nowhere, depending on the heart condition of those participating in the conversation. Thankfully, we are simply called to be faithful, and someone's final response to a faithful apologetic is in the Father's hands and not ours.

Pascal's observations – answering objections

Blaise Pascal was a brilliant apologist and conversational writer (as exhibited in his *Pensées* and *Provincial Letters*), and he also understood that all dialogues about faith are shaped by the limited perspective (or epistemic position) of those involved. It is not just the odd fact here and there that is in dispute but an entire way of perceiving the world. Every one of us has a *synoptic view* of reality that informs how we understand the world around us. The questions that we deem important or unimportant stem from this view. Because of this, we do not need to convince people by arguing about multiple issues separately, but rather, we can share Christ with people as *the medium through which all life can be rightly understood*. The Christ of Scripture is justified in the light of His own evidence. Other important sources of evidence can be understood, interpreted, and presented in the light of our commitment to Christ, but no evidence can be uninterpreted or neutral.

Good scholarship and careful investigation of evidence are important and should never be minimized or undervalued. However, our approach should not be one of frantic attempts to gather a vast barrage of evidence from numerous sources to pour all over the inquirer in hope of tipping the balance in our favor. Such an approach makes one feel that life must be spent perfecting a kind of Christian martial arts, where we always have to find a counter move to beat the opponent, to always be one step ahead. Rather, we should first help the skeptic to face the contradictions of his thinking and his faulty worldview, and then show him the resources of seeing all things in Christ. We can then provide ample evidence, including biblical prophecy and miracles, which becomes compelling when seen in the light of Christ. This was St Augustine's approach in his apologetic epic, the *City of God*. Augustine first demonstrates that the pagan worldview is failing and self-destructive, and in the second part, he invites the reader to see the world in the light of the biblical paradigm. He plots the origin and history of the great City of God under Christ its king. Reading it, one is swept away in the grandeur of an epic that makes life's components fall into place.

In Christ, we see that truth is what corresponds to the mind of God. Truth or facts are not neutral. Life does not consist of *brute facts*, uninterpreted and unrelated – a kind of "bare, mute, reality." All forms of thought are ultimately arbitrary, subjective and without ultimate meaning unless there is correspondence with God's mind. Many have sought to locate and establish truth by its *correspondence* with "reality" or by its internal *coherence*, or through the "success" of ideas when worked out in *practice*. All of these are helpful pointers when examining world-views. However, without a transcendent referent (revelation) beyond our finite minds, we do not know, or at least have no final consensus, about what reality is. So, how can we locate truth as *correspondence* with reality unless we already know what reality is? That is the heart of the question! Furthermore, tests for *coherence* only examine the validity of logical relations and conclusions, but cannot tell us whether we can trust the first premises. And, the *practical success* (pragmatism) of a worldview presupposes a goal. In other words, how do we know if something has "worked" successfully, without knowing what we are trying to accomplish? In order to establish a consensus on any of these tests, we would already have to know the very truth we are seeking to find out! Even if we suggest agreement on the grounds of empirical adequacy or scientific proof, we are assuming a given interpretation of the empirical data.

However, with Christ as our final referent, then all that corresponds to His mind revealed in the Bible corresponds to reality. Ultimately, coherence is not found in human philosophies either. The internal antinomies of non-Christian worldviews can be demonstrated. Coherence is only found ultimately in Christ, in whom and through whom all things cohere. God is exhaustively rational; there is no contradiction in Him. If there were, then rational thought would be meaningless. Finally, all that is *true* will also work out pragmatically, not the other way round. Empirical or scientific data can be biblically interpreted, since God governs everything in this world and works things out according to His plan. Christ and His revelation become then a necessary precondition of knowing and testing truth. Only in Christ, who is the Truth, does truth have a sure foundation. Pascal insightfully guides us in defending the gospel when he writes:

> "Not only is it impossible to know God without Christ, but it is useless also ... I marvel at the audacity with which some people presume to speak of God. In giving their evidence to unbelievers, usually their first chapter is to prove the existence of God from the works of nature. I would not be surprised about this project if they were addressing their arguments to believers, for those with living faith in their hearts can clearly see at once that everything that exists is entirely the work of God whom they worship. But for those in whom this light has been extinguished and in whom we are trying to rekindle it – the pride of faith and grace – such people see nature only by this light and find only obscurity and darkness."[2]

Pascal goes on to say that one might try to argue the case for God from, for example, the regular course of the moon and planets, but in terms of how others will view such arguments without the light of faith, he says,

> "If such an argument were to be presented to them, no wonder they would react and say that the proofs or our religion are feeble indeed, and reason and experience tell me that nothing is more likely to bring it into contempt in their sight. But this is not how Scripture speaks, with its better knowledge of the things of God. On the contrary, it speaks of God as a hidden God, and because nature has been corrupted, He has left men to their blindness. They can only escape from this through Jesus Christ, for without Him, all communication with God is severed."[3]

Thus, it is very important to understand the presuppositions or the paradigm that governs people's thought. *What we believe about different issues depends on the medium through which we see the world.* This medium will govern which arguments are regarded as persuasive or not and how evidence will be interpreted. Furthermore, as Pascal highlights above, that larger perspective is also influenced by factors that are often underestimated, such as our fallen condition, blindness, and hostility toward God. Consider the words of evolutionary biologist and open opponent of Christianity, Richard Dawkins, as he expounds his faith that resists any notion of Intelligent Design in the origin of life:

> "... all of life on this planet is shaped by Darwinian natural selection, which also endows it with an *overwhelming illusion* of 'design.' I believe but cannot prove that ... all intelligence, all creativity, and all design, anywhere in the universe, is the direct or indirect product of a cumulative process equivalent to what we here call Darwinian natural selection. It follows that design comes late in the universe, after a period of Darwinian evolution. Design cannot precede evolution and therefore cannot underlie the universe."[4]
>
> (emphasis added)

Even though grudgingly admitting that he cannot prove that design "cannot" precede evolution and "cannot" underlie the universe, Dawkins is fanatically committed to his religious presupposition to the point that blatant evidence of design is interpreted as an "overwhelming illusion." Thus, his worldview and his religious commitment that must at all costs deny God, determine how he interprets the evidence, in this case, the appearance of design.

Nonetheless, recognizing and showing that we all speak on behalf of a particular worldview is not enough. We cannot be satisfied with just an abstract analysis of people's presuppositions, since the God we are seeking to introduce to people is not theoretical, but is the living God of Scripture. At the foundation of all true understanding is *conversion – a moral, spiritual, and intellectual transformation*. We are not saved by argument or reason, but by faith. In order for us humans to see the world rightly, we need new birth. God wants to use us as instruments in His great work of regeneration, not to win arguments or gloat over embarrassing our opponents, but to welcome people into the hospitality of the City of God.

The condition of our hearers

Reason is given to us as a gift, as a tool our minds inescapably use to think. However, reason unenlightened or unaided does not enable us to understand the big picture. This is because we are creatures and not the Creator; we are finite and limited. We are meant to discover reality as God has made it, not to make it in our own image and thereby live an illusion. Consequently, humanistic philosophies do not arrive at truth, but simply substitute the creature for the Creator. Man must somehow "stand in" for God and speak an infallible word. We pretend that consciousness and reason can account for themselves and function as an ultimate ground or final judge. Either the subconscious or unconscious mind (as in Freud), or the collective voice of the state (as in Marxism and all Hegelian thought) or the biological urge (as in evolution) or the existential moment (as in Sartre) must replace God and define and shape all reality. But, whenever men and women seek to worship the creature rather than the Creator by cutting themselves off from revelation, they inevitably end up with futile, self-defeating thought. They find themselves faced with the impossibility of understanding anything as it truly is in relationship to the whole of reality – they lack a point of unity in the diversity of things.[5]

Since humans have suppressed the truth in their rebellion against God, their eyes are now covered with spiritual cataracts. Humans are lost and alienated from God, and they cannot find appropriate ways of knowing truth simply through reason while disconnected from God and His revealed Word. After all, reason does not supply true premises; it only works on premises that are already given. People are thinkers and know that they must think correctly. Yet, without God, the search for truth proves futile and the quest for happiness is frustrated.

Long before the French existentialists, the writer of Ecclesiastes identified the vanity of life lived without reference to God:

> " 'Everything is meaningless,' says the Teacher, 'utterly meaningless!' What do people get for all their hard work? Generations come and go, but nothing really changes. The sun rises and sets and hurries around to rise again . . . The rivers run into the sea, but the sea is never full . . . Everything is so weary and tiresome! No matter how much we see, we are never satisfied. No matter how much we hear we are not content . . . Everything under the sun is meaningless, like chasing the wind." (Ecclesiastes 1:2–5, 7–8, 14)

However, faith in the God of creation resolves the human dilemma. The tension is gone, because God's revelation supplies true premises by which the world and everything in it becomes intelligible. This faith goes beyond the limits of human reasoning. It sees, describes, and accounts for the human condition as no other view can. *It shows what must be true in order for things to be what they appear to be!*

The great truths of Scripture, upon which we must rest our defense of the faith, are that humans are fallen from their created estate but that they can be redeemed by the Triune God through Christ. And Christ is not merely the redeemer of the soul but also of the entire human person and all of human activity. He has come to redeem our families and communities, our science, literature, art, cultures and philosophy. His redemption covers the totality of human experience. Through Christ, a true epistemology (basis for knowledge) can be established. Christ must always stand at the very center of our message, not somewhere on the periphery, as is so often the case in modern apologetics. It is faith in Christ that leads to understanding where the will, as well as the mind, is fully engaged in shaping new patterns of thought and behavior. As Augustine beautifully stated, "I believe in order to understand." If unbelief results in skepticism and irrationality, our desire should be to show that when our will and imagination are turned towards God, we see things differently, as they truly are. Our objective is to show that without Christ all things are reduced to absurdity and vanity.

Noted atheist Frederick Nietzsche was at least an honest opponent of the God of Scripture, and he readily saw the logical end of what life would mean without God. Proclaiming himself the antichrist and heralding the era of the superman, he claimed to see the abyss with pride. He sought to project himself as the "superman" who was beyond all faiths and all "illusions." The conclusion of this logic is the death of God in human thinking. He wrote: "Our first principles: no God: no purpose."[6]

Furthermore, he stated,

> "'Man must become better and eviler' – so do I teach. The evilest is necessary for the superman's best. It may have been well for the preacher of the petty people to suffer and be burdened by men's sin. I, however, rejoice in great sin as my great consolation."[7]

For him, the great ideals of the Christian faith are illusions, so he relentlessly attacks the idea of hope in or beyond history. His creed is war on all things. In fact, he predicted that there would be "wars, whose like have never been seen on earth before. Politics on a grand scale will date from me."[8] The twentieth century seems to bear out his prediction. Without God, the futility of human existence leaves us at the mercy of this kind of devilry – a true nihilism that makes people sick of the sight of other people. The "superman" who tries to move beyond Christ, being his own god, does not love or liberate, but hates and despises his fellow humans.

By contrast, the great man of faith, Pascal, saw that the living God was no fiction, that He was the Creator of heaven and earth, the God of

Abraham, Isaac and Jacob, the One in whom all things consist. He recognized that human beings are neither "supermen" (capable of transcending all faiths) nor gods, but slaves to their own vanity, pride and selfishness. Therefore, the lives of those seeking to live without Christ and His redemption were reduced to meaninglessness. Both men reached the same conclusion – life without God leads to the death of meaning, law, objective morality, and "true" philosophy. Only evil can reign where Christ is despised. Nietzsche was a moral rebel and was blinded by hate for Christ the Son, while Pascal, a servant of Christ, saw that all meaning, happiness, and virtue was found in Him. Pascal clearly exposes the result of Nietzsche's negation of Christ two hundred years before he was ever born:

> "Without Christ, man can only be sinful and wretched. With Christ, man is freed from sin and wretchedness. For in Him is all our virtue and happiness. Apart from Him there can only be vice, wretchedness, error, darkness, death and despair . . . apart from Jesus Christ we cannot know the meaning of our life or of our death, of God or of ourselves. Without Scripture, whose only object is to proclaim Christ, we know nothing, and we can see nothing but obscurity and confusion."[9]

The power of presupposition

Let us summarize systematically what we have noticed thus far. In logic, a valid argument is offered when the conclusion is entailed in the premise. This implies that the premises are already a form of conclusion. That is, there is no *proposition* without *presupposition*. We all begin reasoning somewhere, taking something for granted, assuming certain things as given. We must put faith in certain beliefs in order to do any reasoning at all. Our most basic assumptions cannot be proven directly, for if they could be demonstrated by criteria beyond themselves, they would not be our *most* basic assumptions. Ultimately then, either God or a form of humanism is our starting point. There is no area of intellectual inquiry that can completely dispense with reasoning, but what many people fail to realize is that all reasoning must make assumptions. This is well summarized for us by Rushdoony: "...before there is a fact there is a faith about facts."[10]

He goes on to point out it is not possible to consider particular facts except in relation to some kind of view of facts. As a result, the most important questions are "Which kind of universal faith can give the *best account* of the facts?" and "What view can give *meaning* to individual facts?" Cornelius Van Til has insightfully noted that:

> "It is impossible to reason on the basis of brute facts. Everyone who reasons about facts comes to those facts with a schematism (sic) into which he fits the facts. The real question is therefore, into whose schematism the facts will fit. As between Christianity and its opponents, the question is whether our claim that Christianity is the only schematism into which the facts will fit, is truth or not."[11]

If it were not for the sovereign Word of God and His eternal plan, all the particular experiences in our lives would be unrelated, because there would be no ultimate framework in which to understand or explain them. This is what Van Til means when he refers to "brute facts" – individual facts that are unrelated to any other fact by an original creative scheme and thereby meaningless. A fact *cannot be interpreted* even when it is considered alongside other "brute" facts. Van Til shows that to believe that individual "brute facts" brought together can add up to real knowledge is like believing that *multiple zeros can add up to something more than zero.*[12]

So, if the God of Scripture exists, there are no "brute" facts. All of our experience is governed and controlled by God's power and pattern and all facts are meaningful, because they are related to God's plan. This means, in the Christian view, to know facts is to know them as God wants them to be known by us as creatures. We are thinking God's thoughts after Him. Therefore, *the God of the Bible gives every fact meaning, so the very idea of neutral or "brute" facts is a denial of God's existence.* Many believe that they are thinking in a neutral or objective way and they demand that everyone must do the same in order to be intellectually respectable. However, as we have seen, it is impossible to be neutral. Someone who believes in neutrality has excluded the God of the Bible from the outset, so she is pre-committed. *Everyone always comes to the facts with a pre-commitment.*

Given this power of presuppositions, the crucial questions to be considered as we engage people in apologetic conversation are, "What must be true to make knowledge, science, and all the fundamental aspects of life meaningful and comprehensible?" or "What must the world be like in order for us to know it and account for our knowledge of it?" The triune God of Scripture is the only meaningful answer to the problem of knowledge.[13] If, for example, science is to have adequate philosophical ground to function, it must assume order. However, when science rejects God, it is forced to locate this order in mindless matter. But how can matter and chance account for any supervening kind of pattern or order? The choice then seems very simple – we must choose between the law and decree of God or the fluctuating decrees of humans who are simply random assortments of atomic particles. Paradigms and patterns are inescapable. We cannot avoid them. Instead, we face the challenge of making an informed choice between them.

Kingdom upside down

To summarize this point, consider that in any apologetic conversation, the worldview of those involved will determine the nature of the conversation and the way individual issues are approached. Sometimes, because the question of worldview is not raised explicitly in the conversation, we can forget how important it is. However, if we do not understand the presuppositions that we all bring to the conversation, we will be frustrated and might feel that we are banging our heads against a brick wall. The key to persuasive apologetic conversations is to understand the lenses through which we all look at the world. At the heart of every conversation about faith, there is a clash of paradigms. Regardless of whether they have thought this through or not, a Christian is presupposing a biblical paradigm and the unbeliever is presupposing one of a number of paradigms that do not include the God of the Bible. The Christian rests the ultimate criterion for truth in the Creator God of

Scripture; the other person does not. So, when discussing some issue, whether abortion, sexuality, science, or the resurrection, it is important to recognize that *what people will accept as fact is dependent upon their religious pre-commitment.* Data that do not conform to their pre-commitment will not be accepted even if accompanied by what we consider powerful evidence. This is because the evidence itself must be interpreted in accordance with their paradigm, which still needs the light of Christ to shine into the darkness.

I will never forget the time when I was delivering a series of apologetic addresses on the Christian faith in London, England. I was in the sixth and final session speaking about the resurrection of Christ. The talk seemed to go very well. At the end, before we were to break into discussion groups one of the skeptics attending the course came to me to ask a question. "That was a great talk", she said. I tried to respond humbly, "Well, thank you very much for your encouragement." "In fact, it was a watertight argument", she added, "but I have a question though." "Please go ahead," I urged her, now feeling very pleased with myself and fully expecting her to ask me what she needed to do to become a Christian. But her question caught me completely off guard, "Jesus was raised from the dead! So what? My uncle George might be raised from the dead. This is a chaotic universe in which anything might happen – perhaps I might be raised from the dead, who knows?"

It took me some time to realize what the problem was. I had been reading apologetics for quite some time at this point and was accustomed to thinking of historical proofs for the resurrection as overwhelmingly compelling. But for those who hold to the idea that history is the result of chance, not a foreordained plan and purpose, no one event can shape or define reality. Even though my argument convinced her that the resurrection probably did happen, she dealt with this evidence, not by seeing it as the final proof of Christ's divinity and the truth of the Scriptures, but by interpreting it in the light of her worldview. The meaning of the event was given by her view of reality. The resurrection was merely a chance occurrence that has no ultimate significance. There can be no "signs" if, in history, all events are equally *in*significant. By the grace of God, this young woman did come to faith in Christ. I learned a valuable lesson about false assumptions in communicating with the non-believer through this. We cannot assume that they share our paradigm.

By first looking at the world as our conversation partner conceives of it, we seek to show how he or she cannot account for our everyday human experience according to that worldview. We can do this by discussing the presuppositions or foundational beliefs themselves from the point of view of our conversation partner. *From within that paradigm*, we can raise objections and highlight internal conflicts that call the whole paradigm into question. For example, as we have seen, humanism destroys the basis of objective morality and real knowledge, while at the same time making truth claims. Take the case of someone arguing for the right to an abortion, insisting that she is "morally justified." But, where does her concept of morality come from if it does not come from God? And why should anyone else accept it if it only comes from her? After graciously highlighting internal conflicts in a perspective that undermine an argument, we can invite the other person to enter our worldview and to look at the world through the lens of Jesus Christ and show how this alone makes sense of our life and loves. We help them to see that by trusting Christ and His authority rather than their own or some other, their understanding will be opened to see the power of the evidence all around them.

The apostle Paul reminds us that although the mind might be able to comprehend Christian arguments, on their own, people cannot properly understand the truth about God.

> "People who aren't Christians can't understand these truths from God's Spirit. It all sounds foolish to them because only those who have the Spirit can understand what the Spirit means. We who have the Spirit understand these things, but others can't understand us at all."
>
> (1 Corinthians 2:14–15)

St Augustine guides us on the right path when he says:

> "The mysteries and secrets of the kingdom of God first seek out believing men that they may make them understand. For faith is understanding's step, and understanding is faith's reward."[14]

Augustine points out that God gives a person a degree of understanding by grace. This enables a person to understand enough that she can decide to take the step of faith. And once she does, she will understand things much more clearly. *Faith brings understanding.* When everything is seen through the lens of Christ, a new understanding emerges and then the evidence becomes utterly compelling. When we show people the world from the view of faith in Christ, the Holy Spirit brings divine conviction. Our message ceases to sound foolish, but rather becomes overwhelmingly persuasive.

Intellectually, one can follow an argument, but only the Spirit can bring us to understand and embrace the truth with our whole being. Our task then, is to help people see the "upside down" kingdom "right side up."

Christians as guides

In John 3:12, Jesus is speaking to a religious teacher, Nicodemus, who is confused by Jesus' language of rebirth:

> "... unless you are born again, you can never see the Kingdom of God."
> (John 3:3)

Jesus says to Nicodemus,

> "But if you don't even believe me when I tell you about things that happen here on earth, how can you possibly believe if I tell you what is going on in heaven?" (John 3:12)

In Nicodemus' mind, salvation came by outward obedience to the detailed requirements of all aspects of the Mosaic Law. His presuppositions concerning how to be right with God were preventing him from understanding what Christ was saying to him. But his problem was not merely a lack of knowledge. In verses 19–21, Jesus helps Nicodemus understand the true reason for his lack of comprehension:

> "The light from heaven came into the world, but they loved the darkness more than the light, for their actions were evil. They hate the light because

> they want to sin in the darkness. They stay away from the light for fear their sins will be exposed and they will be punished. But those who do what is right come to the light gladly, so everyone can see that they are doing what God wants."

Nicodemus had adopted a view that prevented him from seeing the light. Christ challenges his assumptions, " . . . unless you are born again . . . "

In Acts 8, Philip the evangelist is prompted by the Holy Spirit to speak with an Ethiopian eunuch who is reading from the prophet Isaiah. God has clearly been preparing this man's heart, but he does not understand the Scripture he is reading, even though he is a God-fearer who had come to worship the God of Israel in Jerusalem. Many are like this today. They may have some recognition of God, but they do not understand Scripture and they usually assume that salvation results from some kind of personal moral achievement. Philip asks this inquiring man whether he understands the text. The treasurer of Ethiopia acknowledges his need for a guide, so Philip takes this scripture and preaches Jesus to him, bringing color, depth, and context to the man's understanding. It would have been fascinating to be a fly on the chariot wheel during that Bible study! After this remarkable conversation, the Ethiopian official requests baptism immediately.

In Acts chapters 24–26, Paul converses with King Agrippa and imperial Governor Felix. Even though Felix resists Paul's reasoned presentation of faith in Christ, it nonetheless terrifies his conscience. Evidently, this was the reason why he rejected Paul's message (Acts 24:25), since he insisted that Paul leave his presence. Later, Paul has the opportunity to give a lengthy defense before Agrippa and the new governor, Festus. Festus, on hearing the message through the filter of his pagan paradigm, says, "Paul, you are beside yourself! Much learning is driving you mad!" Again, the role of worldview is clear. To him, the gospel is madness. Paul responds, "I am not mad, most noble Festus, but speak the words of *truth* and *reason*" (emphasis added).

The conversations of Scripture not only teach us that paradigms can be powerful obstacles for people coming to the knowledge of God, but also that Christ's power is greater and that He uses our conversations as instruments to bring faith to the heart. The great conversation goes on. It goes on because God began it and sustains it. He is the first communicator, the great conversationalist, the eternal Word who spoke all things into being. Now, He calls us to converse at the family supper table in the house of God in the city of the great King! Let us take this Word to the world in our time and have conversations that count for eternity!

Discussion questions

1. How do you think the average non-Christian views apologetics and evangelism? Do they perceive it as a conversation?
2. Why do you think conversation is so important in apologetics?
3. What do you find most intimidating about apologetic conversation?
4. In what areas would you most like to improve in your conversations?
5. What strikes you most about the biblical conversations discussed in this chapter and how do they help you in thinking about your own approach to conversation?
6. Suggest some questions that would be helpful to ask a conversation partner in order to discover his worldview and underlying questions.
7. Think of an example in which a person's worldview would hinder his or her ability to understand a specific issue about the Christian faith. How could you address the worldview context with him or her in that conversation?
8. If someone asked you how you can believe in a God who allows so much suffering in the world, what might be some of the possible underlying questions of such a person?

Notes

1. Blaise Pascal, *The Mind on Fire, The works of Blaise Pascal*, edited by James M. Houston (Bethany House Publishers, Minneapolis, 1997), p. 152.
2. Blaise Pascal, *The Mind on Fire*, p. 151.
3. Blaise Pascal, *The Mind on Fire*, p. 152.
4. Richard Dawkins cited in, *What We Believe But Cannot Prove*, edited by John Brockman (Harper Perennial, London, 2006), p. 9.
5. For those interested in the ancient problem of unity and diversity and the Christian solution in the doctrine of the Trinity, the following argument may be of interest. The Ontology of the Universe is such that either (a) unity is ultimate and not plurality, or (b) plurality is ultimate and not unity, or (c) unity and plurality are

co-ultimate. 1. If unity is ultimate and not plurality, then knowledge of the universe (even in part) is impossible. 2. If plurality is ultimate and not unity, then knowledge of the universe (even in part) is impossible. 3. Knowledge of the universe is not impossible. 4. Therefore, the ontology of the universe must be such that unity and plurality are co-ultimate. 5. Therefore Christian theism is the case since only Christian theism posits an Ontology in which unity and plurality are co-ultimate – Father, Son and Holy Spirit (nominalistic materialism versus monistic pantheism as paradigmatic examples).

6. Friedrich Nietzsche, cited by R. J. Rushdoony, *The Death of Meaning* (Ross House Books, 2002), p. 124.
7. *The Death of Meaning*, p. 123.
8. *The Death of Meaning*, p. 124.
9. *Mind on Fire*, p. 153.
10. R. J. Rushdoony, *The Mythology of Science* (Ross House Books, 2001), p. 113.
11. *The Mythology of Science*, p. 113.
12. This line of reasoning argues that fact and meaning must be unified by an exhaustive knowledge of reality. This can be formulated into a simple argument for God's existence. (1) If no one has comprehensive knowledge of the universe then no one can have any knowledge of the universe. (If humans are the ultimate reference point, they must know how all the facts relate together.) (2) Only God could have comprehensive knowledge of the universe since humans beings are finite. (3) We have some knowledge of the universe (due to God's revelation both natural and supernatural). (4) Therefore, God exists.
13. This assertion I justify in the chapter "The Faith of Reason," in *Why I Still Believe* (Grand Rapids: Baker Books, 2005).
14. St Augustine, *An Augustine Synthesis* (Sheed and Ward, New York, 1945), pp. 52, 54, 62.

CHAPTER 4

The Apologetics of St Augustine

[This lecture was first delivered at an Augustine Institute apologetics training weekend near Toronto, Canada.]

St Augustine the man: a brief biographical sketch

Although Augustine's name is probably known to most of us, one might ask what relevance a writer living more than 1,500 years ago could have for us in the twenty-first century. Yet, I believe we have much to learn from Augustine (AD 354–430) who, like other influential thinkers, has gone before us to blaze a trail. What is latest is not always the best. C. S. Lewis encouraged us to "read old books" and to "let the clear breeze of the centuries blow through our minds" so that we could avoid the characteristic blindness of our age and learn the lessons of the past.[1]

Born in Thagaste, North Africa in AD 354, in what is now North-eastern Algeria, a city on the edge of the Roman Empire, he grew up in Africa's "Bible belt." His mother was a practicing Christian, but the young Augustine was only interested in his own personal ambition. By Augustine's own admission, he became a "know-all" and rejected the Bible for its lack of eloquence, though he later acknowledged that he was simply too proud to accept its humble words. Thus, he rejected the Catholicism of his mother and set out to find a more rational faith. "Philosophers seek wisdom," says Augustine, "but do not know his name." This was Augustine's experience as he embarked on his quest for the true philosophy.

The second stage in his search for truth was in Manicheism. This philosophy combined *materialism* – that claimed even God was a certain kind of material, visible light – *rationalism* – that denied the role of faith and authority – and *dualism* – that believed everything was composed of either good or bad material, divine light or evil matter. Manicheans despised the body because they saw the soul as a fragment of divine light and the evil body as the product of a conflict between good and evil that gave birth to the world. Much later, after hearing and debating with the leading Manichean and discovering that he was without answers or true wisdom, Augustine became greatly disillusioned and joined the ranks of skeptics who denied that truth could be known by human beings, much like some of our contemporaries.

After his education in rhetoric in Carthage and Rome, in AD 384, Augustine took a post as a teaching orator in Milan, a wonderful opportunity to further his career. Here he was exposed to the thoughtful teaching of Bishop Ambrose who impressed him. Here was a Christian he had to take seriously. He also read the books of the Platonists, which convinced him that the divine was immaterial, omnipresent, and good, in contrast to the materialistic Manichean view. Thus, Neo-Platonism leads him further on his search as he continues to pursue a promising career as a rhetorician and politician.

Not long after, in the late summer of AD 386, at the age of 33, Augustine has his famous conversion to Christianity. He is in a garden, weeping because of his lifestyle and his doubts, when he hears a voice say, "Take up and read." At first he thinks the voice came from children playing a game, but he starts to read the Bible, beginning with the letters of Paul. The first thing he sees is a challenge, to "put on Christ and make no provision for the flesh." This decisive moment transformed his life and he gives himself to God. Between this event and his baptism during Easter of AD 387, he spends some time in philosophical study at Cassiciacum and begins writing some of his earliest polemic and apologetic works – initially in the dialogue tradition of the ancient philosophers, including a unique internal dialog with "reason" called *Soliloquies*. After a short time in Rome, he returns to Africa in AD 388 where he is soon ordained a presbyter in 391. In AD 395, he is consecrated as Bishop of Hippo Regius and in the year AD 400 completes his most popular work, *Confessions*. The sacking of Rome takes place in AD 410, which inspires Augustine to pen his other timeless classic, *The City of God*, which he begins in AD 413. In AD 430, the City of Hippo is surrounded by the vandals and Augustine lies dying inside. And so, at the age of 76, surrounded by his followers reading passages from the penitential Psalms, Augustine goes to be with Christ.

St Augustine's contemporary relevance

The contemporary apologetic relevance of Augustine's work is evident in several areas. First, Augustine had an integrated view of the human person and so a holistic view of the quest for truth and happiness. Today, however, the practical living of everyday life and intellect or thought are so compartmentalized that people often despair of finding something to bind them together. In contrast, Augustine did not see the pursuit of wisdom, truth, virtue and happiness as different and unrelated. Rather, each could not be known without the others. Philosophy is the *love of wisdom*, who is Christ, and wisdom is concerned with living out real life oriented toward God.

In our day, integrated thinking desperately needs to be recovered. People not only need to know what is true, but also how to live and how to pursue happiness. If people are going to embrace a worldview, they will want to know how it works out in practice. Does it connect us to God and others? Does it bring peace, justice, and happiness? Does this truth change the lives of those who embrace the faith? Can I experience this vision of truth in God myself? Augustine helps us answer these questions through the insights of his autobiography, *Confessions*. For Augustine, Christ is the Wisdom of God become human. He brings virtue, truth, and happiness in and through Himself.

Our era shares some striking similarities to Augustine's time. As Christianity grew rapidly in the fourth and fifth centuries, it was seen as a threat by the pagan establishment, and conflict was inevitable. Similarly, there has been a paradigm shift in Western culture over the past 100 years. Global communication and travel have given birth to a multi-faith society that makes any particular religion's claims to truth suspicious in the eyes of the wider culture. The belief that truth is found in Jesus Christ is offensive in a society where no one story is allowed to claim precedence over all others. Many people view this as a "power play" by Christians that marginalizes all those who are not Christians. But Augustine shows us how *God's story*, which he expounds in *The City of God*, and our own stories, which he exemplifies in the *Confessions*, can engage and evaluate other stories with respect, meekness, and persuasive power.

Finally, Augustine's time was, like ours, one of *radical doubt*, in which the ancient skeptics, the academics, prided themselves in doubting everything. Truth, according to them, could not be known by limited human beings bound by so many conditioning factors (relativism). Therefore, almost any god was acceptable except the God of Scripture, and the Roman senate would vote on which gods could be worshiped by the people. Today, any god is again acceptable as long as it does not interfere with anyone else's gods. Augustine's distinctly Christian thought on all these matters can be of great value, for helping us in our time.

Augustine's Christian philosophy

(a) Taking God for granted

Augustine quite rightly refused to take a secular or neutral starting point in philosophy to work his way to theism. Rather he took the truth of Christian theism as his starting point in every aspect of his thought.

Christian philosopher Alvin Plantinga has argued that belief in God requires no proof to be rational, but is in fact a properly basic belief, like that of belief in the existence of the mind, other minds, a real world, and the reliability of reasoning. Properly basic beliefs are foundational beliefs that we must accept without proof in order to make sense of life and experience. When approaching typical questions in philosophy then, the Augustinian philosopher may use all the resources at her disposal, including Christian truth and revelation to deal with such questions.

Critically, the revealed doctrine of the Trinity was foundational to Augustine's philosophical thought. It enabled Augustine to solve an ancient problem in philosophy concerning the one and the many. How could a universe of great multiplicity (the many) be derived from a source devoid of multiplicity (the one)? This problem exists for all non-Christian forms of thought. Ronald Nash notes concerning Augustine:

> "The fact that God is both three and one, plurality and unity, explains how thoughtful Christians like Augustine can explain the coming into being of a pluralistic universe, something Plotinus could only dream of. The problem of the one and the many receives its answer in a God who is both One and Many."[2]

In Confessions, Augustine notes that in some mysterious manner:

> "... the infinite is in itself its own self-same object – at once one and many, so that by itself it is and knows itself and is sufficient to itself without change, so that the selfsame is the abundant magnitude of its unity?"
>
> (Book 13; chapter 11)

Augustine affirmed the existence of eternal realities like truth and goodness, but he denied that they existed apart from God (as in traditional platonic thought). Rather, he insisted that they were grounded in God's mind as eternal thoughts. The Triune God also created this real world of multiplicity and unity – He created it good and able to be known by human beings.

(b) Faith and reason

To Augustine, radical skepticism was self-evidently false. He famously rebutted those who claim that no proposition is true or that no one can know anything with a version of "I think, therefore I am" that long preceded Descartes. Augustine quipped: *"If I am mistaken, I am"*.[3] If one does not exist, how can one be wrong? However, Augustine was no rationalist in the sense that came to dominate after the Enlightenment. He breached the often separated realms of faith and reason. Thus, this classic refutation was not a basis for an autonomous proof of God; it was rather a skepticism defeater. The closest we get to an argument for the existence of God from a philosophical point of view is Augustine's famous argument from truth, which I look at in greater detail in chapter 7.

So, for Augustine, the world could be known, but how is it known? This brings us to Augustine's critical view of faith and reason. He saw faith as an indispensable part of any act of knowing. His defining phrase, *"Credo ut intelligam,"* meaning, "I believe in order that I may understand," formed the basis of his belief that all knowledge begins in faith. This is true not just of religious truth, but of all forms of knowledge. We all believe many things before we can speak of acquiring knowledge. We all believe the testimony of others on innumerable matters, like history, for example. We all *believe* things about our thinking faculties that are *logically prior* to the knowledge we gain *through* those faculties. None of this negates the importance of reason. Reason has a place of central importance in order to examine the coherence and intelligibility of faith assumptions and knowledge claims. Faith and reason are like two blades on a pair of scissors! Even though faith is logically prior, even in terms of trusting reason, reason enables us to validate and strengthen belief. Both blades work together to cut in the direction of truth.

(c) Epistemology – how we know things

Augustine saw that to know *particulars* required a prior knowledge of *universals*. How could one have knowledge of daffodils without having some knowledge of plants in general? We must have some knowledge of universal, eternal, invariant forms such as goodness, truth, "treeness," "duckness" etc. in order to have knowledge of the mutable particulars such as good actions, truthful statements, oak trees, and Mallard ducks. Augustine held that this prior knowledge is the result of *God's illumination* of all human beings. By using the analogy of physical sight and the sun's illumination, he argues that God illuminates the soul and gives mental sight.[4]

God is truth, wisdom, and light; it is in Him, by Him and through Him that we have knowledge. God's illumination plays a role in every act of knowing. Our ultimate source of knowledge is the divine light that shines upon the secondary light of the human mind. Because we are made in God's image, there is a correlation between this derivative light (the human mind) and God, since it reflects the rationality of the Creator. This enables us to grasp, account for, and access the rational structure of the world. Teachers may point us to concepts and stimulate learning, but truths of math are not true because the teacher says they are. They are necessarily true, and I judge the teacher right or wrong as I consult truth within and "see it" for myself.[5]

Negative apologetics

Evil, suffering and free will

By negative apologetics, I mean the effort to respond effectively to objections that may be raised against the Christian, and help the inquirer move past such roadblocks toward faith in Christ. Augustine's ministry as a bishop, theologian, and apologist meant that his distinctly Christian philosophy was brought into conflict with competing worldviews and philosophies prevalent in the pagan and pluralistic context of the Roman Empire. This reality meant that he encountered all manner of questions and objections concerning his philosophy of life. One of these many questions he dealt with in detail was the now famous objection about the existence of evil and suffering in world – how could a good and all-powerful God allow evil in creation?

It is important for us to remember that this is a question every worldview must face, not just Christianity. Every worldview must address the meaning and origin of suffering and evil in the world, since it is a reality we all experience.

When the question is raised as an objection to the Christian view of God, Augustine understood this as a moral complaint against God rather than a legitimate reason to deny God's existence. Unless there is a God, there is no one to complain to and nothing to complain about! Sometimes this problem is formulated *existentially*: I do not like a God that permits these things to happen. This objection is often raised from the experience of personal pain. Sometimes, this problem is formulated *logically*: if God is all-powerful and all-loving, how is it that evil and suffering exist?

Augustine responds to these questions by building a Christian *theodicy* – a justification of God's actions in the world. As in most Christian responses, he seeks to solve the logical question and place the existential one into the context of the Christian story of Scripture.

Critically, the questioner should note that the question itself can only be grounded meaningfully from within a theistic framework, for the non-theist cannot find a basis for moral absolutes nor define good and evil. They are either illusions or exist only as artificial social constructs. Thus, at best, the question can only amount to a complaint about God's dealings, not the existence of a divine being that enables us to judge between what is good and what is evil.

The logical problem

1. God is omnipotent
2. God is omnibenevolent
3. There is evil

There is nothing formally inconsistent in these three premises alone, but we instinctively feel that a good God would want to eliminate all evil, and that is where the problem arises for us. But, are our instincts justified in this case? Could it be a false premise that a good God would want to eradicate every kind of suffering and evil? The answer is yes, so there is no necessary contradiction here. For example, perhaps the possibility of good presupposes the possibility of evil. It is conceivable that God has wise reasons for permitting evil (like protecting the greater good of liberty), even if we do not understand all of His reasons. In other words, the logic problem could be solved simply by adding the premise: "God has wise reasons for permitting evil."

From a Christian viewpoint, God cannot perform what is logically absurd any more than we can. The *coercion* of free choice is not possible! For Augustine, the will would not be a will unless it is in our power to make a choice. It is only because it is in our power that it is free![6] In any case, at what point would we propose that God intervene to reverse our freedom? Should God prevent the evil thought from entering the perpetrator's mind, or stop the murderer's blade as it is about to pierce the victim's chest? This would surely render human experience an illusion and deny that human beings really had a will of their own. It is possible that to create a meaningful world where love and goodness were possible, evil remains always a theoretical possibility in *any possible world*.[7] Perhaps this is the best possible world where human agency is meaningful?

With Augustine's *free will defense* in mind, the objection naturally arose that God is also supposed to foreknow every eventuality, including the sin of our first parents and our subsequent evil actions, yet He still chose to create the world. In that case should He not be deemed finally responsible for evil? Could human beings really have chosen any other course of action than that which God foreknew they would choose? In other words, the objection rests on the premise that God's foreknowledge implies that our actions cannot be truly free, thus undermining the free will defense. First, Augustine argues that God's foreknowledge presupposes that there must be something to know, the power or determination in the will to know – that is, *there must be something not nothing in the will. Therefore, his foreknowledge, far from denying free will, in fact guarantees the freedom of my actions.*[8]

Foreknowledge, then, does not coerce. C. S. Lewis illustrated this point by reflecting on the hypothetical scenario of time travel. If I could get into a time machine and observe what you will have for breakfast on Monday next week and then return to the present with that knowledge, my knowing what you will eat in no way means that I have dictated what you will eat. We all recognize that if I have past events *in my memory*, like what I saw my dad eat for breakfast yesterday, one temporal direction, it does not follow that I caused them. Therefore, simply because foreknowledge goes in the *other* temporal direction, the future, it does not make that knowledge causal. Just because God has all the future in His mind, does not mean that He compels those future events to occur or is the *instrumental cause* of them. In the same way that things do not happen simply because we remember them, things do not happen simply because I foreknow they are going to happen. To know is not to cause. Once known, the event is necessary, but as a contingent event, it did not happen of necessity. In the words of Gareth Matthews,

> "God's foreknowledge that one will act freely will guarantee one's freedom in that action, even though God's foreknowledge of what one freely chooses to do will also guarantee the outcome of one's choice."[9]

Strictly speaking, there is no past, present and future with God, and so no *fore*knowledge as such. In Augustine's Christian theodicy, God grasps all things in one eternal present. Even in our minds, only the present really exists, since the future is not yet, the past is gone, and the present is only the present as it becomes the past – it is here and gone! Yet, our minds stretch to comprehend the past through memory, the present through direct awareness, and the future through expectation. Given God's complete comprehension of all things, both time and eternity, *God foreknows, like everything else, His own actions, but they are nonetheless free.* The freedom of His action is not eliminated by His own knowledge of His actions! So, the idea that foreknowledge must mean coercion and the destruction of free will does not stand up to scrutiny.

Privation – Augustine's second solution to the problem of evil

What is evil? According to Augustine, evil is not something that exists in itself. Instead, it is the corruption of what is good. Since all things are created good by God, it is the corruption of goodness which we call evil. This view contrasts with many Eastern conceptions of good and evil as equal forces or ultimate principles that war against each other. In Augustine's thought, if something lost all *goodness*, it would cease to exist; things exist only insofar as they retain some goodness, since all substance was created good by God. Despite the fact that human beings are fallen and depraved through sin, they nonetheless retain a nature not devoid of goodness, made in *Imago Dei* (God's image) and likeness.

Evil, then, is lack or privation. Only God is unchangeably and perfectly good. All things besides God are finite and changeable. God cannot do the logically absurd and create an eternal, unchangeable being identical to himself. Consequently, as creatures, Augustine argues, our goodness can be increased or diminished. Thus, for good to be *diminished* is what we call evil, and as such it is real. But, unless the creature ceases to exist, some good remains to constitute its being.

Augustine argued that when people turn from God and His goodness, they diminish themselves and tend toward non-being. This leads to despair and meaninglessness. But when we turn toward God and His holiness, good is not diminished, but increased as we progressively reflect more and more what a human being was created to be. That is, we are increasingly "divinized" by our participation in God, becoming partakers of the divine nature as the apostle Peter put it. We do not become God, but we are conformed to the image of His Son, and so reflect the essence of what it means to be human.

Finally, Augustine argued that a picture can be good overall even though it has dark patches in various places. Our problem is that we cannot see the whole. Even though the ugliness of sin examined alone is awful, the eternal picture can still be good.

The great mystery and glory of the biblical faith is that Christ, the Son of God, enters human history, fulfilling God's eternal plan of redemption by participating in the human condition. Christ's miracles of healing and restoration were indicators of God's plan for creation, and in His death, He takes the consequences of sin and death upon Himself by His suffering and death. His physical resurrection guarantees our victory over sin and death and the re-creation of the corrupted order (Romans 8).

Illustrating the direction of Augustine's thought

How might we illustrate then, in broad terms, the general direction of Augustine's understanding of the ultimate questions in human thought? I wonder if you have ever seen a fish out of water. It flips this way and that, gulping for air, its mouth opening and closing as though it were trying to swallow a soccer ball. It can be quite a disturbing sight. A fish flipping about on the bank of a river is a particularly appropriate illustration of the danger of being removed from the environment in which you are meant to be. A fish in this condition is utterly hopeless, helpless, and in dire need of being thrown back into the water from which it came.

Often, we are so accustomed to our environment that we fail to notice it! This is similar to our experience in the presence of a loudly-ticking clock, which at first distracts us, but then we become so accustomed to the sound that we no longer hear it. This process is called habituation. A fish is, apparently, quite naturally and blissfully unaware of its utter dependence upon its life-sustaining environment. It swims, feeds, breathes, and lives, being totally sustained by and in the water and its contents. It would be tough to explain even to a self-aware fish that it lived in a body of water. For this body of water is all it knows. Although certain fish surface occasionally and even jump out of the water, most live entirely in the deep. What alternative existence, then, could these fish compare with their watery one? Every moment of every day, every activity, is taken immersed in H_2O. This is all it knows. As far as the fish is concerned, that is just the way the world is. This watery, life-sustaining environment is taken for granted so it goes unnoticed. The fish is accustomed to the feel of water on its scales, it doesn't know that it moves through water. On the other hand, we humans are very aware of the water's unique sensation when we jump into it. The contrast is especially apparent when we get out!

We, like the fish, are also creatures. But what is our ultimate environment? In what do we swim? By analogy, we face a similar challenge as the fish when thinking about our life-sustaining environment. We are so accustomed to it that we are quite susceptible to being completely unaware of our dependence upon it. That is to say, our living, moving, and existing goes on in such a way that we rarely ask in whom or in what do we live and move and have our being as creatures. The fish is so immersed, encompassed, and enlivened by the water that the water is like the air is to us – *essentially invisible*. We don't divide the air and differentiate its parts. We don't think about it; we just live and breathe it. Our self-aware fish, then, might quite readily deny the existence of H_2O altogether, despite being entirely dependent upon it.

Here is the hook of this slippery illustration. What underlies, as a foundation, all of Augustine's penetrating thought is the view that we *participate in God* as our ultimate environment. This is not a materialist universe where everything is matter and energy. Instead, we are created, sustained, illuminated, and totally dependent upon God in everything. Our ultimate environment is God Himself. God knows and sustains our sitting and standing, our coming and going, our weeping and laughing, our cursing and blessing and our thinking and meditating. We are entirely encircled by the divine presence like fish in water.

When we look at the world, we see the ordered beauty of creation that speaks of God; when we make the *inward turn* and consider the self, our memory, sensation, time, we find God within as that still voice, the inner teacher.

In the Psalms, King David asks himself if there is anywhere to go away from the all-pervading presence of God. Can the highest reaches of space or the lowest parts of the earth's core be remote enough to escape the creator God? Can any point of the compass direct me beyond the distant horizon to a place where God is not? Is there darkness so bleak and black, like the ocean floor, which can hide me from His all-seeing eyes? David's answer is that there is no environment where God is not. God is our ultimate environment. For God Himself created our inward parts and forged us in the secret recesses of the womb:

> "Your eyes saw me when I was formless;
> all my days were written in Your book and planned
> before a single one of them began." (Psalm 139:16 HCSB)

This vision of God as the source, creator, sustainer and governor of all things is too much for David:

> "God, how difficult your thoughts are
> for me to comprehend;
> how vast their sum is!
> If I counted them,
> they would outnumber the grains of sand;
> when I awake I am still with You." (Psalm 139:17–18 HCSB)

The songwriter points out that even in his dreams, God is sustaining him and when he wipes the sleep from those bleary eyes at a sun-kissed dawn, "I am still with You."

Augustine's hero, St Paul, in his oration to the Athenians, tells the "wisdom lovers" of his generation that "in him [God], we live and move and exist" (Acts 17:28).

In his letter to the Ephesians, he describes our God as "... the fullness of the One who fills all things in every way" (Ephesians 1:23 HCSB). The God of creation so surrounds, upholds, sustains, and fills us in every moment of every day that we take Him utterly for granted. His life-giving Spirit is so pervasive and His voice in the heart and mind so constant that we swim through life, living, breathing, and animated by Him, while at the same time oblivious to our utter dependence. Yet, were it possible to pluck us from the river of our life, deprived even for a moment of divine oxygen, and lifted out onto the banks of autonomy and self-reliance, we would be as helpless and hopeless as the gulping fish dying on the shore. In essence, we would cease to be.

We are not unlike the scaly friends that adorn many a tropical tank in our living rooms. We have memories so short that we forget what has just stared us in the face and the daily miracles that typify human experience. *God's presence is so pervasive, yet non-invasive, that many will deny the existence of the water of life – God Himself.* But the very religious denial of God is only possible because of our utter dependence upon God as our sustaining environment.

Augustine commented that it is pointless to argue with those who deny the existence of God, because if they cannot see what is so evident in the internal and external world, our evidence will not convince them of what they are incapable of grasping. Rather, he argues, such people must humble themselves and believe, so that they may come to understand. Because God is within, calling and speaking to our hearts, and not just declaring Himself through His works without, we need only pause in the flurry of daily activity and listen. Here, in this secret place of the heart, we can obey God's injunction "On your bed, reflect in your heart and be still" (Psalm 4:4 HCSB). As we do, we can realize for ourselves the truth of the divine promise: "Be still, and know that I am God" (Psalm 46:10 NIV).

Christian truth and apologetic strategy

Transcendent truth

Before we talk about apologetic strategy in Augustine's two greatest apologetic works, *Confessions* and the great story of Scripture, *The City of God*, we should note a few things about the truth of our story and how we, as believers, come to understand it. We cannot possibly "contend for the faith that was delivered to the saints once for all" (Jude 3 HCSB) if we do not know the nature of our story or have any confidence in its truthfulness. Conviction is crucial to persuasion and we will be found lacking in both areas if we do not really have an unshakable confidence in the story we have to tell.

Central to Augustine's distinctively Christian thought was his view that words are appropriate for signifying truth. First, he argued, it is by faith that we believe truth is bigger than our minds. It is a precondition of knowledge. That is, we believe that there is a "real world" and a "creator of this world" which is distinct from our minds and consequently is unaffected by my subjective conceptions, perceptions and judgments about it. If this were not the case, "solipsism" (the mind alone is all we can know) would be all that is left to us – which would make the entire project of human knowledge utterly futile and every attempt to communicate a "state of affairs" of any kind a self-contradiction. Truth is an inescapable concept.

Augustine argued that a precondition of intelligible experience is that truth is above the human mind. $7 + 3 = 10$ is a truth of arithmetic. We conform our thinking to it, and the same is true of inferential laws of logic. Truth is, then, superior to our minds and is universal or omnipresent – it is in your mind and mine – I hope! Were this not the case, your comprehension of this chapter even at a rudimentary level would not be possible. Ultimate truth must also be invariant. That is, it will always be true and always has been true that "$7 + 3 = 10$." Were this not the case, then we could have no confidence that what is true this minute and the rational laws that apply now, will be true in the next few minutes, next week, next month, or next year.

The Bible tells us that God is truth. Scripture teaches us that without the God of truth, there can be no ultimate truth at all. So, the inescapability of truth that transcends the mind of the individual leads us to the inescapability of the God of the Bible.

As thinking subjects, we know that the very idea of truth involves cognition. Truth is present in our minds. Being an immaterial *mental category*, it is clearly incoherent to speak of eternal, invariant truth as existing in itself (as a pure abstraction floating somewhere in the material universe), we only conceive of truth (real states of affairs) because we have thinking minds. Truth is mediated through the mind. Thus, truth must first exist in an eternal, unchanging, spiritual mind that operates above all our minds. That mind must be God, as a reasoning mind is only found in persons. This was one argument that Augustine formulated for the existence of God.

Words as signs

When we speak with each other and when we read the Bible, words are used to describe thought. Augustine highlighted that words are signs that take our attention to the thing that is signified. So, when we listen to words or read them, we trust that the sign is a sufficient substitute for the thing itself, which is not diminished nor changed by the sign. But, the signs do not really teach us anything (see Augustine's dialogue *The Teacher*), because the sign only has value once we already know its signification. Like listening to someone speak in another language, until those signs are interpreted into signs we know and can understand, we cannot know what is being communicated. For example, if I use a word you do not understand, I need to use several other signifiers that you do understand for you to understand my thought. Unless we observe with the physical eye or the mind's eye what is signified, we cannot understand the sign. I could not possibly understand many chemical or mathematical equations because I do not understand what is signified. When these are explained with other signs, suddenly I understand the sign.

Ultimately, it is God in Christ, who "enlightens every man," who educates the human mind what is the reality represented by signs. In Augustine, God is a precondition of intelligible communication because one cannot describe a given sign without using other signs – verbal and non-verbal to express its meaning. That process cannot go back forever. If God does not enlighten us, then these signs signify either only other word signs (a vicious circle that gives us no ground for meaning in signs), or nothing can ever truly be known to human beings. If there is no God, then words are merely vibrations produced by random atomic activity via chemical and physical processes in the brain. There is no personal, purposeful thought behind signs in this worldview, no mental activity, only brain functions producing the random chatter we call sentences.

Augustinian apologetics uses God-given signs to communicate God's message.

Scripture is God's revelation to us; it is a great epic of his work in history. Its words "draw forth and transport" what God, the Author, has in His mind into the mind of the reader enlightened by Him. Scripture, then, has meaning. It *is* meaning – it carries God's meaning implicitly in it. That does not mean there are no difficulties with things that are obscure and ambiguous because of the difficulties of language. But these challenges spur us on to understanding, rewarding our zeal. Augustine therefore saw great value in obscure passages of Scripture.

We must never forget that human words are God's chosen vehicle for His special revelation to His creatures and they are therefore uniquely and divinely fitted to this task. Because words signify something beyond other words, they can be translated. Although this is not always easy to do adequately, *the very idea of revelation requires that words carry a definite meaning that can be discerned by the reader*. If this were not the case, God's words would not be revelation at all because the revelation could not be identified. The interpretative task is inextricably tied to the idea of revelation. Equally, sin would be impossible if we cannot know we have a true interpretation of God's Word – how can we define sin against God if we cannot understand what He requires?

For Augustine, Christ was the *incarnate Word*, the Logos, who established in history that there is a true interpretation of reality in Scripture. Notice that Jesus rebuked the Pharisees for their sin and error in interpreting Scripture, saying:

> "You are in error because you do not know the Scriptures or the power of God . . . have you not read what God said to you?"
>
> (Matthew 22:29, 31 NIV)

Jesus here presupposes that Scripture is clear– so much so, that His interlocutors are justly deserving of rebuke and the rhetorical question, "Have you not read?" In John 10:35, Jesus defends His own divinity by the use of Scripture, which He declares cannot be broken as He interprets Psalm 82 for them. The apostle Peter, aware of the challenge of correctly understanding some of the apostle Paul's letters, warns his readers that "ignorant and unstable people" are distorting the writings of Paul as they do the other Scriptures, and that this deceptive activity will result in their own destruction. Peter clearly believed there is a wrong way to read Scripture (2 Peter 3:16). If God's Word is not clear in its general substance, then men and women would have every excuse for believing all the wrong things and could not possibly be held guilty before God for rejecting an obscure and ambiguous "revelation." For Augustine, the Scripture is, in an important sense, self-attesting, carrying the key to its own interpretation within itself and to that extent, it is self-interpreting. There is no external key required, beyond the rule of faith and hermeneutic of love for God and neighbor (principles both derived from Scripture).

Augustine emphasized three simple criteria for interpretation of the Bible to be employed when the meaning of a passage is difficult. First, the *intention* of the writer should be ascertained to the best of one's ability. Second, the *context* for the passage should be examined. Lastly, the *rule of faith* should be applied. By the rule of faith, he meant that if an interpretation implicitly or explicitly undermines the orthodox Christian faith as delivered by the apostles and contained in the Church's creeds and tradition, such an interpretation was incorrect. It should also be added that Augustine's humble assessment of himself meant he acknowledged that his literal understanding might not be as literal as it should be. He felt there may be better explanations and acknowledged, "I myself may quite possibly come to a different interpretation that corresponds even better with the words of the Holy Scriptures."[10] We ought to note that his criterion for improvement is a better correspondence with the words of the Holy Scripture.

God has spoken. God has communicated clearly in rational human language in the Scriptures and God is the first language-user. The Word, the *Logos* of God, is the final point of reference for meaning and truth. Furthermore, words have an objective meaning; they are signs that point to something real beyond themselves – the thing signified. Furthermore, as human beings made in God's image, we are capable of understanding and determining, though not necessarily infallibly, what words mean and what is intended by them. The presupposition of all communication and all literature is that we are capable of determining the meaning of another person's words to us. We can employ historical-grammatical exegesis to understand a text. This is essentially the process of formally and carefully doing what we all do regularly and unconsciously in our communication with others, reading a book, or watching television. Those principles that we employ are our hermeneutic – the way we interpret the meaning. So, if we employ a careful method of exegesis with Scripture, taking into account the textual context, the historical situation, the semantics and relationships of the words, we are able to make sense of God's Word. If we hold to the truth of Scripture, and accept that it was given for us to understand by the God of all truth who cannot lie and does not change, we find that many interpretive problems disappear.

Although we do not share precisely the same linguistic and cultural context as the biblical writers, we share a great deal in common simply by virtue of being human beings, language users, made in God's image and part of the same family history. In fact, contemporary western culture has much in common with first-century Rome. More importantly, we share with the biblical writers the gift and presence of the Holy Spirit. The fact that we can understand and translate the ancient text (indeed the fact that translation of the Bible is possible at all) shows that we can understand, and get at the meaning of, words of those who do not share an identical context.

This should give us pause today before we accept that there is no criterion to judge between the true and the false or that orthodoxy itself is a fluid concept. If that were true, no text could carry definite meaning, certainly not a text claiming to be divine revelation. God has revealed Himself in the nexus of His Word, act, and incarnation in history. By the Holy Spirit, the Apostles who knew our Lord and had Scripture interpreted by Him handed down the tradition, the rule of faith, and the New Testament Scriptures from which that rule was derived. This is the "authority of the catholic (universal) church" that Augustine argued supported his own faith. The ecumenical counsels summarized for us the faith of the Church, and Christ as Lord of history has not permitted that orthodox faith to be lost, but has preserved it for all time. Orthodoxy is an inescapable concept and we have not been deceived in our understanding of Scripture for the last 2,000 years. The orthodox faith of the Church provides boundaries, inside which we progress in knowledge, love, and faith and grow in our understanding of His Word.

We are guided by God's Church in history, the Holy Spirit, laws of thought and the historical and grammatical work of those who have labored down through the centuries. To deny the role of tradition and the rule of faith is to posit your own personal and individualistic brand of authority. Andrew Sandlin writes with insight:

> "The Scriptures come to us in human language, but this language was in fact created by God to suit His revelatory purposes. The Scriptures come to us by means of the writing of mere humans, but the mere humans were created by God to serve as vehicles for His revelation. The Scriptures are transmitted to us in human history, but God predestines this history [and mainly His Church in history] as the matrix within which His Word is preserved. The Scriptures address all sorts of topics, heavenly, earthly, historical, ethical, scientific, artistic, and on and on; and the God Who inspired the Word shaped every single aspect of the universe of which His Word speaks. Therefore, we can never speak of any aspect of the Word of God as though it were contingent on the world, any more than we can speak of any aspect of the universe as though it were anything other than contingent on God."[11]

Because revelation and interpretation are bound together, to deny the possibility of truthful interpretation constitutes a denial of revelation, even though that revelation is interpreted by human beings who are fallible and imperfect. In order for us to begin to engage in the rhetorical art of apologetics, we need a firm basis upon which to tell the story – that story being God's authoritative interpretation of reality in His Word, over against the rebellious "interpretations" of fallen men and women. Modern literary deconstructionism (and post-structuralism), which denies there is a common understanding between the author and interpreter, thereby making the reader the creator of meaning, is simply another human device for escaping God and meaning by denying the thing signified. For them, there is no transcendent signification – words signify nothing beyond themselves, and are useless for communicating meaning outside of a particular interpretative community. However, we must assume that they want the general reader to understand their meaning and not distort the words of their books! Ronald Nash summarizes the Augustinian view well:

> "Human language is adequate as a vehicle for divine revelation and for human communication about God because it is a divinely given instrument. God can therefore reveal truth about himself through words."[12]

We come now, having examined the source of our story and its authority, to the question of the competing stories in the world. Here, Augustine comes in to help us with our rhetorical strategy.

Augustine's apologetic classics

In his intriguing book, *Engaging Unbelief*, Curtis Chang refers to the classic status of Augustine's works, such as *The City of God*. Epics like this, he suggests, should not only be preserved but unleashed and retold in our time. This is because they embody the Church's mission. He writes:

> "This mission is suggested in really wonderful epics like the *Lord of the Rings* trilogy or the *Chronicles of Narnia*. In those tales there inevitably comes some moment when our heroes feel overwhelmed and unequipped as they face some daunting challenge. Our heroes can move forward only by encountering some treasure from the past. It might be a cache of ancient weapons: swords and amulets that our heroes need to relearn how to wield. Almost always, those old weapons and tactics turn out to be the only way to overcome the current obstacle. Or the treasure may be a tale of ancient battles – a grand story that our heroes retell. And almost always that story emboldens them to face anew the challenge before them."[13]

Augustine's work can offer us this kind of inspiration, tools that we can use in our own context to help win the day. It is part of the task of apologetics to foster a correspondence between us living today and ancient authors. As Chang puts it:

> "We preserve ancient strategies, swords and songs. We repair and compare them. We treasure them, not to inspect them with evermore minute attention, but to ready them for the day when they will be needed again. We . . . need to be willing to restore and retell grand stories for our day. For we must give the Church stories compelling enough to captivate its challengers. Lose the Epic and you risk losing the Epoch."[14]

There is a tremendous insight for apologetics here. We must not lose the era in the West because of a failure to share and defend the great epic of God's work in history – that is what true apologetics is all about.

Narratives in collision – The City of God's *rhetorical strategy*

The main error that prompted the writing of Augustine's most massive apologetic work, *The City of God*, was that Christianity had essentially caused the problems that now stalked the Roman Empire, especially the fall of the "Eternal City" when the gothic invaders, led by Alaric, sacked and captured Rome. The desire among pagan elites to blame these events on the Christians was very strong. Surely, if the empire had remained pagan, this would never have happened! Augustine's friend Marcellinus appealed to Augustine to answer these charges.

It had been a hundred years since Constantine's famous conversion, after which, following decades of persecution, Christians enjoyed freedom to worship. Many Christians were themselves deeply troubled by the fall of Rome, questioning why God had allowed it to happen just when signs were improving for the Church. Augustine rose to the challenge and twenty-two books and fifteen years later, he finished his epic response, *The City of God*.

Augustine's life took place in a time of great change in history. We now identify this period as the transition from the ancient to the medieval era. Curtis Chang calls the great shifts that threaten the Church's existence "epochal challenges."[15] These are times when Christians feel as if the ground beneath them is shifting, like an earthquake, when the points of reference that guided how they occupied their era start falling around them. These moments can also be called paradigm shifts.

Postmodernity (a somewhat elusive but pervasive mood) represents such a rapid paradigm shift over the past fifty years that it has been disorienting for the Church. This paradigm challenges previously held norms and truths. Chang writes:

> "Thus postmodernity conceives of religion as radically relative, depicts history as a Nietzschean record of the raw will to power and exercises a general hermeneutic of suspicion toward all literature ... the fragmentation

> of Western culture splits Christianity's historical alliance with that culture, while also giving rise to histories that implicate Christianity in a wide range of the culture's ills, racial conflicts, the ecological crisis, battles over sexuality and gender . . . escalating conflict between the Church and the rest of society is a frequent symptom of an epochal challenge."[16]

Augustine's generation stands in a certain historical relation to our time and it is here that our "cloud of witnesses" can help us with appropriate spiritual tools in the current struggle. The indirect rhetorical strategy of *The City of God* is to "Take every thought captive." I am completely indebted to Curtis Chang for his insightful use of Augustine's great work. This strategy as outlined by Chang has three components. The first phase involves entering the challenger's story; the second part requires a re-telling and reinterpretation of the challenger's story and the third move is capturing the re-told story within the great biblical meta-narrative.[17]

Entering

This simply means that when we enter the challenger's story, we seek to relate to them on their own terms and with their own authorities. We put on their lenses; we get into their shoes and mode of thinking in order to find a meeting place in terms of their paradigm and perspective. This is what Augustine does with respect to paganism in the first volume of *The City of God*, citing pagan authorities like Varo.

The story of pagan Rome that Augustine relates is that of a supposedly "Eternal City" that saw itself as established by the gods. Despite the growth of Christianity and the establishment of Constantinople in the Eastern Empire in AD 330, pagan elites still monopolized the institutions of learning, as they do today, and saw themselves as the authoritative interpreters of history. Christianity, in their eyes, had destroyed the beautiful pagan cults and brought the wrath of the gods upon them, much like the way many modern intellectuals blame Christian missionaries for colonial ills today.

Augustine meets this misrepresentation directly, entering the questioner's story with a great understanding of the pagan sources. The book is divided into two volumes; the first is a literal *tour de force* of classical learning where he relies almost completely on pagan sources considered authoritative. He surveys this material and explores it with great skill, highlighting the points of tension, contradiction, and failure of paganism and the absurdity of blaming Christianity for the fall of Rome.

Retelling

From inside the challenger's worldview, we now retell their story from the position of one who has already gained a hearing, and reinterpret it on the challenger's own terms. We seek to show that *our account* of their story – what it implies, where it leads, what it means, where it comes from – is the best interpretation of their story. We rework their story to highlight its tragic flaws, the inherent weaknesses or points of tension that spell its destruction, and focus on the things that highlight their inconsistencies.

Augustine argues that his rendition of the non-Christian story is more true based on the non-believers' own standards. He relentlessly unmasks the pagan pretence of honor and its scoffing at Christianity, by showing that the so-called glories of Rome with their long since defeated gods, were little more than splendid vices revealing only a perverse love of domination and an insatiable greed for human praise and glory. Augustine criticizes Rome for having never been a truly great city because of its lack of justice. No city can be just if it withholds from God the worship due Him. Repeatedly he exposes inconsistencies and half-truths, unmasking selfish power games as he reveals that demons are behind the so-called gods of Rome. This demonic spirit is its "tragic flaw," as Chang puts it, "a weakness intrinsic to one's very nature that will inevitably lead to downfall,"[18] and he identifies not human beings, but spiritual wickedness at the root of Rome's destruction and decay just like it had been in Sodom and Gomorrah. Unlike them, Rome escaped more lightly because of the presence of the Christians and the influence of Christianity on those who sacked the city. It was unusual for invaders to allow places of worship to function as safe havens; but the churches were left alone and so functioned as places of refuge for thousands during Rome's fall. Indeed, not only Christians, but also many pagans also took refuge inside churches.

In another example of reinterpretation, Augustine offers a fascinating survey of philosophy in the Roman Empire and shows how close to the Christian worldview the Greek philosophers had come in Platonism in identifying the one, the true, the good, the eternal, and immutable. But, they refused to accept the logical sequence and see the grace of God through Jesus Christ, where eternal wisdom became flesh, providing the way to God. Instead, he argued, you turn away from these attributes of God to the worship of many demons because of your pride.

By getting inside the pagan worldview, Augustine meets people on their own ground and reinterprets their story as one of human pride. Using their own sources, he unveils and deconstructs the pretense of paganism, exposing its tragic consequences.

Capturing the story

Finally, Augustine models how we can capture the retold story by captivating the mind and heart of the challenger with the biblical epic. We invite them into this story on our terms, calling on them to look at the world through biblical lenses. This takes the form of a great meta-narrative, that accounts for and explains all the other stories. That is, we retell the Christian account in a fashion designed to conform to the reinterpreted story. This final stage involves inviting the unbeliever to see a new view of reality, captivating their hearts with an epic that soars into eternity, reducing their story to a minor subplot with incidental characters in the script of God's great theater that is human history. Chang writes,

> "Like sanded pegs falling into the holes of a massive woodwork, all the reworked aspects of the challenger's story – whether they are the desires of its characters, the flow of its plot or the direction of its dramatic action – now find their final and true place in the gospel."[19]

In the second volume of *The City of God*, Augustine starts mapping a Christian theology of history, using an image found in the Psalms. The two cities are seen as two strands, birthed with angelic rebellion, intertwined in history. To capture the challengers' story, he weaves this wonderful epic in such a way that it resolves the non-believer's difficulties and captivates them. Augustine argues that the biblical story is a faithful record of historic fact. His epic tells of a God who created and governs all things and by His revelation to men and women through signs and symbols appropriate to the times, unveils the "holy ground" of history that has prepared men and women to receive the gospel. Augustine acts as the "unveiler" of the two cities and the distinctions between them. Again, Chang notes:

> "The central dramatic action of City of God, can be aptly labeled 'unveil'. History itself is a series of veiled allusions that require disclosure and interpretation. More centrally, the plot of the metanarrative in volume 2 is driven by the act of unveiling the City of God and the city of men."[20]

The final two books of the second volume paint a picture of a future moment when all history will be finally and fully interpreted in its proper light where the just and unjust will be made ultimately distinct, taking separates roads into eternity.

Augustine's new biblical framework of two cities, two peoples, two destinies, two loves, provides an entirely different narrative net that carries along the pagan story, bringing it to a different conclusion, without destroying its relevance and status. After all, God governs all history and all things therefore serve His purpose. The demonic nature of rebellion against God is revealed in the fall of Satan, the rebellion of our first parents, and the development of the two seeds in history. But, our redemption is possible in the person of Christ. He reveals that the biblical story has far superior explanatory power, and it explains the existence and meaning of the other stories.

Establishing a story's superior explanatory power is crucial to determining whether it can capture all other challengers. A meta-narrative must not only explain an external reality better than other stories; it must also explain the other stories themselves.[21] The gospel resolves the challengers' stories by showing where they break down and that the crucial points of tension can only be resolved in Christ.

In essence, the rhetorical art modeled for us by Augustine in *The City of God* is one of a contest in story-telling. Jesus often dealt with the Pharisees by telling stories that exposed the real nature of Israel's history and so reinterpreted their opposition to Him. For example, the parable of the wicked tenants depicts the Pharisees, who saw themselves as the purest and most enlightened representatives of righteousness in Israel, as wicked servants who would not give God His due, who beat and killed all God's messengers and even the master's son. The Pharisees were in little doubt about the meaning of Jesus' reinterpretation of the nation's history.

The face-off between early Christianity and Judaism produced a contest in story-telling. Which interpretation of Jewish history was correct? Was Jesus' interpretation of a rebellious nation that did not recognize the time of God's visitation, a nation that was supposed to be a "light to the gentiles" and courier of the promises, or the Pharisees' interpretation that was correct? For the Pharisee, Israel as a nation-State was chosen and superior to all by simple bloodline and would once again throw off the pagan oppressor because God was on the side of a national, geopolitical Israel. However, the New Testament re-tells the story of the seed of Abraham, not as a mere bloodline, but as a *spiritual seed of faith* and Christ as the *fulfillment* of all the promises.

Postmodernity, despite its claims, has its own meta-narrative that seeks to trump modernism and its predecessors, interpreting all grand stories as the naked "will to power." Yet, the essential implication of postmodernity is that no story can legitimately evaluate the truth of another, since truth is subjectively and culturally conditioned. Claims to overarching meaning of an absolute or objective character merely hide the motives of violence, power, and control. All such claims are thus to be viewed with suspicion and rejected. Instead, an "infinite openness" to the "other" and resistance to assign definitive meaning to language, literature, or life, is the *only right way* to encounter and understand human thought. This constitutes one of the contradictions inherent within the narrative thought of postmodernity that claims to be nonviolent and rejects the notion of coercion. *One cannot have it both ways.* Either the postmodern account constitutes a true story, capturing and unmasking all others, or it does not. This highlights a radical self-contradiction that collapses relativistic claims by their own weight. By its own narrative structure and way of speaking, it reduces itself to just another power play with absolute intent. If the postmodern claims are true and not false, they become incapable of evaluation, and so cannot offer a critique of the absolute claims of Christianity.

Augustine held that the Scriptures offer an all-encompassing story. Our task is to tell the story in such a way that it takes every other story captive to the obedience of Christ. When stories come into conflict, which story will expose and unmask the other? Is Christ about to be unmasked by skepticism, paganism or whatever other stories are being told in our generation? Augustine wrote:

> "It was by means of the true religion alone that it could be made manifest that the gods of the pagans were nothing but unclean spirits who used the memory of people departed or the images of earthly creatures to get themselves reckoned as gods ... [F]rom their horrible and hateful domination a man is delivered by faith in Him who showed us the way to rise by going to a depth of humility as great as the height of pride from which they fell."[22]

The human city, in its pride, believes that it is the ultimate source of meaning and unity. It is not. It is unable, without the triune God, to find overarching meaning or unity in diversity. Neither Rome nor Byzantium, France nor Britain, Spain nor America is the marriage partner of Jesus Christ. Rather, His Bride is the Church from every nation and every epoch. For Augustine, the resolution of all conflict is possible and human beings possess the basic urge for reunification, but it can only come in and through Christ. Ultimately, this moment fully comes at the conclusion of history when the manifestation of that peace is found in submission to Christ who does us no violence when He subdues our self-destructive pride.

There is the world of difference between willing and grateful surrender and an act of violence. Chang points out that the gospel of Christ involves a very real human surrender that implies no violent coercion. The gospel exposes postmodernism's tragic attachment to pride and self-sufficiency that insists all surrender is obliteration and coercion. There is a self-surrender that is love – the love of Christ that unites humanity to God.[23] This is the gracious conquest of God through Christ at the cross to bring human beings to their destined perfection by love.

Until we acknowledge God as the source of all power and meaning, we live under the tyranny of sin and sinful people who exert the fallen "will to power" and oppress in the name of morality, enlightened rationality and human liberty. Augustine's epic reaches its great conclusion with the biblical story of final judgment where all the apparent ambiguities, power plays, conceits, and confusions are finally brought to rest – a resolution to the epic story that resolves all others into a meaningful conclusion.

Confessions: *a personalist apologetic*

Augustine's approach to apologetics rested on the basic assumption that not only do we all seek truth, but we all desire to know happiness as well. We look for a coherence that adequately accounts for human experience and brings us a happy life. That may sound strange in this current culture, but truth and wisdom are inescapably connected to the human desire for happiness. Even the classic skeptic who claims to doubt everything believes he or she has arrived at the philosophical position that is most "true" and opposes those who deny skepticism. Usually, the skeptic argues that Christian revelation is oppressive and tyrannical. Yet much skepticism results from an existential despair of finding truth. Augustine saw that people act out of desire for joy and happiness yet pursue it in ways that lead to misery since God alone can give the truly happy life.[24] Although people want to be happy, they often do not want happiness God's way. However, since only God can give lasting happiness, their pursuit is in vain.

Augustine noticed that no one wants to be deceived. He argued that very few people would say it is better to be misled than to know the truth. Some people may enjoy deceiving others, but they themselves do not want to be deceived.

> "For if I ask anyone: 'would you rather have your joy in truth or in falsehood?' He would say: 'In truth', with just as little hesitation as he would say that he wants to be happy. And certainly the happy life is joy in truth, which means joy in you who are the truth, God, my light, health of my countenance, my God. This is the happy life which all desire . . ."
>
> (*Confessions*, Book 10, chapter 23)

The idea of the "happy life which all desire," Augustine goes on to argue, is a mental construct and is linked to the idea of truth, which causes us to prefer truth to falsehood – showing that in a certain sense we can't help but love truth and happiness. If we have this perception of both and a real desire for them, why is that people are not happy? Augustine makes his diagnosis:

> "Why are they not happy? Because they are more strongly taken up by other things which have more power to make them unhappy than that, which they so dimly remember, has to make them happy."
>
> (*Confessions*, Book 10, chapter 23)

This answer also helps us begin to understand why it is that, when we share the light of truth and happiness with others in the gospel of Christ, it often leads to their hostility and not to joy. Many Christians seeking to share their faith have asked themselves the obvious question, why does truth so often seem to "give birth to hatred"? Augustine gives this wonderful answer:

> "It is because truth is loved in such a way that those who love something else would like to believe that what they love is the truth, and because they would not like to be deceived, they object to being shown that in fact they are deceived. And so they hate truth for the sake of whatever it is they love instead of truth. They love the light of truth, but hate it when it shows them up as wrong." (*Confessions*, Book 10, chapter 23)

Augustine shows how blind the fallen human mind is in wanting nothing hidden from it while desiring to hide itself. What results is the opposite condition. The truth ends up being hidden from the mind while we ourselves are exposed! The longing for truth and coherence is basic to human beings, even if we are seeking that truth in an attempt to liberate ourselves from the need for coherence. These universal human desires for happiness and for truth are powerful points of contact for Christian apologetics. Augustine's *Confessions* demonstrates how one can use both personal testimony and apologetic persuasion to appeal to the desires for truth and coherence. He uses the analogy of a man on a journey home as a metaphor of finding his way back to God. In an age where many feel lost and disoriented, the theme of *coming home* to Christ is very powerful. Furthermore, Augustine does not approach his discussion of other worldviews with an air of condescension or contempt. Rather, having himself struggled with skepticism, ancient dualism, and Platonism, he relates with compassion, clarity, and understanding to those who are at those points in their journey. He recognizes that it is only by God's grace that he came to have faith in Christ, and that it is by grace that others will come to see the light of Christ.

The *Confessions* recounts the search of a lost, proud man who is graciously led to a road sign-posted "home," where his longings are met in God who was always calling to him from within. The world is just an inn, while the heavenly city is home. *Christ is both the route and the destination* on this journey home – both the way and the goal in Augustine's timeless story. Augustine's story reminds us not to mistake the inn (this world and its pleasures) for home (the manifest presence of God in the New Jerusalem). Just as Augustine's *Confessions* communicates this truth powerfully, so too can our own stories. Each of us has a unique journey through life. Each of our stories was captured by God's. As we share our faith with others, our argument is supported by our experience when it is communicated with authenticity.

Augustine's passion, conviction, and his love for God move and inspire people to this day. It is not only what is said but how we say it that matters as we communicate faith. I taught a course on Christianity in London, England, and a number of young professionals came to Christ. One of them, Charlotte, wrote a short endorsement for my first book that was based on the material from this course. She says, "Encountering this teaching was like having a blindfold removed. Suddenly everything made sense: the way the world is, the way my life is, everything. But even more than the excellent arguments and evidence provided, Joe's obvious love for the truth and for people astounded me and helped me open the door to the greatest love of my life, Jesus." I was genuinely surprised to find that my manner as much as my arguments helped move this young skeptic from indifference to faith.

As a struggling seeker, Augustine read Paul's words during his famous conversion account in the garden, and a "sweet assurance" came over him. The authenticity of his account comes through and touches the heart in *Confessions* Book 8, chapter 12. Certain passages function as "hinges," points around which the focus of the whole book turns. One such passage is found in Book 10, chapter 27:

> "Late it was that I loved you, beauty so ancient and so new, late I loved you! And, look, you were within me and I was outside, and there I sought for you and in my ugliness I plunged into the beauties that you have made. You were with me, and I was not with you. Those outer beauties kept me far from you, yet if they had not been in you, they would not have existed at all. You called, you cried out, you shattered my deafness: you flashed, you shone, you scattered my blindness: you breathed perfume, and I drew in my breath and I pant for you: I tasted, and I am hungry and thirsty: you touched me, and I burned for your peace."

A Christian's love for the truth will always communicate powerfully. At the end of Book 10 in chapter 43, Augustine comes to focus upon the person of Christ: the one who is truth in Himself. The ardor, passion, and conviction of his words speak for themselves:

> "How greatly you have loved us, good Father, who didst not, sparedst not thine only son, but deliverdst him up for us ungodly! . . . otherwise I should despair. For many and great are my infirmities, many they are and great; but your medicine has more power still. We might have thought that your Word was far from any union with man, and we might have despaired, unless it had been 'made flesh and dwelt among us.' "

Numerous volumes have been written on this great work of *Confessions*, and we cannot here even scratch the surface of the richness of this unique Christian autobiography. But we see in these two "hinges" how he seamlessly combines an articulation of his personal *struggle* in the search for truth, beauty, and peace with the presentation and defense of the *answer* to his longing in the gospel of Christ. There is no cold, distant rationalization here. Truth is personal and relational for him, even as he offers the *argument*, almost discretely hidden in the passage above, that without the incarnation we would despair of ourselves.

The *Confessions* is in many respects an extended prayer to God that the reader is given privileged access to. We encounter a man in faith, seeking understanding. Even as he wrestles with philosophical and theological profundities like the problems of evil, time, memory, and creation, they are not abstracted from the man as merely impersonal questions, but are seen as a deeply relational, personal, human encounter with reality. When we communicate the Christian message with personal faith, conviction, and passion as Augustine did, we will be far more persuasive than if we resort simply to cold argument. Christ is, after all, not merely the conclusion at the end of a syllogism. He is the Way, the Truth, the Life, the Beginning and the End, the Living One, our All in All, *the* image of the invisible God, who invites us to be with Him for all eternity!

Discussion questions

1. Why is it important for us to consider the work of great thinkers in history as we approach apologetics?
2. How do you think our own contemporary situation parallels that of Augustine, as it is described in this chapter?
3. What are some ways you could best *enter* and understand the worldview of those around you in order to engage it?
4. What do you think is the most significant or prominent story or worldview accepted by those in your circle of influence?
5. What do you think are the major tensions or implications of that worldview that you could use to *retell* that same story?
6. How can you tell the Christian story in a way that would be most compelling to someone from that worldview? What is it about that worldview that is ultimately fulfilled and explained in Christ?
7. Why is it important to tell our own stories in apologetics instead of just using arguments?
8. What stands out to you as the most important thing you have learned about apologetics from Augustine's example?

Notes

1. C. S. Lewis, *God in the Dock*, ed. Walter Hooper (Eerdmans Publishers, Grand Rapids, 1970), p. 202.

2. Ronald H. Nash, *Life's Ultimate Questions: An Introduction to Philosophy* (Zondervan, Grand Rapids, 1999), p. 146.
3. St Augustine, *The City of God*, translated by Marcus Dods (The Modern Library, New York, 1993), p. 370.
4. Nash, *Life's Ultimate Questions*, p. 153.
5. *Life's Ultimate Questions*, p. 158.
6. Gareth B. Matthews, *Augustine* (Blackwell Publishing, Oxford, 2005), p. 97.
7. This is a contemporary device that Augustine would not have used when considering metaphysical problems.
8. Matthews, *Augustine*, pp. 97–98.
9. Matthews, *Augustine*, p. 99.
10. St Augustine, *On Genesis: The works of St Augustine, A translation for the 21st Century*, translated by Edmund Hill (New City Press, New York, 2002), p. 161.
11. Rousas John Rushdoony and P. Andrew Sandlin, *Infallibility and Interpretation* (Chalcedon Foundation, Vallecito, California, 2000), p. 49.
12. Ronald H. Nash, *The Word of God and the Mind of Man: The Crisis of Revealed Truth in Contemporary Theology* (P & R Publishing, New Jersey, 1982), p. 120.
13. Curtis Chang, *Engaging Unbelief: A Captivating Strategy from Augustine and Aquinas* (InterVarsity Press, Downers Grove, Illinois, 2000), p. 143.
14. Chang, *Engaging Unbelief*, p. 143.
15. Chang, *Engaging Unbelief*, pp. 27ff.
16. Chang, *Engaging Unbelief*, pp. 19–20.
17. Chang, *Engaging Unbelief*, pp. 26–27.
18. Chang, *Engaging Unbelief*, p. 26.
19. Chang, *Engaging Unbelief*, p. 27.
20. Chang, *Engaging Unbelief*, p. 70.
21. Chang, *Engaging Unbelief*, p. 84.
22. St Augustine, *The City of God*, ed. Vernon J. Bourke (Image Books, Doubleday, New York, London, 1958), p. 142.
23. *The City of God*, p. 153.
24. See St Augustine, *Confessions*, Book 10, chapters 22 & 23.

CHAPTER 5

Ethical Dilemmas and Christian Virtue

[This lecture was first delivered at an apologetics conference in Dubai for delegates from across the Middle East.]

> "What should we say then? Is the law sin? Absolutely not! On the contrary, I would not have known sin if it were not for the law. For example, I would not have known what it is to covet if the law had not said, 'You shall not covet.' And sin, seizing an opportunity through the commandment, produced in me coveting of every kind. For apart from the law sin is dead. Once I was alive apart from the law, but when the commandment came, sin sprang to life. The commandment that was meant for life resulted in death for me. For sin, seizing an opportunity through the commandment, deceived me, and through it killed me. So then, the law is holy, and the commandment is holy and just and good. Therefore, did what is good cause my death? Absolutely not! On the contrary, sin, in order to be recognized as sin, was producing death in me through what is good, so that through the commandment sin might become sinful beyond measure. For we know that the law is spiritual; but I am made out of flesh, sold into sin's power."
>
> (Romans 7:7–14 HCSB)

What is ethics?

Imagine a man is selling his seven-year-old family car to a young couple who are buying for the first time, so he points out some obvious defects that might need attention. However, he is aware of other defects and problems with the vehicle only an experienced motorist or mechanic would spot, including some engine trouble and hidden rust. None of these problems would involve immediate expenditure but could be costly to rectify, which would more than limit satisfaction with the purchase. The vendor wants to sell the car quickly and buy a new vehicle, but he also remembers how difficult it was buying his first family car and feels responsible to be as open about the sale vehicle as possible, even though a "bought as seen" mentality governs second-hand car private sales. What should he do?

The challenge of ethical questions

This is a tame example of an ethical problem that could affect anyone. Ranging from minor to major ethical decisions, all of us must face the challenge of right and wrong, good and evil, virtue and vice. In fact, we are all ethicists since we all make moral choices, whether we have given it much thought or not. In terms of the tough, philosophical groundwork, the challenge of ethics comes to us in the form of "meta-ethical questions." Meta-ethics does not address *what* is ethical, but *how we determine* what is ethical. In other words, which criteria do we use in ethics and how do we justify those criteria? These questions go right to the heart of the problem, what does it mean to call an act right as opposed to wrong? What *makes* a right act right? Ethical theories seek to answer these questions.

Ethical theories can normally be divided into two primary categories: **consequentialist** schools of ethics seek to determine what is right or wrong by the consequences of an action; **deontological** schools of ethics believe that we have a certain obligation to particular actions because they are right or wrong in themselves (from the Greek, *deon*, "obligation"). Traditional Christianity is deontological. Actions are deemed right or wrong according to whether they conform to God's law of love, which is a reflection of His character, rather than on what the consequences might be.

The challenge of ethical living

For the Christian, ethical or virtuous living is not of peripheral concern, but is at the heart of meaning of Christianity. Faith in Christ involves radical, spiritual, intellectual and moral transformation (John 3; Romans 12:1–2). According to the apostle John, anyone who claims faith in Christ but does not pattern their life on the "perfect law of liberty" deceives his or herself and is not a believer at all (1 John 1). The Christian faith denies that one knows God at all if the heart is not seeking after and pursuing holiness in daily living. Scripture teaches us that by virtue of people's creation by God, the image of God in them is ineradicable. There is an inward law, impressed upon the mind by the light of the Holy Spirit as part of God's common grace to all men and women. This knowledge formed the referent for the moral judgments of those without the revealed Law of Moses (Romans 2:14–16).

This leads us to understand that we are faced with absolute moral laws in life which should not be violated and for which no justification can be offered. For example, we hold that blasphemy against God is wrong whatever the circumstances. However, we believe that God commands that which brings about the best consequences and He alone is in a position to judge what is best. Therefore, we submit to rather than challenge His Word. To break these moral commandments, which are inscribed in the conscience and in the written law of God, is an affront to the God of all truth and to his image in the sinner and the one sinned against.

Though we know the truth and are required to act upon it, there is a complication; we are fallen human beings. When we reject God, we suppress the truth and often lack the desire to will what is good let alone the ability to act in accordance with it. Even Christian believers, who often have the desire to do what is good, continually fail by doing what we do not want and not doing what we do want (Romans 7:15–25). The Christian description of the fallen and corrupted human will accounts for this universal reality, which both ancient and post-enlightenment thinking are incapable of dealing with.

Scripture speaks of the will as created by God rejecting the illusions of absolute freedom, human autonomy, independence and neutrality. The will is a dynamic power used for righteousness or for unrighteousness – the reasons for which lie within the will, not some external causality. It is tossed and pulled in numerous directions by all kinds of desires. It is either turned ultimately toward God to love Him or away from God to love the self and we notice that our hearts and minds are not the same from one moment to the next; we are forgetful, inconsistent and changeable. The view that reason can tame the passions and govern the will (the ancient teaching of the Stoics rehashed in various forms ever since) proves utterly inadequate in the face of human experience. Thus, the Christian view of ethics emphasizes the need for renewal and transformation in Christ, by the Holy Spirit, who grants us the power *to will* and *to live* a changed life that conforms to His Law-Word.

The scriptural foundations of Christian ethics

The Bible as divine oration

The Bible plays a central role in giving us a foundation for ethics. These God-given Scriptures act for us as a light on our path and equally like a mirror enabling us to assess our progress in the Christian life. The Bible comes to us not with abstract philosophical speculations, but as specific concrete revelation, demonstrating God's holiness and His purpose in order that we should "be perfect . . . as your heavenly Father is perfect" (Matthew 5:48 HCSB). The Bible provides the *content* for our ethical *principles*. Foundationally the highest motivation for Christian living is love – for God and for our neighbor. Yet, rather than simply giving us an abstract, content-less, command to love, the Bible tells us what it is to love (cf. 1 John 5:1–3).

The God of the Bible calls us to *reflect* on His righteousness and to work for justice against injustice. We are to recover the law of God written in the heart (and engraved on the two tables of the Law) in our social environment. Scripture is the final standard by which we measure what is holy and what is unholy, what is ethical and what is unethical, what deserves retribution and what requires restitution. In the Old Testament, God's moral commands given to Moses contained what people should have been able to see through the light of their conscience. This was a preparation for the incarnation of Christ, who alone kept the Law perfectly, and so was the consummation of the Law. After the coming of Christ, the Holy Spirit inscribes the Law of God into the very desires of the hearts of believers (Jeremiah 31:31–34). Through Christ, we are now finally forgiven, free and *empowered* to do with delight that which the Law of God requires – to love God supremely and our neighbor as ourselves. Thus, Scripture, as divine oration, is the mirror for Christian living and should always be our final referent as we confront contemporary ethical dilemmas and value judgments.

The place of God's Law in biblical interpretation

In the Church today, we need to be careful to avoid both extremes of *antinomianism*, which totally rejects the relevance of God's Law for us today, and *legalism*, which focuses attention on a superficial externalism and Pharisaism while ignoring the weightier matters of the Law, the motivations of the heart and the transformation of society. In order to understand the role of God's Law in the biblical worldview, it is important to grapple with the nature and relationship of the two covenants, or the Old and New (or renewed) Testament. For example, it is common to hear people say that we are not obligated to keep all Ten Commandments provided we try to be kind and loving. However, one might rightly ask, "What are kindness and love?" If we ignore God's plumb-line recorded on the tables of the Law, how do we know with our rebellious natures, seared consciences and our remarkable capacity for self-deception what love in any number of situations really looks like? Christian ethics which seeks to avoid the Law of God becomes a subjectivist sea of ethical confusion.

The Psalmist tells us "The law of the LORD is *perfect*, converting the soul" (Psalm 19:7 NKJV, emphasis added). In Deuteronomy we read, "He is the Rock; his work is perfect. Everything he does is just and fair" (Deuteronomy 32:4). Moreover, Paul tells us in Romans 7:12, "But still, the law itself is holy and right and good." God's Law, given to Moses, was written by the finger of God Himself. So Jesus our Lord Himself said, ". . . it is easier for heaven and earth to pass away than for one dot of the Law to become void" (Luke 16:17; cf. Matt 7:17–20). Thus, all contained in the Law is righteous and true!

None of this is to say that we can earn salvation by works of the Law. The Law was given in part to manifest that God is so holy and we so fallen, that we cannot hope for salvation by the works of the Law. It is by means of the Law that sin is seen for what it really is. We all break some of it and are therefore guilty of breaking all of it, as James argues (James 2:10). Yet, although we are incapable of keeping the whole Law in and of ourselves, Christ tells us, "Until heaven and earth pass away, not the smallest letter or stroke shall pass from the Law until all is accomplished" (Matthew 5:18 NASB). So what is the role of the Law in ethics and how does one determine what has been *set aside* (*fulfilled*), and what continues to be binding in the Older Covenant?

Scripture itself teaches us several things about how to apply the Law. Firstly, the Law reflects God's character, and God does not change (James 1:17). Secondly, Christ came not to destroy but to fulfill the Law by meeting its demands with perfect obedience (Matthew 5:17). The book of Romans tells us that the Law of God is a mirror in which we see ourselves and our sinfulness. It highlights the sinfulness of sin and motivates us to turn in faith to God in Christ (Romans 3:20–22; 7:7, 13). The Christian is called to obey the Law in order to grow in *sanctification*, even though justification is by faith alone. It is no less than a call toward moral perfection (cf. Matthew 5:48). For the Christian, the Law of God is perfect freedom and there is blessing in obeying it (James 1:22–25). The Scriptures make very clear that obedience to the Law of God is a mark of a true Christian conversion (1 John 2:3–6). Without obedience, there is no evidence of a real conversion, because in the New (or renewed) Covenant, the same Law that was written on tablets of stone is to be inscribed as a desire in the heart (Hebrews 8:7–13). To obey becomes our desire and delight (cf. Jeremiah 31:31–34; Luke 22:20; 2 Corinthians 3:6). These are the basic principles that govern the relationship between the Old and the New Covenants.

In the New Testament it is made clear that faith establishes and does not diminish the Law (Romans 3:31). God establishes the terms of the covenant and He alone is able to amend, fulfill, or supersede certain temporal provisions. But He cannot set aside His own moral character any more than He can cease to exist. God is holy. He is what He is. However, the specific ways in which He has required His creatures to observe, celebrate, reflect, commemorate and approach His holy presence has been subject to progressive revelation since the fall of human beings from the garden of God. All of this revelation was pointing towards a new perfect fulfillment in the Lord Jesus Christ, who is the focus of the Law and Prophets – Christ is our Prophet, Priest and King who by the incarnation made His "tabernacle" with us.

Thus, I believe our guiding principle of interpretation is one of *continuity* between the old and new covenant unless discontinuity is *specifically indicated*. This was clearly the basic assumption of the apostles in the New Testament. For example, the apostle Peter was shown in a vision of "unclean" animals coming down in a great sheet that the dietary laws, ceremonial cleanliness laws, and the laws of separation from the Gentiles had been fulfilled in Christ, and so were set aside when the fullness of the "shadows" was revealed (Acts 10:9–28). Later Paul had to correct Peter when he separated himself from the "uncircumcised" during an early Church council gathering which discussed which aspects of the Law were to be kept by Gentiles (Galatians 2:11–16). Clearly then, continuity, not discontinuity, was assumed until God set something aside by revelation.

The book of Hebrews, and several passages in Acts and the Epistles, teach that the ceremonial aspects of God's regulations about the temple sacrifices, diet, cleanliness, and separation were illustrative. Their function was to foreshadow, to teach and to remind the people of God's holy and righteous character, their sinfulness, and the need for a covering (atonement) for sin. They were meant to point toward Christ's atonement as the fulfillment of these requirements. Now that Christ had come, these laws were no longer needed. Christ was the Paschal lamb, our true Passover! Christ's body, the new temple, was raised to life and now His living presence is within His people. Thus, when He died the temple curtain separating the people from the holy of holies (the sacred place of God's presence for only the high priest to enter annually) was torn in two. During His earthly ministry, Jesus also foretold the destruction of the temple some forty years before it occurred, a temple that has never been rebuilt; for access to God is no longer through the temple and its sacrificial system, but through Christ the lamb of God who takes away the sin of the world.

This leaves us the ongoing challenge of searching the Scriptures and interpreting them correctly. Although the ceremonial aspects of the Law are no longer necessary, since they were shadows fulfilled in Christ, the moral and civil aspects of the Law are still the perfect standard of righteousness for people and nations.[1]

Augustine and the order of love

When trying to apply these laws, it is helpful to remember that Jesus gives us a wonderful summary of all the Law and the Prophets:

> "You must love the Lord your God with all your heart, all your soul, and all your mind. This is the first and greatest commandment. A second is equally important: 'Love your neighbor as yourself.' All the other commandments and all the demands of the prophets are based on these two commandments." (Matthew 22:37–40)

Without the *hierarchy of love* Jesus refers to here, God's moral commands cannot be understood correctly. Without the foremost injunction of love, seeing God's righteousness and justice as an expression of that love, God would appear harsh in His exacting righteous demands. Love for God and our neighbor are the basis of all ethics, and the commands of God simply particularize this for us.

Love and do as you will

"Love and do as you will," is one of Augustine's most famous sayings on ethics and gives insight as to the essence of the Christian life. Liberty and freedom in Christ are truly realized through the joy of supreme love for God and then love for others, as much as we love ourselves. We love God because He is just and others so that we will be like our Creator and make others around us just, which is why sometimes true love involves discipline. It is only safe to "do as you will" when this order of love is rooted in the heart, for if we truly love God and our neighbor then our will is governed by God's Law and we will act justly. The best way to understand the complex area of ethics was, for Augustine, observing the order of love before everything else.

> "Just as the covetous man subordinates justice to his love of gold – through no fault in the gold but in himself – so it is with all things. They are all good in

> themselves, and capable of being loved either well or badly, they are loved well when the right order is kept, badly when this order is upset . . . hence it seems to me that the briefest and truest definition of virtue is that it is an order of love." (*The City of God*, Book 15, chapter 22)

The biblical understanding of the will is more than merely rational, deliberate choice. The will describes the very essence of what it means to be human – to be moved by love for something. The human heart can only serve one master; it will either love God or self supremely. Our love moves our will, carrying us toward what we love, so *what we love* determines *how we live*. Augustine writes:

> "The body tends toward its own place by its own gravity . . . fire tends upward while a stone tends downward. They are propelled by their own mass and they seek their own places. Oil poured under the water rises above the water, while water poured on oil sinks beneath. They are moved by their own mass and seek their own place. If they are out of order, they are restless, but when their order is restored, they are at rest. My weight is my love, and by it I'm carried wherever I'm carried." (*Confessions*, 13.9)

In a fallen world, we need the work of the Holy Spirit to reorient our will, enabling us to love and will the good contained in His Law (Romans 8:1–2). God has revealed what is good in our hearts (Romans 7:22) and in the revealed commands of Scripture. But we are not righteous simply because we know what is good. We are only justified in calling a person good when their actions are good. It is not just that they claim to know what is good, but because they love the good and manifest goodness by doing it. We are called not just to understand what is good, but to love and pursue that which is good. What is loved affects the will like gravity affects physical bodies it draws us toward the thing loved. This is why loving both God and neighbor are so important.

We cannot create love for God by our own effort. As we seek to obey Him, He works in our lives and gently aids our wills to love by the work of the Holy Spirit. The motivation for our obedience is equally important. If we only obey through fear, we are missing the fruit of the Spirit, who gives life, liberty and joy in obedience, when the Spirit is shed abroad in our hearts (Romans 5:5). As John writes, "Such love has no fear because perfect love expels all fear. If we are afraid, it is for fear of judgment, and this shows that his love has not been perfected in us" (1 John 4:18). To focus only on what we ought not to do misses the heart of Christian ethics. The focus should rather be on what we are to do – to love and delight ourselves in the Lord, to seek first His Kingdom and His righteousness or justice. When we are observing Christ's order of love, loving the Lord first, with our whole hearts, there will be no room left for any other competing loves.

Although there is joy in loving God now, we will not reach the consummation of all our desiring and loving in this life. We are pilgrims looking for a city whose builder and maker is God (Hebrews 11:10). Our loving is also *longing*. Augustine writes, "The whole life of a good Christian is holy desire . . . by longing you are made capable, so that when that comes which you may see, you will be filled . . . God, by deferring our hope, stretches our desire."[2]

Ethical arenas of today

Social ethics

The question of ethics is inevitable; no one can escape it since we are communal creatures. We are not singularities. By definition, ethics concerns how I live with others. All of us were created for and are born into a family and a society. Though the family unit was originally ordained by God as the basic form of human organization and government, the political organization and institutional relationships of society, which are manifest in government of the state, courthouses and so forth, are ultimately consequences of the fall of humanity and necessitated by it. They are God-sanctioned structures (cf. Genesis 9), which are raised up to restrain evil, protect the innocent, punish the evildoer, and so maintain peace and justice as far as possible. Paul writes:

> "Everyone must submit to the governing authorities, for there is no authority except from God . . . For government is God's servant for good. But if you do wrong, be afraid, because it does not carry the sword for no

> reason. For government is God's servant, an avenger that brings wrath on the one who does wrong." (Romans 13:1, 4 HCSB)

Although *perfect* peace and government will never be fully realized in this life because of the reality of sin, all people are nonetheless called to pursue righteousness, justice, peace and equity. As Paul makes clear here, governments and society as a whole are meant to serve God; as such they are held accountable to God's standards, not their own. Therefore, it is only permissible to disobey human government when it contravenes the higher law of God. This was made clear by Daniel's refusal to obey the edict of Darius to stop praying to anyone other than the king and in the New Testament when the disciples refused to stop preaching in the name of Christ despite the authorities' command to stop. An early Church example was Christians who refused to pay homage to Caesar as God who were thrown to the lions for entertainment in the Coliseum as a result.

Since the time of Cain and Abel, love of self and love of God have come into conflict. These loves are manifested throughout history in the functioning of human society. Augustine referred to this as the "City of God" and the "human city," which compete for allegiance amongst human societies. The common good is violated when the right order of love for God and our neighbor is violated. Thus, through its established order, governments seek to uphold the common good. Yet, those who judge and punish must do so with fear and trembling and in reference to the commandments of God's Law. Otherwise, as we see so often, they merely perpetuate the same injustice they are supposed to be preventing. The good of all human society rests on Christ's command to do to others as we would have them do unto us. God's people are called to remind governments and leaders, judges and politicians, that they are not a law unto themselves but are subject to God and divine Law, and will be held accountable to Him for their decisions.

Political ethics

The doctrine of the Trinity is central to understanding community and the function of plurality within unity. In what or in whom do we locate the principle of unity for the political organization of a society made up of many free individuals? How do individuals and family units in society relate to the organizations which make up the governing processes of the state? The state itself in a democracy is a collection of individuals sanctioned by and made up of individuals from the society being governed. Ultimately, however, there are only two possible sources of authority in life and only two ultimate principles by which human societies may be governed. Either we are creatures of God with intrinsic value in a God-ordained order and are under His authority with human authorities acting as vice-regents of that authority, or human beings are ultimate and possess their own ultimate authority creating their own law. If the latter were true, then we would always be under the arbitrary and tyrannical arm of the ruling elite or the dictatorship of the proletariat. Either the triune God is ultimate or humans are.

In classical cultures like ancient Rome or the caliphate of Islam, the state was the principle of unity and locus of authority – it was the final criterion for truth. The Roman senate even ruled on which gods could be worshiped. Caesar was to be worshiped as God; thus, the Roman state was deified. Of course, this led to tyranny. Tyranny is always the result of the destructive presence of sin, which has pervaded human society since the Fall.

Ever since the Fall, human societies have oscillated between emphasizing the individual and the collective in their perpetual struggle for a principle of unity in diversity. Without the ultimate authority of the Triune God and our participation in the Church through true worship and the communion sacrament there is no bond of love that brings together plurality within a wider unity. Instead, there is only an unrelated mass of individuals and thought patterns without a point of unity, or else an overriding totalitarian notion of unity, which cannot tolerate diversity, and so destroys it. Both of these options are seen in the political philosophies produced by humanism that constantly war with each other; we always lean towards anarchism on the one hand, or totalitarianism on the other. One destroys unity; the other destroys diversity. Biblical ethics alone provides for unity in diversity by the will of the transcendent Triune God, whose three persons are held together in unity of being by the bond of love.

Christians should not retreat from this world and its confusion, nor abdicate our responsibility as God's Church, but are to "fill the earth and subdue it," as commanded by God in Genesis 1:28. This involves social engagement and political responsibility. The ultimate good for all will only be found when life is patterned according to the "City of God," based on Christian virtue rooted in true worship, the right order of love. Without this, justice can never prevail. The Church, modeling God's Kingdom, is to be the sign and example of unity in diversity, love and justice, in a world alienated through sin.

Four principles must be considered as we discuss political ethics from a Christian perspective. First, God placed individuals in a communal context from the outset in the relationships of marriage and the family, and this context has an irreducible hierarchical element that needs to be respected. Second, the state is ordained by God to possess the coercive power to be a minister of justice in terms of God's standards. Third, we need to be aware that human institutions are fallible due to the corruption of the human heart and its lust for power and so be realistic about expectations for political institutions, in particular recognizing that it is Christ's regeneration and Law-Word that will make people righteous, not the fact that they are ruled by a "Christian" leader. Fourth, we must recognize that there is a liberty of conscience within biblical bounds. At times, inner convictions are the only recourse in dealing with some ethical situations, like those involving respect for a weaker Christian (Paul's example being food sacrificed to idols), certain aspects of commercial activity, charity and military service.

The psalmist exclaimed, "The earth is the LORD's and everything in it" (Psalm 24:1 NIV), and Christ said, "I have been given complete authority in heaven and on earth" (Matthew 28:18). The prophet Isaiah proclaims, "His ever expanding, peaceful government will never end. He will rule forever with fairness and justice from the throne of his ancestor David. The passionate commitment of the LORD Almighty will guarantee this!" (Isaiah 9:7). The Church is a central part and primary manifestation of the Kingdom that He is establishing, and so we should strive for the coming kingdom in every area of life and all spheres of influence.

Sexual ethics

Sexual ethics must be understood in terms of the origin and purpose of sex – here worldviews come into collision in our culture. If we are animals that arose out of primordial slime and obtained rationality through the cumulative effect of chance, then whatever occurs in nature is ethical since nature is all there is; the only criterion for sexual ethics would be "whatever is, is good." One cannot make value judgments about sexual ethics from the theory of evolution, since there is no outside referent. Any attempt will result in ethical standards that are arbitrary social constructs, which can be revised as society "evolves." Now many societies have abandoned their Christian underpinnings, we see that more and more sexual behaviors are considered permissible, and that there is much less recognition of the sanctity of human sexuality within marriage between a man and a woman.

Christian sexual ethics rest upon the full-orbed Christian worldview of creation, sin, and redemption as the salient facts of history that define human beings. The gift of sexuality is part of our God-given nature, but along with the rest of our humanity, it has been subject to the corruption and distortions of God's original design that bring pain and damage to the human person. God established the marriage relationship between one woman and one man as the *only* legitimate arena for sexual expression. The fruit of this coming together is children – the propagation of the human family who are to rule and subdue the earth under God (Genesis 1; 2:21–25; Matthew 19:4, 5, 6). However, sex was given not merely for procreation, but also for the joy of union, the mystery of two people of different genders coming together as one. Sex is a beautiful, sacred, and joyous treasure for married couples. All other forms of sexual activity mar the image of God in human beings who are made for sanctity. They are ultimately harmful and damaging both to the individuals who practice them and to society as a whole. For example, we are all familiar with the devastation to children caused by divorce and the lack of one or both parents and the devastation to spouses caused by unfaithfulness.

Although clearly environmental, psychological and emotional factors certainly have a role in drawing people into different forms of destructive sexual behavior, we are called to be a people of self-control. All practices that depart from God's ordained order for sexuality work for the ruin of those who participate in them (physical, emotional, spiritual) and for others who are affected by their behavior. As with any sin, we need to respond to sexual sins with compassion for the hurting, recognizing our own sinfulness and need for Christ's redeeming and transforming love. Furthermore, by repentance and faith, the Spirit of God comes in to transform our desires and enables us to govern our passions and express the joy of sexual union in the place ordained for it by God.

Conclusions

The uniqueness of Christian ethics is that it is summed up in love, which is a gift from God. The apostle John tells us that "God is love" (1 John 4:8) and that "God so loved the world that he gave . . . " (John 3:16). All other forms of ethical philosophy assume that we are naturally capable of virtue. However, Christian faith claims that people will never fully know and do what is good nor find truth and happiness without the grace of God.

This is the great divide between classical and post-enlightenment thought and the teaching of the Church. The former views human beings as rational and self-determining, perfectible through knowledge (education), while the latter views human beings as blinded, fallen and ignorant, in need of redemption and regeneration by grace. Humanistic ethics involve pulling yourself up by your own bootstraps. But this has proved itself impossible for millennia! Outward forms of observance or internal search for a god within, such as the Buddhist noble truths and eightfold path or the five pillars of Islam can never address the inward problem of human sin. In Buddhism, all ethical distinctions must break down, since there are no ultimate distinctions in ultimate reality, our current notions of good and evil are an illusion. In Islam, one's interior condition is unimportant; conformity to the pillars, a measure of behavior rather than intention, influences Allah to give entrance to heaven. Even humanistic secularists, who claim only to want the world to be "a better place" (although who determines what better is and by what criterion?), try to locate ethics within a framework of "not hurting anyone," and they find themselves in a losing battle with their own conscience. This is not to deny that non-Christians can do what is right; clearly as beings made in God's image, many people behave morally recognizing through the light of conscience that we should not wrong our neighbor, but Christians believe that true virtue is always oriented toward God. Only the God of the Bible, who reveals His own character and nature as love, manifests His love in Christ and transforms our evil desires by His Spirit. He gives us a new heart by a new birth so that we may be a people of love for God and each other. If it were not for the grace of God, we would all be left to live out the consequences of an ultimate self-centeredness – a hell of our own making. There could be no better summary of Christian ethics than what the apostle John gives us:

> "Dear friends, let us continue to love one another, for love comes from God. Anyone who loves is born of God and knows God. But anyone who does not love does not know God – for God is love. God showed how much he loved us by sending his only Son into the world so that we might have eternal life through him. This is real love. It is not that we loved God, but that he loved us and sent his Son as a sacrifice to take away our sins. Dear friends, since God loved us that much, we surely ought to love each other. No one has ever seen God. But if we love each other, God lives in us, and his love has been brought to full expression through us. And God has given us his Spirit as proof that we live in him and he in us." (1 John 4:7–13)

Discussion questions

1. Describe an ethical dilemma you have had personal experience of, either at first hand or observed. Why was it so difficult to know what to do in this situation?
2. Do you think most people today have a *consequentialist* view of ethics, a *deontological* one, or something else?
3. What do you think are the major ethical questions that people in our society are concerned with today?
4. What insights do we learn from the Bible regarding these questions?
5. How do you think Christians should respond when they disagree about these questions?

6. If you were an atheist, how would you approach ethical questions? Can you see any problems with this?
7. If you were a pantheist and believed that God is in everything, how would you approach ethical questions? Can you see any problems with this?
8. How can Christians most effectively use the fact that morality ultimately depends in God's nature, in apologetics?

Notes

1. For an outstanding study of the role of the Law in Christian Ethics see Greg L. Bahnsen, *Theonomy in Christian Ethics* (Nacogdoches, TX: CMP, 2002).

   For an excellent study comparing *five views* on the role of the Law with each contributor responding to the other, see Stanley N. Gundry (ed.), *Five Views on Law and Gospel* (Grand Rapids: Zondervan, 1996).
2. St Augustine, cited in, Carol Harrison, *Augustine: Christian Truth and Fractured Humanity* (Oxford University Press, Oxford, 2000), p. 97.

CHAPTER 6

The City of God

The end of apologetics

[*This talk brings together two related addresses first delivered at an RZIM Conference in Washington DC and the National Conference of the Christian Legal Fellowship of Canada in Toronto.*]

> "So now, little children, remain in Him, so that when He appears we may have boldness and not be ashamed before Him at His coming. If you know that He is righteous, you know this as well: everyone who does what is right has been born of Him. Look at how great a love the Father has given us, that we should be called God's children. And we are! The reason the world does not know us is that it didn't know Him. Dear friends, we are God's children now, and what we will be has not yet been revealed. We know that when he appears, we will be like Him, because we will see Him as He is. And everyone who has this hope in Him purifies himself just as He is pure."
>
> (1 John 2:28–3:3 HCSB)

> "We shall be in a city of which, my brethren, when I speak, I find it difficult to leave off." (Augustine's commentary on Psalm 84:10)

Keeping it real

Although our thoughts often focus on the apocalypse and new creation when we think of the "eternal city," perhaps we can learn most about the Kingdom of God by looking at how that Kingdom is expressed now on earth. We can see the final bliss of the New Jerusalem as the fulfillment and consummation of that which Christ is establishing by His presence on earth today through us. Thus, He taught us to pray, "Thy Kingdom come on earth as it is in heaven." As we read in 1 John 2:28–3:3, the exact nature of the final state is not fully known. Although we have some limited scriptural information, we are told, "No eye has seen, no ear has heard, no mind has conceived what God has prepared for those that love him" (1 Corinthians 2:9 NIV). Eternity in the "city paved with gold" is the great unfolding, unveiling, completion and fulfillment of God's divine plan – the Kingdom fully realized, paradise regained, the City of God, the New Jerusalem.

The tendency for us believers, given the amount of mystery that surrounds the eternal city, is to abstract this Kingdom from the life and the work of Christ now. This mistaken abstractionism leads to talk about "souls in heaven" rather than whole persons. This dichotomy emerges more from the classical Greek philosophy of human nature than it does from a biblical understanding. The Hebrew term for "soul" referred to persons holistically. Jesus refers to heaven as "paradise," a concrete, material image that signified a walled garden. Furthermore, this life in the presence of God has already begun in the present, and the final fulfillment is not different in *kind*, from what has gone before. All history has this consummation in view and the Kingdom's fulfillment is the perfection in *degree* of God's City in history.

The covenant consummation

Our final state is seen in the Scriptures as the final fulfillment of the covenant of grace with God's people in history. Our history began in paradise, a place of covenant relationship that was broken and where the first announcement of the covenant of grace was given (Genesis 3:15). We are shown heaven as a paradise where the curse is removed and where God's covenant people serve Him forever (Revelation 22:4ff.). Christ's victory over sin, death, and the curse is cosmic and all-encompassing in scope. It was a victory for material creation, not simply for immaterial "souls."

Our final state is not the "heaven" where those who are dead in Christ live now. They still await the full realization of the Kingdom. All of creation longs to be clothed with heavenly glory. Those who are alive, while not wishing to die, nonetheless long for mortality to be swallowed up by life (2 Corinthians 5:1–5). The Spirit given to us is a down-payment and foretaste of this re-creation. We are still waiting for our adoption as children, the redemption of our bodies, when the totality of covenant life in the City of God is fully realized.

The tale of two cities

One of the best images and pictures of the historic meaning of God's Kingdom in the world is found in Augustine's description of two cities and their conflict in history, culminating in the vindication and glorious realization of the City of God and the terrible judgment against the rebellious human city. In a letter to a friend about his intention to write *The City of God*, Augustine says:

> "There are, then, two loves, of which one is holy, the other unclean; one turned toward the neighbor, the other centered on self; one looking to the common good, keeping in view the society of saints in heaven, the other bringing the common good under its own power, arrogantly looking to domination . . . [W]ith these two cities intermingled to a certain extent in time, the world moves on until they will be separated at the last judgment.[1]

As he reflects on the fall of Rome in AD 410 and its causes, Augustine contrasts the temporal and transitory blooming of human empire – the city of the world in rebellion against God or the secular city – with God's people, the city of God from the time of Abel to the present.

Another classic of Christian literature that reflects on the biblical epic begun in God's paradise is John Milton's *Paradise Lost*, published in 1667. This work was prompted by the demise of Oliver Cromwell in seventeenth-century England. Milton was a devoted supporter of Cromwell and had hoped that Cromwell would bring about a Christian commonwealth of righteousness and justice. But after Cromwell's death and the return of the monarchy with Charles II, Milton felt old and blind in a world crumbling in ruin about him. He lamented the demise of a dream that had seemed so close – a kingdom of righteousness and justice, an illustration and growing manifestation of the Kingdom of God. He wrote *Paradise Lost* as he reflected on the fate of England. Soon, many more puritan Christians left for America to seek to build a true, independent republic to manifest the liberties and responsibilities of the City of God. Later, having been told by a friend that he had written only half the story, Milton penned *Paradise Regained*

These great works point us with hope toward the nature of the Kingdom of God. In the same way, the Scriptures, through the temporal and conditional promises to the people of Israel concerning the geographical location of the Promised Land, foreshadow the inheritance of the *entire world* for the covenant people in Christ. So here, we have a biblical, *concrete* analogy, in the history of Israel, a nation constantly in conflict with the pagan city.

Augustine highlights the antithesis between the two cities and the final state of both the righteous and the unrighteous. The progress of the city is not the progress to be attached to any specific national entity or empire. The City of God is much bigger and more glorious than that. He is not perturbed by the fall of Rome, despite the apparent set-back to the process of Christianization. For him, peace and justice, the two great aims of human society, are only realized in and through the Commonwealth of Christ. Babylon, the biblical image for the city of rebellion against God, can only offer a false semblance of peace and justice that rests on a partial and tentative agreement between selfish wills in constant opposition to each other. The peace and justice of the City of God is due to the perfect submission and joyous obedience of the subjects to Christ and His revelation, expressed in love to one another. Augustine rightly shows that the fallen nature of human beings outside Christ is revealed in the desire to live for self as the center of one's own world, believing the delusion that you are self-created and sustained. In the presence of God, a transformation is taking place that is moving toward completion throughout history. Love for God and for one's neighbor is the goal of the new society of kings and priests.

The Psalms reveal this same antithesis:

> "Rise up, LORD!
> Confront him; bring him down.
> With Your sword save me from the wicked.
> With Your hand, LORD, save me from men,
> from men of the world,
> whose portion is in this life:
> You fill their bellies with what You have in store,
> their sons are satisfied,
> and they leave their surplus to their children.
> But I will see Your face in righteousness;
> when I awake, I will be satisfied with Your presence."
>
> (Psalm 17:13–15 HCSB)

Two types are people are considered here – people of the world and covenant people. One group's goals and desires are all in this life. They are satisfied with the things of the world alone, so God fills them now with what is finally in store for them – more of the same – a self-absorbed universe of separation from God. But for the covenant people, David says, "we will see his face in righteousness." For the believer, the presence of God and the likeness of God are synonymous, so we will not only see God, but be transformed by Him. "Blessed are the pure in heart, for they will see God" (Matthew 5:8 NIV). "Everyone who has this hope in him purifies himself, just as he is pure" (1 John 3:3 NIV). Paul tells us both about the progress and nature of our transformation and reminds us that though we do not now see the kingdom fully realized in the temporal realm, the unseen reality of the City of God is an everlasting Kingdom:

> "We all, with unveiled faces are reflecting the glory of the Lord and are being transformed into the same image from glory to glory; this is from the Lord who is the Spirit . . . we do not focus on what is seen, but on what is unseen; for what is seen is temporary, but what is unseen is eternal."
>
> (2 Corinthians 3:18, 4:18 HCSB)

Thy Kingdom come – childhood and maturity

What does it mean, then, to live now as a citizen of the City of God, as a child of this Kingdom that *has* come and is *still coming*? As I was growing up, I had a firm belief in the Kingdom of God even though my understanding of it and the sophistication of my expression was naturally limited. Equally, my sphere of authority and responsibility in "Kingdom life" was very limited. This is proper, as we consider it something of a tragedy if a child is made to bear adult burdens and responsibilities. Growing up in a strong Christian family, I was taught the great truths of the Christian faith. However, the realm of application for these truths was limited in my experience to my immediate person, my ultimate salvation, heaven, and the sharing of the gospel with my school friends. My life was circumscribed by realms of authority in the family home, in school, and in the church we attended. At that stage of maturity, I could not understand or express a comprehensive application of this faith in the coming Kingdom of God.

Today, as an adult, some of the hedges of protection and authority that guided my life are no longer present. I am now a husband, father, employer, and defender of the faith, with God-given responsibilities. Hence, very quickly, my spheres of authority and the realms in which I am to apply God's Word and its *material authority* (as opposed to its formal authority) are greatly expanded.

It is not only a tragedy when a child is forced to be an adult prematurely; it is also tragic when an adult has never left the sphere of childhood. When able-bodied people of sound mind have never left home, gone out to work, or broken the ties of childish dependence, we recognize this as stunted growth. It is a "failure to launch," to be and do what they were created to be and to do under God – they are people with no regency under God.

Christians can also become stuck in the realm of childish faith and vision, failing to grow in the understanding and application of what they believe. The apostle Paul wrote of the distinction between childish and mature thinking by comparing it to knowing in part and knowing more fully. There is a maturing process whereby we move from seeing things partially to seeing with clearer perception: "It's like this: When I was a child, I spoke and thought and reasoned as a child does. But when I grew up, I put away childish things" (1 Corinthians 13:11).

One of the big distinctions between adulthood and childhood is *comprehension*. As we grow, we see new connections between things, thoughts, and persons, and so our understanding becomes more comprehensive. I see this in the different stages of my two daughters' development. At five years of age, one has become very articulate and she comprehends when I read her a story. These stories are becoming increasingly complex. I often cannot read the same story at the same time to both my girls because my other daughter is three years old and she can lose interest before the end of the first page of a book suitable for my eldest daughter. Likewise, my five-year-old easily becomes bored with the simpler and shorter books for toddlers, because she has matured beyond them.

One of the great challenges of our day is to move beyond thinking, speaking, and reasoning as toddler Christians. We need to begin to make the necessary *connections* in order to gain *a comprehension* of the spheres in which God calls us to operate as mature believers in His Kingdom. God's commission to men and women from the beginning of creation was to "Multiply and fill the earth and subdue it. Be masters over the fish and birds and all the animals" (Genesis 1:28). Furthermore, Psalm 8:4–9 reads:

> "What are mortals that you should think of us,
> mere humans that you should care for us?
> For you made us only a little lower than God,
> and you crowned us with glory and honor.
> You put us in charge of everything you made,
> giving us authority over all things –
> the sheep and the cattle
> and all the wild animals,
> the birds in the sky, the fish in the sea,
> and everything that swims the ocean currents.
> O LORD, our Lord, the majesty of your name fills the earth!"

Men and women were created to have comprehensive vice-regency under God. This is sometimes referred to as the "dominion mandate" by theologians and is still in force. God has never rescinded this commission. The Kingdom of God comes in and through the person of Christ and His redeemed people as they trust in and serve their Lord.

Our faith is a comprehensive faith that applies to every aspect of human life. If the kingship of Christ was recognized and applied in every realm, our individual lives, families, workplaces, society, and nation would be transformed as a result. Our childish neglect and retreat from the task of vice-regency under Christ the Lord has meant that we have often failed to engage communities, culture, government, and institutions with the law and gospel of Christ. Our sphere has remained the sphere of a child. Instead of making necessary connections from biblical truth to all areas of life, such as the home, law and justice, politics, education, the arts and cultural life, we have allowed our faith to become privatized in this increasingly secular context. It has become a personal, not a public matter, concerned only with the soul and the salvation of the individual. But, the Psalmist claims that God is Lord over more than just our souls:

> "The earth is the LORD's, and everything in it.
> The world and all its people belong to him.
> For he laid the earth's foundation on the seas
> and built it on the ocean depths." (Psalm 24:1–2)

In Matthew 28:18–20, Jesus effectively reaffirms the mandate to exercise regency and establish the Kingdom and City of God:

> "Jesus came and told his disciples, 'I have been given complete authority in heaven and on earth. Therefore, go and make disciples of all the nations, baptizing them in the name of the Father and the Son and the Holy Spirit. Teach these new disciples to obey all the commands I have given you. And be sure of this: I am with you always, even to the end of the age.' "

As a child, all I could understand from these verses was that I should be telling people about Jesus. I was concerned about my friends and wanted them to know Christ. I wanted them to go to heaven. I wanted them to know the joy that I knew. As important as this is, it was only part of the greater picture. There were more concepts to be grasped, connections I needed to make and responsibilities I needed to take on. The evangelical church has been greatly concerned about personal salvation and going to heaven. And while these are important concerns that should not be forgotten, to focus on them alone overlooks the comprehensiveness of our faith. Christ is not merely concerned with saving individual souls, but also with saving *people as whole communities*. He wants to redeem marriage partners, whole families, and the generations to whom His promises apply. He does not simply want to remove people from the world into heaven, but He wants to bring heaven to people through the Kingdom of God: "May your Kingdom come soon. May your will be done here on earth, just as it is in heaven" (Matthew 6:10). This world is His and He has come to redeem it – this includes our philosophy, literature, music and science, our institutions and laws – every aspect of life so that, as Paul tells us, "whatever you do, whether you eat or drink, do it all for the glory of God."

Engagement or retreat?

Sometimes Christians talk as though Jesus is only concerned about delivering a tiny band of defeated holdouts out of a world run by Satan and into heaven. But Jesus tells Peter that hell's gates will not be able to hold against the advance of God's people (Matthew 16:18). This is not the gates of hell pressing down God's Church. Consider for a moment the picture of gates running towards you, crushing and threatening, with cowering, almost defeated followers underneath. No! the picture is the other way round, not a few believers just surviving the onslaught, but rather God's people are the advancing army besieging the gates, applying the victory of Christ at the cross so that hell's gates cannot resist the "increase of His government and peace" (Isaiah 9:7). Since, as Jesus taught, the strong man who is Satan has been bound and stripped of his authority, we now take from Satan by Christ's authority all that he has stolen and ruined, restoring and reconstructing all things in terms of Christ's lordship. He is not going to abandon His creation in despair, but He has a sovereign plan for victory in history, called the "Kingdom of God," the City of the Great King. As we have already noted, one day we will be fully adopted as God's children and our very bodies will be transformed and redeemed (Romans 8:23).

When the Church retreats from engaging with culture, it is a sign that the growth of the Church has been stunted. Institutions, arts and sciences, schools, legislatures, and governments are surrendered to humanism and the Church is no longer involved in the apologetic task – contending for the faith in every area of life and offering a reasoned defense. In effect, this is an abandonment of the Great Commission. The call to be comprehensive in our application of the faith is a call to maturity out of infancy. It is a call to take the Word of God for what it says:

> "In the last days the mountain of the LORD's house will be established at the top of the mountains and will be raised above the hills. All nations will stream to it and many people will come and say, 'Come let us go up to the mountain of the LORD to the house of the God of Jacob. He will teach us about His ways so that we may walk in His paths.'" (Isaiah 2:2–3 HCSB)

To live in terms of the eternal city now, proclaiming Christ's resurrection to contemporary society in appropriate terms for *our* culture is to affirm a real plan of God in time – the central teleology of the historical process. The biblical Christian is neither an abstractionist, taken up purely with ideas and avoiding applying faith to the particulars of life and work, nor caught up in a pietism that abandons the world for a purely future heavenly state. This line of thought is a direct descendant of Greek dualism and the early Christian heresy of Manicheism, so vigorously opposed by Augustine, which saw the material world as not merely secondary but *essentially evil*, a product of a principle of darkness warring with that of light in the cosmos. Instead, the Christian is to recognize that the Pilgrim City of God in the world, whilst not indulging utopian dreams of human betterment without Christ's regenerating work, nor confusing God's Kingdom with temporal human empire's or institutional membership, must live life completely in terms of Christ's lordship – manifest most gloriously in God's Church. The more people embrace the lordship of Jesus, the more transformation takes place in the world – towns cities and nations.

The Christian faith represents a direct challenge to the modern state's claim to sovereignty and lordship, because it claims that Christ is King and sovereign over all. This faithfulness to Christ's lordship is what led to the confrontation between the imperial state and the early Church in the Roman Empire under Caesar. For the Roman emperor's claim for himself was nothing less than divine status and absolute lordship – a divinized state, the cult of Caesar as God. All subjects, including Christians, must offer incense to Caesar or be accused of atheism, sedition, or superstitious abomination. Our Christian forebears were thrown to lions, burned alive and made sport for the mob in the Coliseum for their faithfulness to Christ's lordship! They were good citizens but refused to acknowledge any Lord (authority) above Christ; neither must we.

God's plan for victory

Each perspective, whether Christian, Islamic, or humanist, is a blueprint for the future. Augustine's monumental apologetic work, *The City of God*, became something of a blueprint for the Christian Middle Ages. Those years were by no means perfect, but much good can be said of them. In Anglo-Saxon England before the Norman invasion, the Christian Church provided a structural hierarchy where the foundations of freedom, justice, liberty, and righteous rule were already laid, paving the way for many of our modern institutions of government, such as democracy, that we now take for granted in the West. However, in the last two hundred and fifty years, the Christian vision and blueprint of the future has slowly been replaced by a utopian humanistic one. This is simply another tower of Babel. Humanists believe that if we just invent and pass enough laws to alter people's environment, they will be transformed. This notion is essentially salvation by the state: a counterfeit redemption by positive law-making. It is a myth because the root of the human problem is sin in the heart and will, not people's environment or lack of education. It is only when sin is dealt with that people are transformed and their environments are changed. The future envisioned by the Scriptures toward which Christians are to strive is a society under God where there is justice, peace, and equity.

In a letter to Vincentius around AD 407, St Augustine argued that we as God's Church, since the ascension of Christ, live in the millennial age of the Church where the prophecy of Daniel 7:27 is going to be fulfilled:

> "The kingdom, dominion, and greatness of the kingdoms under all of heaven will be given to the people, the holy ones of the Most High. His kingdom will be an everlasting kingdom, and all rulers will serve and obey Him." (HCSB)

In a later section of his letter, he writes:

> "Truly, if past events in the prophetic books prefigured future ones, both the age of the church under the apostles and the present age of the church were prefigured in that King named Nebuchadnezzar (Daniel 3). What was prefigured when this king compelled the pious and just men to worship an image and, when they refused, sent them into the flames (Daniel 3:1–23) was fulfilled in the age of the apostles and martyrs. What was prefigured in the same king a little later, when, having turned to honoring the true God, he decreed in his own kingdom that whoever blasphemed the God of Shadrach, Meshach, and Abdenego would be subject to appropriate penalties (Daniel 3:96–96) is being fulfilled now." (Letter 93, section 9)

Only by relearning Scripture and revitalizing a concern for God's present and coming Kingdom will we be able to head toward this future. God's plan is for the blessing of all nations. In the days of Abraham, God promised him that all the nations of the world would be blessed through his offspring. This was fulfilled through Christ. Only biblical faith provides hope for our children, our society, and our nation.

As we apply our faith in Christ and His Kingdom comprehensively, to all aspects of life, clashes are inevitable and there will be a cost. The plight of many Christians in our day and throughout Church history demonstrates that these costs can be severe; however, the rewards are eternal. Whenever God's Law and human law come into conflict, it is our duty to obey God's Law. The apostles demonstrated this to the Jewish authorities in Acts 5:29: " . . . we must obey God rather than any human authority."

There are several important biblical examples where God sanctions, and indeed blesses, disobedience to illegitimate human authority, such as the midwives' disobedience to Pharaoh in Egypt and Daniel's disobedience to Darius' edict in Babylon (cf. Exodus 1:15–21; Daniel 6). Noted theologian John Stott writes, "If the state commands what God forbids, or forbids what God commands, then our plain Christian duty is to resist, not to submit, to disobey the state in order to obey God ... Whenever laws are enacted which contradict God's law, civil disobedience becomes a Christian duty."

According to God's Word, we are made in God's image and do not derive our value and meaning from the modern state. Let us stand fast upon God's Word without compromise so that justice will reign on the earth. To serve God's Kingdom is to serve the Kingdom without end where final victory is assured.

> "The earth is the LORD's, and everything in it.
> The world and all its people belong to him.
> For he laid the earth's foundation on the seas
> and built it on the ocean depths ...
> Open up, ancient gates!
> Open up, ancient doors,
> and let the King of glory enter.
> Who is the King of glory?
> The LORD Almighty –
> he is the King of glory." (Psalm 24:1–2, 9–10)

God's plan in Scripture is for redemption and restoration through Jesus Christ. His call is that the Church work for this Kingdom in every sphere of life. "For the earth is the LORD's and everything in it!" The primary means of the Kingdom is apologetic and evangelistic persuasion (regeneration not revolution) since the Kingdom of God cannot be imposed by physical force and is not identical with Christianization. The Kingdom of God is to be received and entered into with joy. As we "persuade others" and the Kingdom grows, Christian truth, values and law will be embraced and received, transforming a decaying humanistic culture. Inquisitions are *not* the way of Christ.

When His Kingdom comes

When I was a child, the purpose and goal of the Kingdom of Heaven confused me. I wanted to be a child who lived in the New Jerusalem and I hoped for Jesus' return before I grew up. I thought that when I became an adult I would not want to frolic with lions (I was wrong about that; the thought is still very appealing). Later, I wondered, would heaven become boring eventually (how many times can one sing the same song)? But, Scripture indicates several related aspects of the new heaven and new earth: vision or contemplation, transformation and dominion. St John tells us what we do know: "We know that when He appears, we will be like Him, because we will see Him as He is. And everyone who has this hope in Him purifies himself, just as He is pure" (1 John 3:2–3 HCSB). These have been some of the most precious verses of Scripture to me. This text combines all the components that make for human beatitude, the blessed life, the "rest in Thee" of which Augustine speaks.

First, the vision of God in the face of Christ implicitly involves *divine contemplation* and emotional and intellectual fulfillment. Secondly, it is a *transformation* – we shall be like Him! And thirdly, we are given the gift of *dominion*. Whoever has this hope purifies him or herself because "He [Christ] is pure." Interestingly, Scripture teaches that to govern one's self is better than ruling a city. To have mastery over self is to apprentice for the governance of kingdoms. The person who cannot rule himself or herself can truly govern nothing.

Thus, praising and serving God together with the community of believers is the business of heaven. The need for community is met by the community of the Trinity as we are enfolded in His free, unshakable embrace. For all eternity, we will each be perfected according to our God-ordained potential. This city is for the whole person, including a resurrected body now incorruptible and perfect according to its potential – the body that we experience now, free from all imperfection.

As God's people, we are the Bride of Christ. We are married in a mystical union with Christ, utterly fulfilled in the perfect society and community. Each of us will be complete and fulfilled according to our bodily, intellectual, and spiritual potential. Thus, although we are one in

Christ, that does not mean uniformity or equalitarian humanism. We are all different; there will be unity in diversity and no one will envy others or desire their position, role or reward since no one will lack anything essential to perfect fulfillment in the image of Christ. What a glorious vision it is! Job stated it: "In my flesh I will see God" (Job 19:26 NIV). It is the miraculous fusion of understanding and love, which will surpass what we now know of them individually. Although we will never know God as God the Father, Son and Holy Spirit know each other, only to our fullest human capacity, this miraculous fusion is the perpetual novelty of heaven. Heaven is an active and loving mutual embrace of Creator and creature: to see, know, love, serve, and praise forever. Augustine writes:

> "But faith gives way to sight, which we shall see, and hope gives way to bliss itself, which we are going to arrive at, while charity [love] will actually grow when these other two fade out. After all, if we love by believing what we cannot yet see, how much more will we do so when we have begun to see it? And if we love by hoping for it, what we have not yet attained to, how much more when we have attained to it?"[2]

There will also be an identity of work and rest. There will be much work to occupy us, exercising the creation mandate to rule and subdue. Before the curse, Adam was to work, but after the curse, toil and wearisome labor were added so that rest and work rarely coalesced. Those who long to retire and see heaven as eternal retirement are misguided. God both works and rests, and we rest in His perfect work.

Many of us find it equally hard to conceive of community and service in the coming City of God because false notions of equality and uniformity have taken root in our worldview. If everyone were equal in every way, we would have no need of others, because we would each have the resources and talents of all people. In fact, we are dependent upon numerous others and therefore interdependent. We give and receive service because of our diversity. We need one another. We do not stand alone, but community is necessary. We are a "communion of saints" and "members of one another." Because of our fallen condition, we are all prone to seek an illegitimate dominion over each other and to promote selfish ambition and vain conceit, rather than mutual accountability in community. These attitudes inevitably result in division and disharmony. Hell is the final realization of the earthly city of rebel men and women, a place of perfect disharmony where every person is his or her own god in total isolation, incapable of community. If we cannot serve God, we cannot serve each other. Sinful people who live in pretended self-sufficiency serve neither God nor others and are finally not served by anyone. Their own choice becomes their hell.

But the covenant joys of heaven are beyond human articulation. Augustine tries:

> "God will be the source of every satisfaction, more than any heart can rightly crave, more than life and health and food and wealth, glory and honor, peace and every good – so that God as St. Paul said, 'may be all in all.' He will be the consummation of all our desiring – the object of our unending vision, of our unlessening love, of our unwearying praise." (St Augustine, *The City of God*)

The White City and the defeat of Mordor

With great pathos and imagination, Christian writer J. R. R. Tolkien's glorious fantasy, *The Lord of the Rings*, puts beautiful words into the mouth of the white wizard, Gandalf, concerning the journey beyond this life. He and one of the hobbits seem to be facing imminent death behind the doors of the Citadel, and the hobbit expresses his fear of the end. Gandalf says,

> "The end? The journey doesn't end here. Death is just another path, one that we all must take. The grey rain curtain of this world rolls back and all turns to silver glass. Then you see it ... White shores, and beyond, the far green country and to a swift sunrise."

So then, what sort of a City and Kingdom are we inheriting and how are we to respond? Let us conclude by hearing the Scriptures:

> "Instead, you have come to Mount Zion, to the city of the living God (the heavenly Jerusalem), to myriads of angels in festive gathering, to the

> assembly of the firstborn whose names have been written in heaven, to God who is the judge of all, to the spirits of righteous people made perfect, to Jesus (mediator of a new covenant), and to the sprinkled blood, which says better things than the blood of Abel." (Hebrews 12:22–24 HCSB)

Given that this is a *living reality*, a concrete truth, what kind of people ought we to be as we fight the good fight of faith and run the race marked out for us? Let us hear the Scriptures again on the matter:

> "Therefore, since we are receiving a kingdom that cannot be shaken, let us hold on to grace. By it, we may serve God acceptably, with reverence and awe; for our God is a consuming fire." (Hebrews 12:28–29 HCSB)

> "Therefore, through Him let us continually offer up to God a sacrifice of praise, that is, the fruit of our lips that confess His name. Don't neglect to do good and to share, for God is pleased with such sacrifices."
> (Hebrews 13:15–16 HCSB)

Finally, let me remind you again how St John exhorts us as spiritual children and as soldiers in this battle:

> "So now, little children, remain in Him, so that when He appears we may have *boldness* and *not be ashamed* before Him at His coming."
> (1 John 2:28 HCSB, emphasis added)

The halls of our fathers

Close your eyes for a moment and imagine Christ coming in His glory – the myriads of angels, the firstborn whose names are written in heaven, and the saints of old made perfect, the great cloud of witnesses! Do you want to be *bold* on that day, *unashamed* at His coming because you have fought the good fight, remained in Him, offered yourself as a living sacrifice on the battlefield of righteousness, truth and mercy, for the glory of the City of God?

Again in Tolkien's myth *The Lord of the Rings* ("The Return of the King"), the great King Théoden of Rohan, one time captive to the evil wizard Sauroman the servant of the dark Lord, is released from the spell by Gandalf the White and girds on his armor. Ashamed of his previous weakness, captivity and impotence and determined to save Rohan and Gondor from the armies of darkness, he is found fighting in a series of great battles that eventually lead to the deliverance of the White City and realm of Gondor. In one of the last conflicts of the story, after heroic conflict with darkness, he is finally thrown down by his enemies and as he lies dying beneath his horse on the battlefield, Théoden utters these last words to his niece who crouches over him in tears:

> "I go to my fathers in whose mighty company I shall not now feel ashamed."

I do not want to be ashamed of my life and service in the Kingdom of Christ when I stand among the great saints and martyrs of the golden city in the New Jerusalem – nor do you! Therefore, let us keep the faith and lay down our lives for the City of God, for, "we are God's children *now*, and what we will be has not yet been revealed. We know that when He appears we shall be like Him, because we will see Him as He is" (1 John 3:2 HCSB, emphasis added).

Discussion questions

1. How do you think that the way our worldview addresses the question of our ultimate destiny makes a difference in our lives? How would the following beliefs affect your life if you accepted them?
   (a) This material world and natural forces are all that is real
   (b) Your life is merely one moment in an ongoing cycle of rebirth
   (c) Your individuality and the particulars of your life are an illusion from which you need to escape by being dissolved into ultimate reality
   (d) Your destiny might be wonderful or horrible depending on the unknown will of God and the balancing of all your deeds
   (e) Martyrdom is the only way to guarantee entrance to heaven
   (f) You are going to leave this material world behind to go to heaven: an ethereal realm distinct from reality as we know it

(g) God's Kingdom is going to be a renewal of the goodness of His creation and the establishment of justice and peace
(h) Your destiny depends on how you respond to Jesus Christ
(i) Your destiny depends on how well you follow your religion or conscience

2. In what areas of life do you think you have neglected to apply your faith? What are some of the implications of your faith for this area of life?
3. How do you think the Christian hope for eternity can function effectively in apologetics?
4. Throughout Christian history, the Church has struggled with how to *engage the culture* around it without *compromising its identity*. With what areas in our culture do you think the Church needs to engage more? What areas do you think pose a real danger for us in terms of compromising our identity?
5. What things do you find most difficult to understand about the Christian view of eternity or the Kingdom of God?
6. When you think about eternity, what do you find most captivating about the hope Jesus offers?

Notes

1. Carol Harrison, *Augustine: Christian Truth and Fractured Humanity; Christian Theology in Context* (Oxford University Press, 2000), p. 199.
2. St Augustine, *Teaching Christianity: De Doctrina Christiana*, translated by Edmund Hill, edited by John E. Rotelle (New City Press, Hyde Park, New York, 1996), p. 125.

PART TWO

Persuasions: Crafting our Defense

CHAPTER 7

God Does Exist

[The paper was first delivered as the opening thesis at a formal debate on the existence of God at Carleton University, Ottawa, Canada.]

Seeing is not believing

Everyone comes to the question of God's existence from a worldview context. We all have a system of interconnected beliefs through which we interpret evidence and answer questions of ultimate concern. These beliefs constitute our worldview, which, in turn, governs our views about the core questions of *origin*, *meaning*, *morality* and *destiny* that human beings have always asked. These beliefs are often undefended because they are held to be so basic that they need no defense. Often they are cherished personal beliefs and determine, for any given individual, what is the acceptable *kind of evidence* for the issue under discussion. In disputes about God, the origin of the universe, the source of morality, or historical evidences for the miraculous, it is not simply isolated facts that are in dispute but an entire way of looking at the world. It is the very nature of "the facts" that is in dispute, not where a given fact leads. If we have a pre-commitment concerning the *nature of which facts we accept*, we have already decided where they will lead. There are no neutral facts. Facts are always interpreted in light of a wider framework of belief.

Although the Christian view of belief in authority involves convictions formed on sufficient ground, people often think that to believe or to accept authority in questions of religion is totally unacceptable and an example of credulity. But all beliefs that human beings hold are not simply ignorant credulity. If "belief" is wrong, if there is something unacceptable about belief without certain proof, then it is unforgivable to believe a friend's word, a witness's testimony, a spouse's vow, a business handshake, or any other kind of unproven claim or unsubstantiated promise. I do not see the truth of my wife's marriage pledge to me in her mind to verify it empirically, but I believe it on faith. That does not render my belief to be unreasonable or foolish credulity, because it is not believed without reasons that have earned my trust in her. We believe countless things solely on authority, because we have grown to trust the source. Do you know your parents are your parents? Have you had your DNA checked to make certain? Furthermore, does not belief or faith often prepare our minds for seeing something clearly for ourselves? Years ago, I believed my philosophy teacher could help me understand different logical arguments. This conviction brought me to his classes, and very soon the "penny dropped" and I *saw it for myself.* Belief consistently prepares us for knowledge. In the Christian view, belief in God prepares us for the knowledge of God and love of God assures us of it.

Some argue that belief in God is irrational or irresponsible, because it is not self-evident, and it can reasonably be doubted psychologically. If we agreed with this argument, most of our knowledge in ordinary life would be irrational and irresponsible including belief in the external world, the existence of other minds, and the reliability of memory. These things are not *inferred* by other beliefs but are taken as basic to our knowledge structure. The statement, "I had breakfast at 8 am this morning," is not inferred from other more basic beliefs, but it is still knowledge even though it is not self-evident.

From a different perspective, others argue that something need not be self-evident, but it is still wrong to believe anything based on insufficient evidence, especially religious beliefs. Guilty until proven innocent or the "presumption of atheism" is considered by such people as the only right position. But, again, this would undercut most of our everyday knowledge. We believe many things rationally, properly, and justifiably without proof or evidence. As noted above, the beliefs that there are other minds, that we are persons not androids, and that the world continues to exist when we are not around, are all examples of beliefs that we hold without evidence. Furthermore, the evidentialist thesis itself is self-defeating. *The idea that it is wrong to believe anything upon insufficient evidence is not established on sufficient evidence. It is simply assumed.*

Equally, the popular doctrine that all significant knowledge is empirical in nature is a belief that fails its own test, since that statement itself is not empirical and cannot be verified. Furthermore, many of our most important claims are not empirical observations, such as moral truth or even laws of rationality and logic. Thus, there is no evidence for such a claim. Instead, it is a dogmatic assertion that limits investigation from the outset.

In the light of the many things we believe which can be doubted and for which we cannot offer direct empirical proof, it is important not to put God in the wrong family of beliefs. Some beliefs, like belief in the earth's rotation, are evidence-essential. If this belief lacked relevant evidence, we would reject the theory as irrational. But many other rational human beliefs are *not* evidence-essential; they do not require supporting evidence or arguments to be rational.

There is no good reason for denying that it is rational, reasonable, and acceptable for people to believe in God without being able to prove it to someone else. Although there is no successful direct argument to prove the existence of other people's minds, we believe it to be a perfectly rational assumption. I am convinced that belief in God is of the same kind, the same family of beliefs, as the belief in other minds. A worldwide poll conducted in 1991 found that the global figure for atheists was 4.4% and that for agnostics was 16.4%, leaving almost 80% believing in God.[1]

Just because the vast majority of people believe in a supreme being does not make it so, but it does suggest that there is an important difference between *knowing* and *showing* that God exists. We have belief-forming mechanisms that shape our beliefs under certain conditions. For example, "I had tea this afternoon," or "my wife loves me" or "I remembered my fourteenth birthday today" are all claims that cannot be proved, but they are warranted directly by circumstance. Christian philosopher Alvin Plantinga writes:

> "Our cognitive faculties [are] designed to enable us to achieve true beliefs with respect to a wide variety of propositions – about our immediate environment, about our own interior life, about the thoughts and experiences of

> other persons, about the past, about our universe at large, about right and wrong . . . and about God. These faculties work in such a way that under the appropriate circumstances we form the appropriate belief. More exactly, the appropriate belief is formed in us; in the typical case we do not decide to hold or form the belief in question, but simply find ourselves with it."[2]

Citing the belief in the physical existence of a tree and remembering what you ate for breakfast in the morning, Plantinga notes, "In these and other cases I do not *decide* what to believe; I don't total up the evidence . . . and make a decision as to what seems best supported; I *simply believe*" (emphasis added).[3]

Consequently, arguments or proofs are not necessary for belief to be rational – if that were so, as we have seen, most of our knowledge would be complete irrationality – but arguments can function as triggers that, with other dispositions, can produce the conviction that God exists. It is for this reason that I offer arguments for God. Not because I believe I need them to be rational, but because I want others to come to know the God whom I know and love.

What standard of proof should we need when considering whether God is real? This is not a question in the field of geometry, in which exact standards are applied. No philosophical beliefs are supported by that kind of evidence. My arguments will not lead you deductively or inescapably by direct appeals to facts to the conclusion that God exists. Rather, they will attempt to focus attention on the inner and outer world of our experience to show that certain features are what we should expect if the Christian worldview is true; at the same time highlighting the self-destructive nature of disbelief in God.

Person to person – or not?

Our world and experience demands some kind of explanation. To stop looking for an explanation would be to stop being human! Arguments for God are explanations or reasons for the way the world is. Ultimately, there are only two types of explanations for reality: *personal* and *impersonal*. So, when an impersonal explanation fails to do justice to a phenomenon like morality, we seek a personal explanation instead. Philosopher Richard Swinburne writes:

> "When a detective argues from various bloodstains on the woodwork, fingerprints on the metal, Smith's corpse on the floor, money missing from the safe . . . to Jones having intentionally killed Smith and stolen his money he is arguing towards an explanation of the various phenomena in terms of the intentional action of a rational agent."[4]

Thus, in the detective work of those making a case for Christian theism, Swinburne notes that,

> "When the theist argues from phenomena such as the existence of the world or some feature of the world to the existence of God, he is arguing . . . to an explanation of the phenomena in terms of the intentional action of a person . . . a theistic explanation is a personal explanation. It explains phenomena in terms of the actions of a person."[5]

To die of natural causes or to be murdered involve these two different types of explanation. When archaeologists see Mount Rushmore over against the white cliffs of Dover, it is intuitive that the former needs an explanation involving human causality since an impersonal, scientific one, such as the action of wind or water, does not adequately explain the heads of the presidents appearing in the rock. However, when scientists at the SETI (search for extra-terrestrial intelligence) project with their listening devices hear random background noises generated in space, they ignore it as naturally occurring. What they are searching for is a signal containing a pattern that, like prime numbers in sequence, requires personality or rational agency as an explanation. The question is, then, which set of conditions best explains the features of our inner and outer world, even those things we take for granted? Is an impersonal explanation adequate?

A causal argument

Have you ever asked the question, "Why is there something instead of nothing?"? We are driven by human experience to seek a reason for our existence and for the world around us. Physics and astronomy strongly suggest, to the best of our current knowledge, that the universe is expanding and that it had a beginning. Thus, the evidence suggests that the universe began to exist and that it was created from nothing. The atheist holds as an ultimate axiom of faith that *all that is just popped into existence from nothing (a point at which all known laws break down) and by the agency of nothing.*

But does this faith make sense? Intuition tells us that from nothing comes nothing. So why does something exist? Surely, there is a reason, a first cause that brought this universe into existence. Simply put, this argument has often been structured as follows:

1. Anything that *begins to exist* requires a cause
2. The universe *began* to exist
3. The universe has a cause

This line of reasoning makes the argument that, in this case, the ultimate cause for the universe must be uncaused, and changeless – neither beginning to exist (uncaused) nor itself a system of events and changes (changeless).

Another way of looking at the question of cause is to consider *sufficient reason*. Whatever exists, human experience shows, demands explanation. If nothing existed, no reason would be required. But, since we are here, we rightly ask, why something rather than nothing? Anything that is *contingent* finds its explanation or sufficient reason in something other than itself and so its *non-existence* is possible. It is not the *ground* of its own existence. In our world, we have not yet encountered anything that is not contingent. Rivers, cars, mountains, atomic bombs, and human beings all need an explanation – a reason beyond themselves that account for them.

So, it is reasonable to argue that if nothing exists in our world without sufficient reason since it is contingent, there must be a sufficient reason for the universe as a whole. The series of reasons for contingent things could be said to stretch back infinitely in time, but this is counter-intuitive, and no matter how far back one goes the whole series is still *contingent* and still requires a sufficient reason outside the series. There must be *a sufficient reason for the world other than the world.* The only solution to this quest for sufficient reasons is a necessary being that *contains its own sufficient reason* for existence. There must be something not infected with contingency, something that is *necessary* that could serve as the explanation for the entire series of contingent events and causes. Although some non-theists do not like the question, and argue that we do not need to ask a question like that since our knowledge ends with physical causes in the world, their response is inadequate and deeply unsatisfying. It *is* a legitimate question to ask for a sufficient reason for the world – an ultimate ground, a logical first cause. Why does the world exist? In the end, contingency cannot explain contingency!

However, although some may claim that appealing to God simply replaces one question of causality with another (i.e. who made God?), this misses the point. We do not need a sufficient reason for a *necessary being* because, by definition, such a being is uncaused or self-caused. Its sufficient reason is contained in itself. God exists by His own nature. To be a necessary being is simply to be not dependent for your existence upon something else. We have already seen that the world could not be this necessary being. Philosopher Richard Taylor comments:

> "For we find nothing whatever about the world, any more than in its parts to suggest that it exists by its own nature. Concerning anything in the world, we have not the slightest difficulty in supposing that it should perish, or even that it should never have existed in the first place. We have almost as little difficulty in supposing this of the world itself . . . it would seem then, that the world . . . is contingent and dependent upon something other than itself for its existence . . . it must depend upon something, for otherwise there could be no reason why it exists in the first place."[6]

Some have claimed that this argument from the contingency of the universe's component parts to the contingency of the universe itself commits what is called the *fallacy of composition*. The fallacy of composition argues that something which is true of the parts must be true of the whole. For example, I might build a perfect cube out of rectangular individual bricks. Just because the parts are rectangular does not mean that the whole possesses the same property. However, the fallacy of composition is what is known as an informal fallacy, meaning that the particular content of the argument determines whether an inference from parts to whole is valid or not. In other words, while it is sometimes fallacious to reason from the parts to the whole, it is not *always* wrong to reason from parts to whole. For example, if all the individual tiles in my kitchen floor have the property of being green, then it is perfectly reasonable to conclude that the floor as a whole has the property of being green. The argument from contingency that I have outlined is of this type so the critics have not successfully identified a fallacy.

Arguments against naturalism

The Christian theistic view of human knowledge is that the universe is created by God according to a specific design plan. Our minds have been constituted in such a way by God that under the right conditions they lead to true-belief production. Since we have been made in God's image, our minds are designed to relate to the real world. Theism thus provides a personal explanation for knowledge and rationality.

Accounting for rationality

Let us assume for a moment that the Christian worldview is not correct and try to examine the implications of the naturalistic, impersonal explanation of many non-theists. Simply stated, if we hold that human beings are the product of *undirected naturalistic evolutionary processes*, do we not have very good reason to doubt our own minds? A naturalistic account of human origins gives no basis for thinking that our belief-forming processes give us anything like an accurate picture of the world since there is no designed rational structure in the mind or the world. We have arisen, with all our cognitive faculties, from irrational animals. Thus, the basis for reliable thinking processes is sufficiently weak that it makes sense to doubt one's own conclusions. If one has reason to doubt our belief-forming processes themselves, then one has reason to doubt all one's beliefs, including the belief that naturalism is the best explanation for human origins! Thus, the naturalist holds an implicitly irrational position that can only lead to extreme skepticism about all knowledge.

In a universe without God, how can we be sure of any of our rational capabilities, like logic, mathematics and value judgments in ethics? Pascal writes:

> "...we cannot be sure that these principles are true (faith and revelation apart) except through some natural intuition. Now this natural intuition affords no convincing proof that they are true. There is no certainty, apart from faith (revelation), as to whether man was created by a good God, an evil demon, or just by chance, and so it is a matter of doubt, depending on our origin, whether these innate principles are true, false or uncertain."[7]

Is this human "software" to be trusted? Unless it is the creation of a good God, can it be relied upon? If theism is true and God relates our thoughts to a real world of experience, then these faculties, though not infallible, can be depended upon. For example, my car is a well designed vehicle for the purpose of transportation. However, it sometimes skids on ice, stalls in the rain, or develops an electrical fault etc. Though my vehicle for transport is not perfect (flawlessly free from all failure or error) it is far better than no transportation at all! In the Christian view the human mind is a well designed vehicle of knowledge, whilst, like my car, not totally free from the possibility of error.

Clearly, to rely on your reason is ultimately an act of faith and not of reason; it is not an empirical observation or self-evident axiom.

So, the relevant question remains how are we to make intelligible sense of our use of reason? There are only three possibilities.[8] First, we could appeal to something *sub-rational*, like animal instinct and evolutionary processes. But, how can a sub-rational *inferior* validate a rational *superior*? This makes no sense at all. It is comparable to asking your pet cat whether you have filled in your tax return correctly. Second, could reason be validated *directly* by another piece of reasoning – a reasoned argument for reason without recourse to God? Clearly not! This just begs the question since it is reason we are trying to validate in the first place. Consequently, the only remaining possibility is an *indirect validation* by something *super-rational* – faith in God and His revelation. Only belief in God and His assurance that we are made in His image as rational persons, capable of understanding the world and knowing truth, gives us any basis to trust our reason.

The mind/brain problem

Another serious problem with naturalistic atheism has to do with the distinction between our physical brain and our minds and thoughts. Is all thought merely chemical brain processes? For example, as Roger Sperring once asked, can the meaning and information content of the words on this page be explained purely in terms of the physics and chemistry of the ink and paper? Do meaning and thought have chemical and physical properties occupying space with location like all other material phenomena? Yet, on the atheist account, this is essentially what we are to believe about the human *mind* – that it is explicable on physics and chemistry alone. Michael Robinson writes:

> "If there is no God, we are just molecules in motion, and we have no sense and no mind; we are just the random firing of chemicals in the brain. If our minds are composed only of physical matter, then our thoughts are, (as Doug Wilson wittily quipped in his debate with atheist Dan Barker), just 'brain gas' . . . If our minds are just the result of chemical reactions, then in the debate over pop cans, God's existence can rightly be settled by shaking the two soda pop cans simultaneously. Labeling one can 'atheism' and the other 'theism'; after shaking the cans, the one that fizzes the most wins the debate. If our minds are simply the fluctuations of proteins, neurotransmitters, and other brain biochemicals, then an intellectual debate is equivalent to the chemical reactions that occur when one shakes up a couple of cans of soda."[9]

Materialistic and naturalistic accounts of the mind destroy knowledge and the intelligibility of our experience.

If a friend asked you, "Where did that thought occur in your body?" you would think she was mad, because *mental events* do not have a location nor occupy space. Thoughts and neural events are related but they are not identical. Mental events are known but not in the same way that physical events are known, because the thinker has privileged access to his own thoughts. Even if you were to crack someone's head open to observe her brain, you would not be able to access her thoughts because they are not physical events. The privileged nature of our thoughts strongly suggests that they are not physical properties.[10]

We cannot explain exactly how mind and matter interact in the human person but if we can find even *one thing* that is true of mental events and not of material events, physicality no longer holds, since we would see that mental and material events are not identical. We have seen that physical substances have weight, location in space and chemical and electrical properties, but my thoughts and mental events do not! Furthermore, mental events are self-presenting, which means that we are aware of them directly and immediately in our consciousness. As Augustine astutely observed, the mind is more aware of itself than anything else in human experience, but the mind is never represented to us *by* anything else like memory or sense experience of physical objects. The mind is simply the immaterial "I" that we never think of as a physical property.

Identity over time

Another problem that appears to render atheism self-defeating is the problem of human identity. Only the theistic position can give us any reason to be certain of who we are and any confidence that we are the same person we were in the pictures we see of our childhood. This may sound like a ludicrous suggestion to many people, but consider this – our physical bodies are changing every moment. Our skin replaces itself once a month. Stomach lining is replaced every five days. The cells in the liver are replaced every six weeks. Our cells are in a constant state of flux. In seven years, every atom in a person's body has been replaced.

So, does that mean that every seven years a person has transformed into someone entirely different? If only the physical or material is real, then it is hard to avoid that conclusion. With every atom replaced by a new one every seven years, in what sense is a twenty-one-year-old the same person he was at fourteen unless God provides a spiritual basis for personhood? In a world without God, I am not married to the same woman I was nine years ago since every molecule of her physical being has changed.

How can we trust our memories or have confidence that they are giving us any truth about the past since all our brain has been exchanged three times by the time we finish university? We may not be able to prove it directly, but we each know full-well that even though we have matured and grown in life through our experiences, we are still the same person. The "I" that we knew as a teenager is still the same "I" that looks back with fondness and frustration at those earlier years. In fact, our early experiences often shape us for the rest of our lives!

Even though we cannot explain the means by which mind and matter interact with and affect each other, we have good reason to believe that they do. Mental stress is known to be a cause of ulcers, and emotional trauma can cause post-traumatic stress disorder and even temporary blindness, as seen in numerous cases in war. A head injury can alter somebody's personality when brain connections are damaged. To believe that both mind and brain are real and are interconnected has greater explanatory power than to believe that mind is reducible to the physical brain alone. Similarly, though we do not know what energy is, we still believe it exists because of its explanatory power. Christian theism holds that we are a unity as persons and that our bodies and minds are significant components of our identity that cannot be understood separately.

Moral argument

My final argument against naturalism here is a form of moral argument. Without God, morality has no *objective basis*, so it is reduced to subjective personal preference. Few people can tolerate this notion when they understand its full implications. Without an objective basis for morality, nothing is wrong in and of itself. Right and wrong are simply labels humans have decided to use and there is no objective way to distinguish between good or bad systems of morality.

Two views dominate the moral thought of atheism. The first, **ethical subjectivism** is the view that whenever people say something is morally good, they mean that they like it or approve of it. This morality is based on the inner feelings of the speaker. Moral judgments are nothing more than approval or disapproval, like or dislike. On this view, all moral judgments are correct because they refer to nothing more than the opinion or subjective state of an individual or group. What one likes is good; what one dislikes is bad. On this basis, moral truth may change radically from one circumstance to another, based on the individual's emotional state of mind, personal desires, or even physical condition at the time.

The second view is **ethical relativism**, which holds that moral beliefs are dependent upon one's culture and historical epoch because we derive our morals from our family and surrounding culture. However, just because we learn something does not make it correct. I learned that two plus two is four, but that does not mean that someone who disagrees with me has an equally valid truth. We learn some things that are true and some that are false. The fact that different cultures in different times may disagree about a moral question does not negate the existence of morality that transcends culture. To conclude that because moral judgments differ there is no moral truth is a glaring logical fallacy.

In an effort to escape radical subjectivism, the atheist often appeals to evolution to anchor moral values in something beyond personal preference. Nonetheless, it remains to be seen how an ethical "ought" can be derived from a biological "is". Philosopher Stephen Evans writes:

> "The moral order does not seem to consist in any such things [i.e. instincts and feelings]. It is not an instinct, because it is itself the standard by which we judge our instincts to be good and bad. And it is not merely a social impulse or feeling. People who have dulled their consciences often are in fact obligated to do things, yet have no such feelings of obligation whatsoever . . . feelings and real obligations cannot be identical."[11]

If no one moral code is better than another because they all lack a transcendent referent, we cannot make any moral judgments about tyrants, oppression, prejudice, or anything else. If a minority is oppressed with the permission or approval of a majority, like the slave trade in the British Empire or the United States, there is no ultimate moral standard by which to condemn that oppression as wrong. In fact, in the case of the trial of Nazi war criminals including Nazi doctors, government officials, and the military high command, their legal defense at Nuremburg rested on the claim that they had broken no law of their land. They also appealed to the eugenics program operating in North America and parts of Europe as the model they were following.

Equally, there is no basis for moral improvement if morality is subjective. The eventual abolition of slavery in the British Empire and the United States, the development of voting rights for women, or the ending of child labor in England was not an indication of moral advancement, just moral change. No one can condemn or praise either period, nor criticize the actions of another if we are just matter in motion, slime that evolved rationality. Morality is merely a social construct in this worldview. Therefore, it is not *objectively evil* to abuse little children because there is no objective good or evil, only a "blind, pitiless indifference" as Richard Dawkins has put it. Clearly, these notions make little sense and lead to what appears to most people as an evidently false conclusion. Again, we see that naturalism lacks adequate explanation for this essential aspect of human experience and makes moral judgments rationally impossible.

Argument from truth

Another important theistic argument first made its appearance in the work of St Augustine. It was his only attempt to formulate a direct argument for God's existence and is known as the **argument from truth**. It has been developed since by other Christian philosophers.[12]

One of the preconditions of any meaningful communication between people is the metaphysical assumption that we all share the same rational categories in our minds. One important question concerns how can we account for this remarkable conviction? Can the existence of what we call truth be accounted for adequately by a naturalistic explanation as opposed to a personal one? This seems implausible because, as we have seen, a naturalistic account bypasses mind and the intelligence while truth is in essence an issue of mind – a mental category. This argument can be outlined as follows:[13]

Truth exists

It is not difficult to refute the position that "there is no such thing as truth." All that is needed is to inquire whether that statement itself is true. If it is, truth exists. If it is not, truth exists.

Truth is unchangeable

What is true at any time will always be true. True propositions are eternally true. The proposition "two plus two equals four"[14] or the proposition "I visited my friend on 24th January in Ottawa" will always be true. If truth were changeable, then even naturalism might only be true today, but untrue tomorrow and so it is hardly worth any allegiance.

Truth is eternal

Even if the whole universe were to cease to exist, truth would still endure. It would be impossible for truth to cease to be, because even if it were possible for truth to die, it would always remain true that truth had died. Thus, to deny the eternality of truth is self-defeating.

Truth is mental

The existence of truth presupposes the existence of minds. Without the mind, truth cannot exist, because truth is a proposition, a meaning, a thought, a mental construct. Materialism fails here. For naturalism, all thought (logical reasoning) is the result of mechanical necessity. But changes in atomic arrangement (physical motion), can be neither true nor false, they are what they are. One physical motion cannot be "truer" than another. In naturalism, there is no mind to offer a "physical explanation" of reality! If there is no mind, there is no truth, and therefore materialism cannot be true. With no mind, no such thing as logical reasoning from necessary laws exists. By inference, the materialist cannot provide a valid argument to justify his position. Philosopher Gordon Clark clarifies the futility of the atheist position:

> "If a truth, a proposition, or a thought were some physical motion in the brain, no two persons could have the same thought. A physical motion is a fleeting event numerically distinct from every other. Two persons cannot have the same motion, nor can one person have it twice. If this is what thought were, memory and communication would be impossible . . . it is a peculiarity of mind and not of body that the past can be made present. Accordingly, if one can think the same thought twice, truth must be mental or spiritual. Not only does truth defy time; it defies space as well, for if

communication is to be possible, the identical truth must be in two minds at once. If in opposition, anyone wished to deny that an immaterial idea can exist in two minds at once, his denial must be conceived to exist in his own mind only; and since it has not registered in any other mind, it does not occur to us to refute it."[15]

Truth is superior to the human mind

Truth is not subjective or individualistic – certain truths are universal. Beliefs may vary, but truth does not. Our minds do not judge truth but rather truth judges our minds, as we have all experienced in math class. If truth and the mind were identical then it would be changeable and subject to error, rendering rationality and knowledge impossible. Truth must then transcend reasoning and any individual or collective minds. Therefore, there must be a mind higher than the human mind in which truth resides.

Truth is God

Truth must be grounded on something real. This ground cannot be perishable or accidental. Since truth is eternal and immutable it must be grounded in an eternal and immutable mind. Only God possesses these attributes, so God is truth. The propositions that may be known are the thoughts of God – a personal living God.[16]

A transcendental argument from the preconditions of debate

My final argument asks what a debate about God's existence assumes at the outset. All reasoning assumes the validity of certain logical principles. Most of us call it common sense! Philosophers identify these principles as laws of logic or inference. These laws, we readily assume, enable us to differentiate between right and wrong inferences in our thinking. The laws of identity, non-contradiction, and excluded middle are foundational examples of these laws. For example, either God exists or God does not exist. Both of these propositions cannot be true; there is no middle way. These simple rules of inference are abstract and immaterial. They must be invariant and universal in nature if we are to retain rational argument.

They are necessary to the extent that we have to use them in order to refute them. They are not dependent or changeable and we cannot conceive of them not existing in any possible world. Can a naturalistic worldview adequately account for such trans-subjective rules of inference? How can a materialist have an immaterial, invariant law of inference in her worldview? If they are merely consensual, then what if a different culture has a different consensus about rationality? Could they be reasoned with? Once again it seems that the atheist is at a loss to even account for a debate about God's existence – the atheist's worldview if consistently applied would preclude the possibility of meaningful debate.

God does exist

The biggest problem facing the atheist is that deep inside we each know that there is a Creator and that we are the creatures. Because of this, we cannot find the true interpretation of reality by ourselves, for we neither create, control, nor sustain ourselves or our environment. If we begin like Descartes, with ourselves acting as the ultimate source of truth, we have nothing to which we can point with proper confidence. If the individual human mind must be author of truth and establish it without God, then, as we have seen, truth as something beyond the individual would be destroyed – we would be left in a sea of never-ending skepticism. Truth presupposes God.

As a result, our minds cannot be the ultimate standard. We need a transcendent point of reference, a referent outside of ourselves. We need, after all, revelation. The claim of Scripture is that truth has come down from God to us so that we are not left with our futile, abstract, and wearisome speculations. The Gospel of John opens in the following manner:

> "In the beginning, the Word already existed. He was with God and he was God. He was in the beginning with God. He created everything there is. Nothing exists that he didn't make. Life itself was in him, and this life gives light to everyone. The light shines through the darkness, and the darkness can never extinguish it." (John 1:1–5)

God has spoken truthfully, though not exhaustively in Scripture. It is on this basis that we, as subjects, can know an absolute, objective truth with as much certainty as our human weakness is capable of. This does not mean that we know truth absolutely or exhaustively or with perfect objectivity. Exhaustive, absolute knowledge is for God alone, and so the humanistic dream of grounding truth independent of God is futile. The skeptic, in flagrant self-contradiction is found to need an exhaustive metaphysical knowledge to assert that God cannot be known or that it is irresponsible to believe in God.

Revealed truth does not depend on our IQ, logical ability, or the exacting interpretation of our sense experience. It rests upon God who shares knowledge with us. In God's light, we see light. Our rationality is a derivative and secondary light, illuminated by Christ. The Christian argument in its essence is that *truth, reason and logic, math and science, morality, personal identity, dignity, language and learning, communication, motion and love only have an adequate explanation and foundation when we acknowledge that a personal God exists and has communicated with us in creation, in our rational nature, and in the Scriptures.*

Scripture teaches us that we have all been made in God's image and that deep down we know that we are creatures God made. Because of this, we cannot help living by and simultaneously believing in the validity of our identity over time, reasoning, logic, language, science, and moral truth. This is in spite of the fact that what unbelievers profess to believe about reality would destroy the possibility of human reasoning altogether. We live in the rational world of a rational Creator God and as such can succeed in our use of logic and science only because God has so constituted this world and us in it.

What must be true for my human experience to be what it appears to be and not to be rendered total nonsense? What must be true about reality in order for rationality, laws of inference, causality, truth, science, morality, and every other meaningful aspect of my experience to exist in the first place? What can make sense of life and love, good and evil, justice and injustice?

The proposition that God created and governs the universe cannot be subjected to scientific tests. It is a religious proposition. Its alternative is the religious negation of the Creator. You must make your choice as to which faith you will live by.

What light do you have in your life to illuminate all of the facts? What is your authority? On what basis do you trust that source of knowledge? What presuppositions can make sense of this discussion? Ultimately, we have to decide if we find a personal or an impersonal explanation most satisfying. Which makes intelligible sense of experience – moral consciousness, guilt, love, justice and truth? Many of us know deep inside that our own answers do not satisfy, but we resist God's claim on our lives and avoid facing the tough questions honestly because we are afraid of meeting God and afraid of God's demands on our lives.

Christ emphasizes that only those who seek God find Him, and furthermore, that all those who truly seek Him will certainly find Him. Thus, both rationalism, which denies the need for the search, and skepticism, which denies the final encounter with truth fall short of Christ's promise. The great problem facing the skeptic is not lack of evidence or inadequacy of reasons to believe, but rather, his or her own attitude towards God. We tend to find only what we want to find, and will see only what we want to see. C. S. Lewis writes:

> "Men are reluctant to pass over from the notion of an abstract and negative deity to the living God. I do not wonder . . . it is always shocking to meet life where we thought we were alone . . . An 'impersonal God' – well and good. A subjective God of beauty, truth and goodness, inside our own heads, better still. A formless life force surging through us, a vast power which we can tap, best of all. But God Himself, alive, pulling at the other end of the cord, perhaps approaching at an infinite speed, the hunter, king, husband – that is quite another matter. There comes a moment when the children who have been playing at burglars hush suddenly: was that a real footstep in the hall? There comes a moment when people who have been dabbling in religion ('Man's search for God'!) suddenly draw back. Supposing we really found him? We never meant it to come to that! Worse still, supposing he had found us? So it is a sort of Rubicon. One goes across; or not. But if one does, there is no manner of security against miracles. One may be in for anything.[17]

Belief of some kind is inescapable. Faith is a necessary aspect of the life of every human being and authority is a governing reality in all of our lives. We can trust in Jesus Christ not because of philosophical certainty derived from arguments, but with confidence because of the overwhelming evidence of His existence that He has provided for those who will seek with an open heart. The skeptic offers nothing but his or her cynicism. Christ offers life, light, and knowledge if we will seek Him.

Jesus does not try to shield our feelings when He tells us that we are blinded by our moral hostility to God. He offers Himself to us as the Healer and the Cure. He is the lens through which to see all of life. This lens, like glasses, is corrective. It shows things as they really are. I invite you to put on the lens of Christ and see if life does not become clearer.

Ancient Greek atheist, materialist and atomist, Democritus, said that the truth about the universe can be summed up in two words: "atoms" and the "void." Jesus said, "I am the way, the truth and the life." We make the choice between Jesus and the void.

Discussion questions

1. If you believe in God, what do you think were the biggest factors in forming this belief?
2. List some of the things you believe without proof.
3. List some of the things for which you accept a natural explanation. Why?
4. List some of the things for which you need a personal explanation. Why?
5. Which of the arguments laid out in this chapter do you find most convincing? Why?
6. Of the people you know who do not believe in God, what do you think are the biggest reasons for this?
7. Pick one of the arguments in this chapter and describe how you might explain it to the average person who has little interest in abstract arguments. How can you explain it in a way that person could understand and relate to?

8. This chapter argues that when it comes down to it, we cannot prove many of our most basic assumptions about life and thought. But, we believe these things because they have *explanatory power* to make sense of our world and our experience. How is the concept of explanatory power helpful in apologetics?

Notes

1. *International Bulletin of Missionary Research* – January 1991.
2. Alvin Plantinga, cited in, R. H. Nash, *Life's Ultimate Questions: An Introduction to Philosophy* (Zondervan, Grand Rapids, 1999), p. 284.
3. *Life's Ultimate Questions*, p. 284.
4. Richard Swinburne, *The Existence of God* (Clarendon, Oxford, 1979), p. 20.
5. *The Existence of God*, pp. 22, 93.
6. Richard Taylor, cited in, Ronald H. Nash, *Faith and Reason: Searching for a Rational Faith* (Zondervan, Grand Rapids, 1988), p. 130.
7. Blaise Pascal, cited in, Peter Kreeft, *Christianity for Modern Pagans: Pascal's Pensées, edited, outlined and explained* (Ignatius Press, San Francisco, 1993), p. 107.
8. Ibid., p. 111.
9. Michael Robinson, *God Does Exist?* (2006), p. 45.
10. Nash, *Life's Ultimate Questions*, pp. 373–374.
11. C. Stephen Evans, *The Quest for Faith* (IVP, Downers Grove, 1986), p. 47.
12. Philosopher Gordon H. Clark was one champion of this argument in the form I use here. This can be found in detail in his book, *A Christian View of Men and Things* (Trinity Foundation, 1989).
13. My main source for this argument is, Nash, *Life's Ultimate Questions*, pp. 296–298.
14. In everyday life, that is. In quantum physics adjustments need to be made, also when using numbers to a different base, such as binary where the only numbers are one and zero, the math that makes my computer function.
15. Gordon H. Clark, cited in, Nash, *Life's Ultimate Questions*, pp. 297–298.
16. I have depended completely on Gordon H. Clark and R. H. Nash for this useful development of Augustine's argument from truth.
17. C. S. Lewis, *Miracles* (Fount Paperbacks, 1974), pp. 97–98.

CHAPTER 8

Glory, Rubbish and the Human Race

Confronting the human paradox

[*The lecture was first delivered at The Peoples' Church, Toronto, Canada, with a wider television audience in mind.*]

> "The human heart is most deceitful and desperately wicked. Who really knows how bad it is? But I know! I, the LORD, search all hearts and examine secret motives. I give all people their due rewards, according to what their actions deserve ... O LORD, you alone can heal me; you alone can save. My praises are for you alone." (Jeremiah 17:9–10, 14)

Anesthetist or realist

A common objection in contemporary Western society is that Christianity is essentially divorced from life, neither practical nor particularly useful. It may be of some limited interest to those interested in spirituality, ancient beliefs and mystical thought, but it is not about real life. The Bible is falsely yet consistently thought of as a compilation of unreliable history and a great deal of mythology. Many assume that carefully looking at its message would be a waste of time. In my experience, many who strongly object to the Christian faith have never even read one of the Gospels in the New Testament. Life is busy. There is so much to occupy us and hold our attention. There is also much to entertain. Why should we consider this old message? The Old and New Testaments of the Bible are so restrictive and old-fashioned, it is assumed, how can their message possibly be relevant to us in the Western world with all our sophistication and advancement?

Some of today's thinkers will reluctantly concede that Christianity at least has some psychological benefit – this, they say, may be true of religion in general. A healthy spirituality is useful in order to get you through life's problems and aids a quick recovery from illness. Religious devotion gives people a little relief from the anxiety of life, in a similar way that golf or tennis, yoga or meditation can do. Hence, the Christian faith may be tolerated and is not problematic so long as believers keep their faith to themselves and regard it as a purely private matter, but any attempt at propagating your own personal perspective as the truth is a gross violation of the contemporary, unquestioned doctrine of equal tolerance for all views.

Taken to an extreme (popularized by Richard Dawkins, Christopher Hitchens, Sam Harris and others) some people think of Christianity as a dangerous, even evil form of self-delusion, while others view belief as a psychological crutch for those unwilling to face life in all its stark reality. In other words, Christianity does for the intellectually weak what intoxication and drug use does for others. It provides an artificial atmosphere to give temporary escape from life so that you can forget your troubles and feel comforted.

Atheist fundamentalist Dawkins in his recent book, *The God Delusion*, makes a highly questionable attempt to re-popularize the atheistic argument for the non-existence of God offered by anti-religious German philosopher Ludwig Feuerbach. He argued (in 1841) that God had been invented or dreamed up by human beings to give intellectual and spiritual consolation. Karl Marx equally held that people need this God delusion because of their economic and social alienation – thus a socialist revolution would naturally put an end to religion. Sigmund Freud famously located the source of the "God Delusion" in the human longing for a stable father figure; an infantile wish we would shed as we grew up. Oxford Professor and author of *The Dawkins Delusion*, Alister McGrath, in addressing the mocking notion that belief in God is like belief in a teapot orbiting the sun summarizes these similar arguments in the following way:

> "There is no God.
> But lots of people believe in God. Why?
> Because they want consolation.
> So they project or objectify their longings, and call this God.
> So this non-existent God is simply the projection of human longings."[1]

Obviously this kind of argument can cut both ways.

> There is a God.
> Some people don't believe in God. Why?
> Because they are afraid of being accountable to a supreme judge after death.
> So they project this wish onto reality and call it atheism (no God).

This sort of argument has limited logical force (though some rhetorical), so another form of argument is increasingly popular – again used by Dawkins. Belief in God is conveniently written off by many such contemporary apologists for atheism as a by-product of evolution, a "mystical gene" if you will. The "religious" pre-supposition is naturalism and so a natural explanation must be given for belief in God – it thus pre-supposes its own conclusions. Dawkins has argued that religion (not distinguished from belief in God i.e. what of non-theistic faiths?) is an accidental by-product (epiphenomenon) or *"misfiring of something useful."* But how is this consistent with his view of a universe without design or purpose; without a design plan, characterized in his own words as manifesting, "blind pitiless indifference"? Oxford professor McGrath rightly asks,

> "How can Dawkins speak of religion as something 'accidental', when his understanding of the evolutionary process precludes any theoretical framework that allows him to suggest that some outcomes are 'intentional' and others 'accidental' ... for Darwinism, everything is accidental. Things may have the appearance of design – but this appearance of design or intentionality arises from random developments."[2]

The atheist worldview propounded by the likes of Dawkins which seeks to make overarching sense of everything in terms of biology has a hard time accounting for the very notions of *"misfiring"* and *"intentionality"* (purpose), never mind providing a rationally grounded arguments against the existence of God. Simply asserting that "brain modules," and thus brain activity is a possible cause of religion hardly refutes the existence of God – after all, brain activity is a necessary condition of *all* human experience and behavior, even that of Dawkins! It is simply impossible for the scientific method, psychological or otherwise to validate or refute the idea of God's existence.

It is difficult to see how the idea that belief in God is "wish-fulfillment" is even psychologically valid, for although cognitive bias is a fundamental of human psychology, it is not primarily manifest in believing what we would like to be true, but rather in maintaining the status quo of beliefs – holding to something for the value of its conserving a worldview rather than destabilizing our thinking. I would love (wish) to have a giant yacht and second home in California – that doesn't mean I believe that to be true. I can wish for many things (the ideas of which might bring comfort) that never bring me to the delusion that I possess them – that they are now parked in my garage!

Is the issue relevant? Does it make you happy?

Another common assumption is that the question of the truth or falsehood of a given belief is not as important as its pragmatic success in your life. This is increasingly seen as true with respect to all belief systems – does it "work" pragmatically for you? This is the only important issue – does a particular belief "work" for you? The truth status of your belief is not relevant, and probably cannot be ascertained – its effect is what counts. Ironically, this "soft" skepticism usually maintains that its own stance is unbiased and practically self-evident. Allan Bloom writes:

> "The relativity of truth (for college students in American culture) is not a theoretical insight but a moral postulate, the condition of a free society, or so they see it. The point is not to correct the mistakes and really be right; rather it is not to think you are right at all. The students, of course, cannot defend their opinion. It is something with which they have been indoctrinated . . ."[3]

Many falsely suppose that the elusiveness of truth is a new realization, and only the brave who are prepared to question the old norms can face up to it. Truth has fled the universe, so all culturally relative religious beliefs must be deconstructed and exposed for the power games they really are. Postmodern thinker Foucault, whose ideas helped shape the mood of our time, articulates this view. Truth is a purely human product, a kind of regime of constraint, developed only for its functionality. He writes:

> "Truth is a thing of this world: it is produced only by virtue of multiple forms of constraint. And it induces regular effects of power. Each society has its regime of truth, its 'general politics' of truth: that is, the types of discourse which it accepts and makes function as true . . . "[4]

Skepticism is thus seen as the only safe position to hold today. Kelly Monroe notes that people "feel safer as doubters, than as believers, and as perpetual seekers rather than eventual finders."[5] Friedrich Nietzsche, after announcing the death of God, viewed truth, especially Christian truth, as,

> "A mobile army of metaphors, metonyms and anthropomorphism's – in short, a sum of human relations, which have been enhanced, transposed, and embellished poetically and rhetorically, and which after long use seem firm, canonical, and obligatory to a people: truths are illusions about which one has forgotten that this is what they are; metaphors which are worn out and without sensuous power. To be truthful means using the customary metaphors – in moral terms: the obligation to lie according to a fixed convention, to lie herd-like in a style obligatory to all"[6]

Nietzsche saw "herd moralities" of good and evil as human perspectives shaped by a raw "will to power." His definition necessarily dissolves a real distinction between truth and lies. He argues that truth claimants "lie" according to "fixed convention" in a "herd-like" fashion; but surely this accusation would mean that truth can be distinguished from the lie! Yet he denies truth has external validity. It is obvious that his definition must include or exclude itself. If it includes itself it can be safely ignored as part of the "army of metaphors." If it excludes itself then Nietzsche is in possession of truth and defeats his own statement. There is no way to escape truth.

Interestingly, returning to the contemporary pseudo-scientific polemics of Dawkins, we see that though his philosophy of scientism differs widely from Nietzsche, the notion of God (the ground of all truth) as an illusion reappears as another form of "herd lying" not in terms of metaphors that have become canonical but as nasty "belief" viruses that have infected and diseased the mind of the group. This is Dawkins' explanation for why the greater part of the world's population believes in God and have become victims of the delusion. Unlike most of us, Dawkins is free from such contamination and his writings are the cure! Unlike real viruses, Dawkins' special viruses cannot be identified, observed, or there manner of functioning analyzed – they are not subject to scientific tests at all; they are a "polemical construction" with a rhetorical value for lambasting those things Dawkins doesn't like. As it turns out in an incredible illogical and unscientific subjective judgment, only religious (theistic) ideas are viruses, not all ideas!! Rational, science based beliefs are not mental viruses! Who decides what beliefs are rational, evidence based and scientific? Dawkins of course!

Again McGrath responds poignantly:

> "Every world view – religious or secular – ends up falling into the category of 'belief systems', precisely because it cannot be proved directly. That is simply the nature of world views and everyone knows it. It prevents nobody from holding a world view in the first place, and doing so with complete intellectual integrity in the second. In the end, Dawkins' idea simply implodes, falling victim to his own subjective judgment of what is rational and true. It's not an idea that is taken seriously in the scientific community, and can safely be discarded."[7]

The same is true of his hypothetical "meme" (the equivalent of a gene, but in cultural rather than biological evolution) which he would have us believe has infected all theists by "leaping" into their brains. No such phenomenon has ever been observed and there is no testable model – it is another essentially biological notion dreamt up to support *universal Darwinism*, that seeks to dismiss the fields of anthropology and sociology (not to mention theology) in one fell swoop. Anthropology and sociology that study cultural development see no need for the "meme" in accounting for human beliefs – it is simply a redundant concept. The mainstream scientific community view it as a "flaky" idea at best.[8] The reception in the serious philosophical world is not much better. Noted atheist and professor of philosophy at Florida State University, Michael Ruse, has said, "*The God Delusion* makes me embarrassed to be an atheist." Hypothetical, unobserved, non-empirical, conceptually redundant entities are hardly the stuff of science so perhaps we require a "meme for believing in memes in the first place,"[9] which naturally means that Dawkins and co have been infected (with other belief memes) and their judgments cannot be trusted. Wasn't the problem with believing in God that He cannot be demonstrated by the scientific method, thereby making belief in Him irrational?

Hobby or drug

Skepticism and fundamentalist atheism aside, on the face of it, there is some element of truth lurking in an aspect of these general criticisms that view religion as a drug or hobby. There can be no doubt that many who claim to be religious, even Christian, treat their faith like a hobby, a sport, or a drug. However, the honest inquirer must be careful, for just because some people abuse and misuse the Christian message, that does not invalidate it. Most people's understanding of Christianity is a misunderstanding, which leads naturally to objections that are based on false assumptions. The actual objective of the Christian message is not to help you soothe away your trouble, but to highlight and expose the root of our common problem and then to remove and overcome it. In the Bible, the solution to our individual and corporate problems is found in the person of Jesus Christ. His life, teaching, death, resurrection and historical impact certainly warrant more serious attention than the insanity experienced and subsequently inspired by the work of Nietzsche. Anyone taking the time to examine the message of the Bible will quickly discover how false the many popular misunderstandings really are. The Christian message is no anesthetic to dull the ache of human existence – there has never been a more realistic outlook confronting human beings as they really are.

Deceit and delusion

Ravi Zacharias has written a folktale from India for children called the *Merchant and the Thief*, in which a poor fruit seller becomes envious of the wealth and possessions of some merchants in his town. He begins to steal from the market and from his customers. Before long, he decides he must steal something very valuable to overcome his poverty. He knows that one wealthy merchant went to visit his family in the town of his birth, a week's walk to the west, once a year. He knew the merchant would carry his most precious jewels with him rather than leave them to be stolen in his absence. So, posing as a merchant himself, he caught up with the wealthy jeweler on his journey and befriended him, traveling with him along the road.

The jeweler was suspicious of strangers and had devised a plan to protect his precious jewels. For several nights, they shared a room at the inns en route. The innkeeper would give them each a mat, a pillow, a basin, and some soap. The thief suggested they take turns to go and wash on the balcony of their room while the other set out his bed and thus have some privacy while undressing and preparing to sleep. The thief deceptively offered to go first, fully intending to find and take the jewels, then slip away into the night, when it was the merchant's turn on the balcony. But while the thief was taking his turn to wash each evening, the merchant carefully hid his jewels.

With speed and care, each night, the thief looked everywhere in the merchant's bag, in his clothes, under his bed and pillow, but couldn't find them. This went on for four days until the last day of the journey, when the thief's frustration had reached its limit. On this last day, to put him out of his misery, the rich merchant put his hands on the thief's shoulder and said, "I know what you have been up to, searching for my jewels while I was washing my face. I know you are a thief. So I hid them every evening where you would least expect to find them. You slept on them each night, for I put them under your pillow!"

This clever and humorous story illustrates well the corruption and deceit endemic to the human condition. Even in reading this simple tale of an envious and corrupt man who sought to justify lying and stealing because of his poverty, we almost feel sorry for the devious thief as he is outwitted by the ingenuity of the jeweler.

One incredible feature of the Bible is that it portrays people as they really are, at their best and at their worst. It never shies away from exposing the truth about the human condition – the folly, the indifference, the hypocrisy and the baseness of people's life and behavior. Scripture is not always pleasant reading. You will find all of human nature in the Bible – ugliness and beauty, vices and virtues. Consider those who are wise or in high positions in all their heroism, pomp and glory; the same ones are seen groveling in immorality and vile debauchery. Yet in Scripture we see equally the marvelous possibilities – the glory, genius, and beauty of virtue open to these incredible beings called men and women. We see these wonderful attributes and yet at the same time, this shame and awful potential, due to a corrupt heart.

Some time ago, I read a story on the front page of a Canadian national newspaper, the *Globe and Mail*, the horror of which lodged in my mind. A man from British Columbia had shot and strangled his six children to get revenge on his wife and then cut his own throat in front of her. In the light of such horrific incidents Philosopher Thomas Morris asks:

> "How can the same species produce both unspeakable wickedness and nearly inexplicable goodness? How can we be responsible both for the most disgusting squalor and for the most heartbreaking beauty? How can grand aspiration and self-destructive impulses, kindness and cruelty be interwoven in one life?"[10]

The Bible tells us the truth about ourselves and that can make people feel uncomfortable. A recent lead article in Canada's *Macleans* magazine entitled "How Canadian are you?" claimed more than 30% of Canadians were most uncomfortable around evangelical Christians, a similar percentage as other top "untouchables" like drug addicts and child abusers. Christians are by no means perfect but does that account for why so many people would respond like that? One compelling answer for such an extreme reaction is the biblical one – the human ethical hostility towards God. The Christian faith and the holiness of God, bring us face to face with the stark truth about ourselves. It unswervingly confronts us with our deceitful hearts and moral deficiencies. No book matches the Bible for its forthright realism. Bible study is no idle pastime or hobby. No secular psychology or anthropology can compare with the Bible for diagnosing our ills and yet simultaneously accounting for our great strengths. How could they measure up, since they do not acknowledge the true God and therefore fail to diagnose the human problem correctly? In his woeful understanding and hatred of the biblical text, Dawkins identifies the God he does not believe in as,

> "A petty, unjust, unforgiving control freak; a vindictive, bloodthirsty ethnic cleanser; a misogynistic, homophobic, racist, infanticidal, genocidal, filicidal, pestilential, megalomaniacal, sadomasochistic, capriciously malevolent bully."[11]

This is quite a *moral outburst* from a writer who admits that his Darwinian atheism can't provide a stable basis for transcutural, non-subjective ethical judgments – a man who occupies a universe in which there is no good or evil, justice or injustice! Can you really have it both ways? He has clearly never met the Jesus Christ of the Gospels, the eternal Son of God (according to Christians). Dawkins hasn't described the God of the Bible at all nor diagnosed the human problem, *but he has inadvertently described the moral condition of men and women in their treatment of each other and that is the essence of the problem that the Christian gospel of Christ faces head on.*

God's or cosmic garbage?

A large number of people agree that we should enjoy life while we can. Eat, drink, and be merry, for tomorrow we die. "I hope I die before I get old," was how one rocker of the sixties put it. Oblivion is coming when our misery and the ordeal of this life will end, so we ought to make the best of the time we have. We don't know what reality is, so live as you please, and don't be confined by religious claims. In *The Search for Signs of Intelligent Life in the Universe*, Lily Tomlin writes:

> "I refuse to be intimidated by reality anymore. After all, what is reality anyway? Nothing but a collective hunch. My space chums think reality was once a primitive method of crowd control that got out of hand. In my view, it is absurdity dressed up in a three piece business suit. I made some studies and reality is the leading cause of stress among those in touch with it. I can take it in small doses, but as a lifestyle I found it too confining."

This rejection of divinely appointed structure and order sums up the cultural climate of our day. The Bible gives us a radically different perspective, one that has that peculiar ring of truth about it. It tells us this life is not all there is, and that our reality rooted in time is defined by eternity. Yes, it acknowledges and expounds the great tragedy of life like no other book, but it also tells us that death is not the end, but a transition into a new final destiny. This is not a comfortable thought for many. The eternal state is something they would rather not think about. Scripture exposes and analyses life with unmatched clarity. Listen to how it accounts for the combination of glory and rubbish characteristic of human life. The psalmist writes,

> "For you made us only a little lower than God,
> and you crowned us with glory and honor.
> You put us in charge of everything you made,
> giving us authority over all things." (Psalm 8:5–6)

And yet Jeremiah could write with equal truthfulness, "The human heart is most deceitful and desperately wicked. Who really knows how bad it is?" (Jeremiah 17:9).

It was this apparent paradox that led the seventeenth-century Christian, scientist and philosopher, Blaise Pascal, to write,

> "What sort of freak then is man! How novel, how monstrous, how chaotic, how paradoxical, how prodigious! Judge of all things, feeble earthworm, repository of truth, sink of doubt and error, glory and refuse of the universe ... know then, proud man what a paradox you are to yourself. Be humble, impotent reason! Be silent, feeble nature! Learn that man infinitely transcends man, hear from your master your true condition, which is unknown to you. Listen to God."[12]

Consider, who really knows you but yourself? We do not share many of our thoughts and desires or even some of our actions with our nearest and dearest for fear of being repugnant to them. These inevitable secrets create an awful sense of aloneness and alienation that is part of the human condition. To be fully known by anyone would be frightening because of our vulnerability to their knowledge. Such knowledge is power that could wound our friends and delight those who resent us and use that knowledge to harm us. Ask yourself how many friendships would survive if we really knew what friends said about us when we were not around.

Has this ultimate sense of loneliness ever struck you? It seems we have two selves. The real person and the one we seek to project are often quite different. We know all too well what we are "really like." We often fear that the person we really are will deservedly be rejected. We are so often ashamed of what we are because we know what we could and should be. Even in our supposed moments of openness, we are perpetually shielding our true selves.

The prophet Jeremiah reminds us that some of our thoughts and desires are so deep-seated we can even deceive ourselves about our character and motives. In our self-assessment we twist, distort, and color many things in our favor. So he asks regarding the deceitfulness of the human heart, "Who can know it?" (Jeremiah 17:9)

Many of us are concerned not so much with what is right or wrong but with how much we can get away with. This is well illustrated by the many financial scandals that make the news. We hear constant rumors of abuses of power. For example, some Canadian officials are fiddling their expense accounts, some European Union bureaucrats are creating imaginary companies to extort money and again some UN officials are accused of bribery or misusing their positions. It seems we trade on illusion. The fact that we do not know what is in others' minds keeps society functioning rather than disintegrating. Our society works so hard on impression. We must face it. Many of our motives and desires are hidden. We are an enigma to ourselves. Our measure of happiness is largely due to the facts that are not known about us. Jeremiah rhetorically asks, "Who really knows how bad it is?"

Dispossessed kings

Yet this is only half the story. Despite our penchant for moral failure and deception, we are also capable of great things like art, poetry, music, mathematical and scientific genius, literary and philosophic brilliance, technological advancement, and surprising acts of self-sacrifice, altruism, and moral reform. Consider, for example, the Canadian commuter who jumped onto the train tracks in front of an advancing train to help an elderly woman who had fallen. He held her against the wall, putting himself in the way of the train as it bore down on them. Or think of the bravery and selfless courage of firefighters at the scene of 9/11 or of British commuters helping the injured after the bombing on 7th July, 2006. Consider the heroism of which humans are capable, the love that moves us, the music that lifts us and the moral excellence that periodically manifests itself.

Human nature is a contradiction and a mystery. Consider the ways in which fellow human beings have treated one another. Ernest Gordon's book, *To End All Wars*, tells of an army chaplain giving himself to be crucified in a Japanese labor camp for another soldier who was antagonistic to the Christian faith. However, others are capable of committing mass murder and genocide in the name of progress. While one captured soldier stops to aid a fallen comrade in the infamous "death march" from Bataan, indoctrinated Japanese guards make sport with the Philippine onlookers, women and their babies, by having live bayonet practice, tossing infants into the air and running them through. According to US pilot William E. Dyess, exhausted American soldiers who were forced to surrender the Philippine fortress of Bataan, were simply shot as they fell to the road on this "death march" in April 1942.

> "I never can forget their groans and strangled breathing as they tried to get up. Some succeeded. Others lay lifelessly where they had fallen. I observed that the Japanese guards paid no attention to these. I wondered why. The explanation wasn't long in coming. There was a sharp crackle of pistol and rifle fire behind us. Skulking along, a hundred yards behind our contingent, came a 'clean-up squad' of murdering buzzards. Their helpless victims, sprawled darkly against the white of the road, were easy targets."[13]

The human history recorded in the Bible reflects, like secular history records, the greatness and the horrific distortion of our original nature. We retain a weak instinct of the moral splendor we were meant to exhibit, but we fumble in the darkness of our own weakness and corruption.

What does this tell us? The Christian faith claims that human beings have fallen from our true, original state, that which God created us for and intended us to be. The history given in Scripture tells us that there is no accounting for the paradox of humanity without the deep history of our fall from paradise. Because of the Fall, we need to be rescued. We need to be healed. We need to be mended, for we are broken people. The Bible makes us face ourselves and then it makes sense of who we are. This is no drug, no comfort blanket, no illusion. This is the very essence of what it means to face reality. Any tenable worldview must confront reality and in order to do so it must deal persuasively with the paradox of human life – yet only the Christian story is able to do this convincingly. Non Judeo-Christian perspectives uniformly fail either to define (as in atheism), acknowledge (as in Buddhism), or confront (as in existentialism) the actual, real existence of evil and account for it.

We know that we are dissatisfied with ourselves and deep down we know we need to change. We nurture unrealized hopes, unquenchable desires, and experience unexpected frustration that nothing on earth can satisfy. We feel like dispossessed kings and queens; dethroned and stripped of our original assets. Somehow, we know we were made for more than this. We are conscious of our greatness, our distinction from animal life, of human intelligence and godlikeness, and yet we are equally aware of our weakness, failures, and deplorable thoughts and actions. Our own consciences condemn us.

Perhaps you are wondering why I have focused on the negative aspect of the human condition. Does this mean I have too low an opinion of human beings? Not at all! This is the paradox. It is the truest indicator of being made in the *imago Dei* (the likeness of God) that we are capable of recognizing how weak and wretched we are. If we had never been corrupted, we would today enjoy universal peace, joy, innocence and contentment. We would have no sense of failure, loss, or alienation. But in our greatness, our godlike apprehension our moral sensitivity and rational capacity, we *are* unhappy because we have an aspiration of holiness, truth and happiness that we are powerless to achieve. We are not completely devoid of knowledge, yet, in ourselves, we find much doubt. These are just a few of the contradictions in our nature that were so effectively highlighted by Pascal. The Christian message explains that these conflicts indicate that we have fallen from relationship with God. Wrong-doing and rebellion entered into the world and ruined that unbroken communion and relationship with our Creator, Life-giver and Joy. Now, our hearts are deceitful, corrupted, and alienated from God. The Bible alone allows us to understand the human paradox. In it, we see our godlikeness, our resemblance to God. We bear His imprint in our own nature and yet we are also aware of the corruption that is in the human heart caused by sin. These truths, when presented together, indicate both hope of recovery and foster an appropriate humility.

Historically the human paradox has certainly been manifest in those who claim religious beliefs as well as those who do not. But Jesus Christ taught us "love your enemies and pray for those who persecute you, so that you may be sons of your Father who is in heaven. For he makes his sun rise on the evil and on the good, and sends rain on the just and on the unjust" (Matthew 5:44–45 ESV). If you are struck on one cheek He taught, turn the other! He did no violence, but suffered violence and there was no deceit in His mouth. Yet at times people have done wicked, unjust things in the name of Christ. Therefore we must ask are they consistent with His life, example and message?

In Cambodia, Pol Pot eliminated millions in the name of atheistic socialism. Lenin considered the eradication of Christianity as central to an effective socialist revolution and established means for its elimination by the "protracted use of violence." Such people saw themselves as accountable to no other moral authority than the state – since for them there is no transcendent moral authority by which the actions of a state can be judged. History proves that the Soviet authorities deliberately and systematically destroyed the vast majority of churches and priests during the period of 1918–41. This was done in the name of an atheist agenda. The question is does atheism have the moral authority, philosophical framework and moral resources to condemn such actions as evil, wrong and reprehensible? Subjective judgments of taste and preference don't make them wrong. Relativistic judgments about culture and history cannot condemn them as finally evil. How can you derive an ethical *ought*, from a biological *is*? There is no transcendent referent to show that these actions are evil.

The Christian theist, however, does have the framework and resources for such ultimate ethical judgments in the character and nature of God, manifest in His Law and ultimately in the person of Jesus Christ. It was this faith that provided the moral and legal framework upon which this country (Canada, but also the United Kingdom and United States) with their remaining liberties and justice were founded. When God is rejected society can only "transcedentalize" ideas embodied by the state (Hegel's pantheism and atheistic socialism). In such a case we are in perpetual grave danger.

Crowned with life

The prophet Jeremiah reminds us that God is deeper than all our pretence. When we congratulate (or console) ourselves by imagining that our thoughts are known to no one but ourselves, we forget the all-pervasive presence of God. The prophet reminds us that God "searches all hearts and examines the secret motives" (Jeremiah 17:10). He sees to the very depth of our being – nothing can be hidden from Him. We are like an open book to His all-seeing gaze. We can mislead our friends, even the world, but we cannot mislead God: "For there is going to come a day of judgment when God, the just judge of all the world, will judge all people according to what they have done" (Romans 2:5–6). In the light of all this, Jeremiah finally gets to his prayer because he sees his own heart and recognizes his own need: "O LORD, you alone can heal me, you alone can save" (Jeremiah 17:14).

This is no superficial self-help therapy. He is not content to fool or delude himself and others, but he humbles himself and faces the truth. Yes, he is horrified to look in the mirror. Despite his best human efforts, he feels wounded, broken, and in need of God's help. There is nothing in himself that he can depend on. He is tired of make-believe, and he is tired of trying to cure himself, so he prays with sincerity of heart, "Heal me, Lord. Save me."

Thus, the Christian message, the good news, begins here, with total realism – it goes to the very root cause of misery and death, our own sinfulness. We need to begin here, seeing ourselves the way Jeremiah saw himself. We need to let go of our cleverness and vain self-effort and see that we cannot save ourselves, that we cannot be what we were created to be without the intervention of God. Only when we recognize this are we in a position to receive the divine solution to our malady, Jesus Christ. With the disposition of a child and with humble hearts and open minds, we need to come to Christ for forgiveness and healing. Pascal writes:

> "The Christian faith teaches men these two truths: There is a God whom men are capable of knowing, and they have a corrupt nature which makes them unworthy of him ... It is as equally dangerous for man to know God without knowing his own sinfulness as it is for him to know about his sinfulness without knowing the redeemer who can cure him. Knowing only one of these aspects leads either to the arrogance of the philosophers, who have known God but not their own sinfulness, or to the despair of the atheists, who knew their own wretched state without knowing their redeemer."[14]

This is the reality of this message: that through the death and resurrection of Christ, we can come to God by faith. We can receive forgiveness and cleansing and by God's indwelling Spirit, we receive the power for a changed life. A new synthesis begins where the paradox of human glory and rubbish is resolved, as the fire of His glory in us burns up the refuse of sin.

It is in part through the careful examination and living experience of the human condition, this paradox of glory and refuse, that God calls and pursues us. It may be that our internal conflict and alienation, even from ourselves, does us a great service; for in it, we hear the voice of God calling us from the decomposition of sin and all its futility – the very footsteps of God behind us, pursuing us and calling us back to Himself.

And even though we may flee from God, He pursues us still, for He is relentless and as constant as the Northern Star. I am reminded of Francis Thompson's great poem, *The Hound of Heaven*, an apt reminder of this comforting truth:

> "I fled him, down the nights and down the days;
> I fled him, down the arches of the years;
> I fled him, down labyrinthine ways
> Of my own mind; and in the mist of tears
> I hid from him, and under running laughter.
> Up vistaed hopes I sped;
> And shot, precipitated,
> Adown Titanic glooms of chasmed fears,
> From those strong feet that followed, followed after.
> But with unhurrying chase,
> And unperturbed pace,
> Deliberate speed, majestic instancy,
> They beat – and a Voice beat
> More instant than the feet –
> 'All things betray thee, who betrayest me.'
>
> Halts by me that footfall:
> Is my gloom, after all,
> Shade of his hand outstretched caressingly?
> 'Ah, fondest, blindest, weakest,
> I am he whom thou seekest!
> Thou drawest love from thee, who drawest me.' "[15]

Discussion questions

1. What current examples best illustrate the rubbish that we are capable of?
2. What current examples best illustrate the glory that we display as bearers of God's image?
3. In what way do these contrasting features of our humanity highlight the explanatory power of the biblical narrative? In what way do they show that the biblical story makes sense of our world?

4. How does the biblical description of human nature compare with worldviews that believe:
   (a) we are essentially good
   (b) we are neutral and conditioned by environment
   (c) we are essentially selfish or even evil
5. How do you think this chapter can help you in apologetic conversation?

Notes

1. Alister McGrath, *The Dawkins Delusion* (London: SPCK, 2007), p. 28.
2. McGrath, *The Dawkins Delusion*, p. 30.
3. Alan Bloom, *The Closing of the American Mind* (Simon and Schuster, New York, 1987), p. 25.
4. Michel Foucault, "Truth and Power", in *Power/Knowledge: Selected Interviews and Other Writings, 1972–1977*, ed. Colin Gordon; trans. Colin Gordon, et al. (Pantheon Books, New York, 1980), p. 131.
5. Kelly Monroe, *Finding God at Harvard* (Zondervan, Grand Rapids, 1996), p. 15.
6. Friedrich Nietzsche, *On Truth and Lie in a Extra-Moral Sense, The New Nietzsche*, ed. D. B. Allison (Dell, New York, 1977), p. xvi.
7. McGrath, *Dawkins Delusion*, p. 41.
8. Ibid., p. 43.
9. Ibid., p. 44.
10. Thomas V. Morris, *Making Sense of it All – Pascal and the Meaning of Life* (Eerdmans Publishing Co., Grand Rapids, 1992), p. 129.
11. Richard Dawkins, *The God Delusion* (London: Bantam, 2006), p. 31.
12. *Making Sense of it All – Pascal and the Meaning of Life*, p. 137.
13. M. J. Cohen, and John Major, *History in Quotations* (Cassell, 2004), pp. 835–836.
14. Blaise Pascal, *Mind on Fire*, edited by James M. Houston (Bethany House Publishers, Minneapolis, 1997), pp. 148–149.
15. From: "The Hound of Heaven," *The Lion Christian Poetry Collection* (Lion Publishing, Oxford, 1995), p. 32.

CHAPTER 9

It's About Time

[*First delivered at a student mission event at Oxford University.*]

> "He has made everything beautiful in its time. Also he has put eternity in their hearts, except that no one can find out the work that God does from beginning to end." (Ecclesiastes 3:11 ESV)

> "You are before all the past in the sublimity of your ever-present eternity, and you are above all future things because they are still to come, and when they have come they will be past; but thou art the same, and thy years fail not . . . your today is eternity, and so it was that you begot one who is co-eternal with you to whom you said: This day have I begotten Thee. You made all times and before all times you are; nor was there a time in which there was no time." (St Augustine)

Telling the time

The wise philosopher-king, Solomon, writing the remarkable book of Ecclesiastes, leads us to expect great mysteries in understanding time and eternity as it relates to human experience. Ecclesiastes 3:11 is from a beautiful passage that reflects on God's mysterious providence (His working and governance). This exquisite Hebrew poem summarizes the beauty and appropriateness of attitudes to actions and events when they occur in their appointed seasons. Solomon's insight has lost none of its force right through to the present. Time remains an enigma. The Christian philosopher and theologian, St Augustine, was repeatedly taken up with the mysteries and the problem of time,

> "How can it be that there are two times, past and future, when now the past is no longer and the future is not yet? However, if the present were always present and did not pass into past time, it obviously wouldn't be time but eternity. If time present – if it can be time – comes into existence only because it passes into time past, how can we say that it is, since the cause of its being is its ceasing to be? Therefore, can we not truly say that time *is* only as it tends toward non-being?"[1]

You may need to read that more than once. This short extract highlights the conceptual difficulties and paradoxes of the nature of time. It will come as no surprise to find that scientists and philosophers have puzzled over the nature, origin and meaning of the space-time universe. There is no end to speculation about the *origin* of our temporal reality and how it is that conscious human life has come to be capable of reflection on the passage of time. One of life's greatest mysteries is the nature and origin of *time* itself.

Many scientists today believe that the space-time universe came into being in the finite past at a moment of creation – that is, with time, not in time. Generally, the universe is no longer thought of as eternal but as something that began to be. Of course, without an observer, motion cannot be measured against a referent anyway. So, prior to the universe, there could be no time as we know it and with no observer, no human experience of it.

It is not my purpose here to detail or refute various rival theories about time, but to note that this whole field of study is still today a matter of great controversy and dispute. Exactly what is time? What precisely is its relationship to eternity and are these questions that can be answered? Can we describe the infinite, and what relationship does it sustain to the finite? These problems have, so far, been insoluble for the finite mind of human beings. Indeed, this is what the wisdom literature of the Bible leads us to expect, because we are dealing with the "mysteries that belong to the Lord." The infinite, transcendent, Creator God of Scripture whose "ways are past finding out" and who "dwells in unapproachable light" is beyond human intellect. The absolute, triune personality of God is incomprehensible unless He reveals himself: "No one can find out the work that God does from beginning to end." For the Christian, then, God's self-revelation in Scripture must be the starting point for knowledge. Christ is our ultimate criterion for truth. As the ultimate criterion, He cannot be proved by a criterion more ultimate than Himself. In such a case, He would not be ultimate.

I cannot prove to you *directly* the origin and true nature of time. I cannot inductively reason up from the facts of experience to demonstrate the triune God of Scripture as the author of time, for we may have a disagreement about the very nature of facts. For many people, all facts are uncreated or self-created, and ultimately unrelated, derived from an impersonal void of chaos. However, for the Christian, all facts are created by and therefore dependent upon, the personal God of Scripture. As Augustine put it, "This world could not have been known to us unless it existed, but it could not have existed unless it had been known to God."[2]

What we can do here, is consider some of the implications of the biblical and non-biblical views of the origin and nature of time and examine what follows in terms of meaning and purpose – for I believe that only the biblical view of time provides meaning and makes intelligible anything we do in time.

Time and again

The Bible reminds us of the existential reality of passing moments – these moments come to us all. There is "a time for every purpose" (Ecclesiastes 3:1 NKJV). Regardless of our philosophical views on these matters, we are all conscious of time. We remember our childhood as past and think of death as future and experience now in the present. Augustine again speaks of our apprehension of time existing within the mind,

> "Even now it is plainly evident that there are neither times future nor times past. Thus it is not properly said that there are three times, past, present and future. Perhaps it might be said rightly that there are three times as such,
>
> 1. A time present of things past
> 2. A time present of things present
> 3. A time present of things future.

> These three do co-exist somehow in the soul, for otherwise I couldn't see them. The time present of things past is memory. The time present of things present is direct experience. The time present of things future is expectation."[3]

We are then aware of three aspects to our lives: the past, some of which is present in our memories – the present, as you read this line – and the future, expectations we have that depend very much on memory of the past.

In more concrete terms, we have all been conceived and born into this world and a moment will come when we will die. That is the ultimate statistic: one out of one die. Life takes place between these points in our apparently linear reality.

Reflecting on this space-time existence Albert Einstein once noted ... "It might appear possible to overcome all difficulties attending the definition of 'time' by substituting 'the position of the small hand of my watch', for 'time.' "[4] Einstein did think time was real and external but conditioned by (or relative to) the position of the perceiver, so its measurement must be local.

Look briefly then at your wrist watch. Your watch is a measure of moments, the succession of events. Already the moment at which you began to read this paragraph is history. Now consider the quantity of time we call a second. We are told the following happens, on average, every second – four and a half cars are manufactured, two thousand square meters of forest is wiped out, three people are born, one and a half people die, three point two million cubic meters of water falls as precipitation, two point six million cubic meters of that falls on dry land. In a single second, *Concorde* could fly six hundred and eleven meters. The space shuttle *Columbia* flies at a ground speed of seven point seven kilometers per hour. On its orbit around the sun, our planet travels thirty kilometers. Two point four million red blood cells are produced in our bone marrow, our lungs move two hundred cubic centimeters of air and four billion impulses are exchanged between the cortical hemispheres in our brain. A lot happens in a second. This succession of events we call time. And we have developed ways to measure time from small quantities, fractions of a second, to large quantities – centuries and millennia. Yet the puzzle remains, what exactly are we measuring? Is time subjective, objective or both? You have heard the proverb "a watched pot never boils," but regardless of our perception the duration actually remains the same each time we boil a kettle in our kitchen (although water boils at different temperatures depending on altitude, and so takes different times in different places).

Old timer

It is not so much the philosophical problem of time but its apparently destructive effects that often concern us most. The existential reality of time is troubling. Time seems to pursue us and hunt us down. We feel stalked by the passing years. Time, it seems, is *running out*, or rather, we are gradually *passing out* of the world of time. Although this reality hits home more as we grow older, reflection on it brings the same feeling whether we are spotty teenagers or pensioners in the twilight years riding toward sunset. I am always struck by the vivid and poetic description of old age marking the slow decay of time in Ecclesiastes 12; a passage that prompts us to remember our Creator by focusing attention on our mortality and the short span of our earthly pilgrimage:

> "Remember also your Creator in the days of your youth, before the evil days come and the years draw near when you will say, 'I have no delight in them'; before the sun and the light, the moon and the stars are darkened, and clouds return after the rain; in the day that the watchmen of the house tremble, and mighty men stoop, the grinding ones stand idle because they are few, and those who look through windows grow dim; and the doors on the street are shut as the sound of the grinding mill is low, and one will arise at the sound of the bird, and all the daughters of song will sing softly. Furthermore, men are afraid of a high place and of terrors on the road; the almond tree blossoms, the grasshopper drags himself along, and the caperberry is ineffective. For man goes to his eternal home while mourners go about in the street. Remember Him before the silver cord is broken and the golden bowl is crushed, the pitcher by the well is shattered and the wheel at the

> cistern is crushed; then the dust will return to the earth as it was, and the spirit will return to God who gave it." (Ecclesiastes 12:1–7 NAS)

In the classic movie, *Star Trek Generations*, a fascinating story unfolds exploring the mystery of time and the human desire to defeat it. The film centers around a fictional anomaly in space called the nexus – a temporal "ribbon phenomenon" that pulls you into a place where the ordinary flow of time seems meaningless. This phenomenon can also read your thoughts so in this "nexus" you are placed into your ideal world to live out your dreams endlessly. A place where the temporal order is suspended – an interesting heaven parallel. In one portion of dialogue, Captain Picard is trying to talk some sense into the villain, Soren, who is going to destroy millions of lives by exploding a star, altering the ribbon's course toward his location, just to get back into the nexus – he will do anything to get back. Why? Soren, our villain, evocatively describes time as a predator that is stalking you, gaining on you, closing in to make the kill. But, he says of the nexus, "time has no meaning there, the predator has no teeth." This popular film explores one of the greatest mysteries of human existence: time – its origin, meaning, purpose and end.

Stretching your mind

So, have we moved any closer to understanding time? Can we gain any more clarity? The *English Chambers Dictionary* defines time as "the continuous passing and succession of minutes, days, and years." This does not really tell us what time is at all. It just tells us how we have measured time. Augustine's most famous remark about time was stated as a humorous question: "What then is time? If no one asks me I know what it is. However, if I wish to explain time to him who asks, I don't know."[5] He was highlighting the fact that time is so very difficult to for us to contemplate. When we do, we are overwhelmed by a sense of the weakness of the human intelligence. We cannot put this reality into words; even though we largely assume we know what it is when we are not asked to explain it. Furthermore, we cannot sum it up with an equation. Einstein's theory of relativity has not brought the expected breakthrough.

It must be conceded that time appears like a riddle to us, an inscrutable mystery. It leaves us with puzzles and paradoxes, so we ask an important and very human question, from whence did time originate and will we be able to move beyond confusion and semantics when we talk about it? I find Augustine's conclusion helpful and compelling, giving important clues about the nature of God.

> "It's in you, O mind of mine, that I measure periods of time . . . I measure the periods in you. I measure as time present the impression that things make on you as they pass by and what remains after they have passed. I don't measure the things themselves that have passed by and left their impression on you. This is what I measure when I measure periods of time."[6]

Augustine is suggesting here that measurement of time is primarily a function of the mind, because even if we did not have atomic clocks or revolving heavenly bodies we would still have an internal perception of the flow of time – a kind of internal chronometer. In a sense, time is the stretching or extending of the mind. The present, the now, has no duration, but from here the mind stretches to anticipate the future and remember the past. The future does not have an existence, except in the mind of God, and neither does the past as it is gone; the present does not abide – so what do we measure but the extending of the mind? This brilliant observation gives us a small glimpse of the mind of God and eternity – the intersection between the temporal existence of human beings and the non-temporal existence of God. Our finite, limited minds stretch only a little, but if they could extend to encompass all the future and the past we would have knowledge of all time. Perhaps this imagined circumstance points to the vastness of the mind of God who knows not only all time simultaneously, but all eternity also! This may help you to begin to see what the writer of Ecclesiastes was saying when he wrote, "He has planted eternity in the human heart, but even so, people cannot see the whole scope of God's work from beginning to end" (Ecclesiastes 3:11).

Lucky timing

We are limited in our alternatives when considering the nature of time. We have essentially a choice of two. Firstly, we are creatures made by God in His image, living in the space-time world and capable of perceiving a flow of time that has real meaning and purpose, or else we (who have minds that perceive and measure time) are ultimately products of chance, any "god" that may or may not exist is finite, in the world of time and correlative to the world. The popular "big bang hypothesis," a contemporary origins story, though affirming a beginning for the universe, is fraught with mathematical problems that have been creatively solved by invoking "hypothetical entities" to make the hypothesis workable. It has no real explanatory power to tell us how the space-time continuum came into existence from nothing, by blind mindless processes acting on nothing! All the laws of physics are said to break down at the quantum singularity, the entity which must be accepted by faith by those who reject a faith commitment to God. Hence an explanation that is no explanation helps us neither philosophically nor personally, since the origin of time is deeply significant to us all; for only as we come to understand its origin can we contemplate the *meaning and purpose* of time and how we should use it. If all is random, irrational and thus ultimately meaningless as some suppose, then we may just kill and waste time, for this is what time does to us. Consider the following poem:

> "Once upon a point of infinite density, Nothing that was Something went boom. Then there was Everything. Everything eventually named Something 'Matter', the tragic character in our story. Sadly, Matter had no mind, yet this makes our tale or the more amazing!
>
> Now Matter had only one companion, the hero of our fable, a mysterious stranger of unknown origin called Chance. Chance, though blind, was a brilliant artist. Chance taught mindless Matter to paint, and paint our pupil did. Matter painted a universe from center to rim on the canvas of a vacuum. And lo, innumerable galaxies emerged filled with infinite wonders, beauty, order and life. The inspired brush strokes of ignorant Matter, guided by the hands of blind Chance, created together a cosmic masterpiece. But as Matter and Chance were working away they failed to spot our villain, Time.

> Time crept in unnoticed back at the boom and was extremely wound up about being stirred from his sleep. Time determined there and then to wind down again and thus rub the masterpiece out – as soon as he got hold of that chance! Chance, being blind, didn't see time coming and mindless Matter was helpless to intervene.
>
> Now, time ruins the painting little by little and brags that by chance it's just a matter of time before the canvas is blank and the boom will swoon and Everything, that was Something, will be Nothing again. Once more, upon a pointless point of infinite nothingness, with no time for chance to matter anymore."[7]

This is one view of the origin and end of the space-time continuum. Is the eternal God a reality beyond time and space or is the blank void behind everything? To which authority should we go for guidance? Should we be led merely by physics textbooks or humanist philosophers? Unfortunately, their observations, though at times helpful, are not far-reaching enough. Although many concede today that time as we know it has not always existed since it came into existence at the beginning of the universe along with space and matter, few are willing to acknowledge the God of Scripture who is "before all time" (Jude 25 HCSB). Instead, many skeptics simply try to dodge the question by asking "Does not God need a cause as well?" If God does not need a cause, why should the universe need one?

Time's arrow

The cosmological or causal line of reasoning has some value here. In the observations of everyday life, in our naïve realism, we notice that nothing comes from nothing. We also observe that *effects do not seem greater in quality and quantity than their cause*. If we apply this line of thought to our finite universe, it suggests that all space-time reality was brought into existence by one who is truly personal (with a mind, for we, as the effect, are personal with minds), all-knowing (greater than the sum of all human knowledge), all-powerful (greater than the sum total of created energy) and, most importantly, infinite (greater than the reaches of space) and timeless (since time as we know it came into existence with the motion of the space-time universe). Otherwise, we can make little sense of what exists and must resort to asserting that reality just came into existence without mind and without cause. If God exists, He is not a finite, changing event or series of events like our universe that requires a cause to be intelligible. He is uncaused and unchanging, the source and ultimate cause of all effects.

If Augustine is right and time is primarily the measuring of the human soul and ultimately the divine mind, then God's mind stretches to encompass all time (past, present and future) and eternity in His eternal, unchanging present. So then, if we want to know about who we are and how to use our short time on this earth, we should seek the One who brought time and our ability to experience it into being. The only alternative to belief in God is the infinite nothingness of impersonal existence and a lack of meaning and rationality to the universe at every level. The very essence of the search for a cause of time is the quest to discover the reason for time. Without God, there is no ultimate reason for anything. On such a view, "Time is the reef upon which all our frail mystic ships are wrecked."[8]

God's timetable

Unlike the books of many contemporary philosophers, the Bible begins, "In the beginning God created the heavens and the earth" (Genesis 1:1). Or, to put it in a manner that might elucidate my point, "In the beginning was infinite information calling the space-time continuum into existence." Time, on this basis, is not an eternal cycle, not infinite. It had a finite beginning, and as we know it, will have an end. "Not cycles but sequence; not fate, but providence; not chaos, but order; not caprice, but pedagogy."[9]

The same is true of the physical world we live in. Governed by God's providence, the cosmos is running down, decaying, wearing out. We call this principle "entropy." Yet despite the evident decay of time, the creation all around us reveals something of the divine watchmaker in the intricacy, beauty, order, complexity and diversity of life. As William Blake once powerfully asked,

"Tyger, tyger burning bright
In the forests of the night,
What immortal hand or eye
Could frame thy fearful symmetry?

When the stars threw down their spears,
And water'd heaven with their tears,
Did he smile his work to see?
Did he who made the lamb, make thee?"[10]

The Author of the space-time universe, the Creator of heaven and earth, according to the Bible, is the triune God: Father, Son and Holy Spirit (John 1:1ff.). This I take on faith in the authority of Jesus Christ. The Scriptures tell us, "By faith we understand that the universe was created by the word of God, so that what is seen has been made from things that are not visible" (Hebrews 11:3 HCSB). It is a rational and intelligible religion to believe that Christ, the wisdom of God, an "immortal hand and eye," shaped our universe; it is a religion of pure irrationality to assume that blind chance is the author of it all. It is worth noting that there is no known natural law through which matter can give rise to highly specified, coded information. This is similar to believing that an explosion ripping through a lumber yard could create the Taj Mahal. It is hard to imagine a more counter-intuitive assumption.

In the Bible, Jesus teaches supernatural creation. He claimed to be the Author of the world, the beginning and the end, the self-existent one (Revelation 1:8) and confirmed His claims by demonstrating incredible power over the creation. This is admirably documented in the Gospel accounts from His turning water into wine to walking on water and raising the dead. In the biblical worldview, time, whatever time is, belongs to God. Scripture affirms that our times, the successive moments of life, are in God's hands. Jesus addressed this very thing when He asked, "Who of you by worrying can add a single hour to his life?" (Matthew 6:27 NIV). We cannot extend the time we have, and we do not know when our time will end, but we can use it foolishly or wisely. In fact Jesus taught we can *invest* our time in eternity, a place where time does not run down, or we can face the consequences of wasting it without regard for God.

If God is indeed the Lord of all time, then the meaning of time is defined by eternity. Time has a goal, a divine direction. Our time has real purpose because of the all-inclusive plan of God which ranges across all the ages. Seeing this, we have a wisdom that can help us understand the meaning and purpose of *our* time here on earth. As the Bible admonishes us in Psalm 90:12, "Teach us to number our days aright, that we may gain a heart of wisdom" (NIV).

Time saver

The English poet Steve Turner poignantly reminds us: "These are the good old days. Just wait and see!" Like camp and college days, before we know it, *today* will become one of our good old days. Time waits for no one and it is flying by. Looking at time from a perspective that excludes the God of Scripture is rather depressing. Have you ever considered that *much of our life is spent trying to find something to do with the time that we rush through our lives trying to save?* We never seem satisfied with the present and are always caught up with experiences from the past or expectations of the future. Consider this penetrating observation of Pascal,

> "Let each one examine his thoughts, and he will find them all occupied with the past and the future. We scarcely ever think of the present; and if we think of it, it is only to take light from it to arrange the future. The present is never our end. The past and the present are our means; the future alone is our end. So we never live, but we hope to live; and, as we are always preparing to be happy, it is inevitable we should never be so."[11]

Will we ever be truly happy in time? Our thoughts always turn to the future to try to improve our reality, but is it a future we have no guarantee of reaching?

Sir Walter Raleigh (1552–1618), the English Commander, historian, and poet wrote an untitled poem the night before his execution:

> "Even such is time, which takes in trust
> Our youth, our joys, and all we have
> And pays us but with age and dust

> Who in the dark and silent grave
> When we have wondered all our ways
> Shuts up the story of our days."[12]

This highlights an important and tragic truth. The Christian faith does not reject or ignore this reality of life and death. On the contrary, we are described as like grass that is here today and gone the next. The beloved English hymn writer, Isaac Watts, notably reminds us of this biblical worldview:

> "Time, like an ever-rolling stream,
> Bears all its sons away;
> They fly forgotten, as a dream
> Dies at the opening day."[13]

Jesus affirmed that "heaven and earth will pass away" (Matthew 24:35 NIV). The apostle Paul writes: "This world in its present form is passing away" (1 Corinthians 7:31 NIV). History as we know it is working toward an end. We cannot lend, store, skip or bank time to gain more. We cannot freeze our bodies when we die and be certain of being given another period of life, nor can we travel through time – it is a one-way system! But if our time is a gift from a God who is there, two things become true that move beyond Raleigh's prognosis. First, our time has real significance and meaning despite our physical death. And secondly, time has a new destination, eternity. Thus, with the biblical origin of time and its destination in mind we can begin to see *why* our time has real importance and significance; time is not ultimate but is defined by eternity. What you do and who you become [in time] matters to God and it matters to other people. What we do has a real lasting effect on people, not just ourselves.

Just "in time"

There have been many significant moments, pivotal events, in history. Certain events stand out to Western historians such as the Reformation beginning in 1521, the origin of modern democracy during the English Civil War beginning in 1642, the Great War starting in 1914, the England football team winning the World Cup in 1966 (a personal favourite of mine!), the first heart transplant in 1967, the first steps by a man on the moon in 1969, the dismantling of the Berlin Wall in 1989. These notable events illustrate significant turning points or times of breakthrough that changed the world forever. The most important event of all, from which all of these pivotal moments derive their date, is found in Galatians 4:4: "When the right *time* came God sent his Son" (emphasis added). Although many societies have their own calendars, the BC–AD dating system is understood throughout the world. Time and eternity fused at a single moment when humanity's God became human and came among us. The Creator of time and Lord of eternity became one of us (see John 1:1–10). There has never been a more important moment in human history. The world would never be the same again! Augustine tries to find the words to describe this epochal revelation of Christ at the incarnation:

> "The Lord has made all things, and yet He takes his stand among the very things He's made. He's the Revealer of His Father, and at the same time He's the Creator of His mother. He's the Son of God born of the Father without a mother; and He's the son of man born of a mother without a father. He's the Day as the angels count time; He's the Clock as human beings tick off the day. He's the Word of God before there were timepieces; He's the Word made flesh who stopped the clock when he was made flesh."[14]

Time's up

He came into time to reveal eternity. The ministry of Jesus the God-man focused in on people's relationship with God, explaining that the way we live in time shapes our present and determines our eternity. In the box-office hit, *Gladiator*, the hero, Maximus, rallying his cavalry for battle, tells them, "What we do in life echoes in eternity."

The time God gives us in the present, affects not only our earthly life, but our future beyond this life also. Our decisions become *infinitely* important. Most important of all is how we decide to respond to God and His Son Jesus Christ. When the writer of Ecclesiastes tells us that there is a time for everything, this includes God's call to us to get our attention!

Jesus explains the significance of this in one of His many parables about time and its eternal significance – for time's importance is not diminished but reinforced by the ultimate of eternity.

> "A rich man had a fertile farm that produced fine crops. In fact, his barns were full to overflowing. So he said, 'I know! I'll tear down my barns and build bigger ones. Then I'll have room enough to store everything. And I'll sit back and say to myself, My friend, you have enough stored away for years to come. Now take it easy! Eat, drink, and be merry!' But God said to him, 'You fool! You will die this very night. Then who will get it all?' Yes a person is a fool to store up earthly wealth but not have a rich relationship with God."
>
> (Luke 12:16–21)

Here, a rich man sets himself up for life and decides to take an early retirement and live only for himself, presuming that his time and his money are his own. That very day, as he boasted in his heart of what he was going to do, God says that his time has come. The folly of such a misdirected life is exposed.

It is so easy to ignore these issues and live selfishly for ourselves, ignoring God. Our rich man in the parable made the fatal error of presuming upon time. He thought his time was his own. He thought it belonged to him. He was mistaken. He was rich in wealth and pleasures on earth, but he was spiritually impoverished. He was not aware of the need to prepare for eternity. He was not ready for the "undiscovered country." Time had made the kill and he was unprepared to pass through the jaws of death. The message Christ came to bring was one of life – beginning now and reaching on beyond time into eternity. He did say, "Heaven and earth will pass away", but He added, "My words will never pass away" (Matthew 24:35 NIV). What words? We can read them in the Scriptures. Jesus said, "I am the resurrection and the life. Those who believe in me, even though they die like everyone else, will live again" (John 11:25).

What is it we are to believe? Through Christ's incarnation in time, His death for our wrong-doing, and His bodily resurrection defeating sin and death forever, we can find forgiveness for all of our failures and know joy everlasting in the unseen world without end. Our consciences can be cleansed and our shame washed away, as we put our trust in Christ Jesus, believing that He is Lord of the universe who died to bring us to God and was raised to give us life eternal. The Bible teaches that this is the most significant and important decision we can make in time. The Author of time, the One who will bring time as we know it to an end calls us to come to Him for new life. The apostle Paul puts it simply for us: "For the wages of sin is death, but the free gift of God is eternal life through Christ Jesus our Lord" (Romans 6:23).

Timeless

The British dramatist Tom Stoppard noted: "Eternity is a terrible thought. I mean, where's it all going to end?" This humorous quip raises a potential misunderstanding about eternity and the nature of God. As we have seen, God does not run by the atomic clock for atoms are part of reality He has created. He is not bound and limited by the space-time universe He has made. Terms like "past" and "present" and "future" lose their meaning where God dwells. There is no "there" and "then" with God, only "here" and "now," an eternal, dynamic presence of this moment. God transcends our time axis and sees the rolling ages at a single glance. Even we can imagine looking on events that happened thousands of light years ago. A light year is a measure of distance, defined by the distance light travels in one year. If we could look through a telescope from a star 1,000 light years from Earth we could witness the events of the turn of the previous millennium. If we could travel at limitless speed from star to star we could experience a certain contemporaneousness of all past events. God's time is an eternal *now*. Filling "all in all," He spreads undivided and operates unspent.

Consequently, eternity is not physical time stretched out infinitely like a conveyor belt. It is a new quality and a new dimension to life that will endure forever. Though impossible to fully comprehend, we all have this internal sense of God and eternity somewhere in our consciousness. "God has set eternity in the human heart, but he cannot fathom what God has done from beginning to end." Yes, we are presently limited to time; we cannot see what God sees. His sovereign work from beginning to end is a mystery to us and so only apprehended by faith in the heart:

> " 'My thoughts are completely different from yours,' says the LORD. 'And my ways are far beyond anything you could imagine. For just as the heavens are higher than the earth, so are my ways higher than your ways and my thoughts higher than your thoughts.' " (Isaiah 55:8–9)

Yet we possess a sense of eternity, knowing deep down that life goes on beyond the veil of time. Of course, eternity is only heaven because God gives it meaning, purpose, and endless joy. Eternity without God is what the Bible calls hell. Hell is ever-present self-absorption and isolation, living with the fruit of the delusion that humans are their own god.

From time to time

An unspeakable gift is given to those who trust in Jesus – a new quality of life. God Himself, by the presence of His life-giving Spirit is the gift, the new quality that fills our lives. "Those who have the Son," said Jesus, "have life in all its fullness" (John 10:10 REF). So, there are only two destinies that lie before each of us to choose. Jesus was clear about this:

> "All who believe in God's Son have eternal life. Those who don't obey the Son will never experience eternal life, but the wrath of God remains upon them." (John 3:36)

As we pass our days on earth moment to moment, from time to time, this pressing question does occur –will I inherit the wind when I die, or will I inherit *the whirlwind* for a life lived in rebellion against God? However great, rich, famous or powerful one may be, none can stem the sands of time. All succumb to the ceaseless erosion of time. But, what then? Will anything last?

> "O Time the fatal wrack of mortal things,
> That draws oblivious curtains over kings,
> Their sumptuous monuments, men know them not,

> Their names without record are forgot,
> Their parts, their ports, their pomp's laid in th' dust
> Nor wit nor gold, nor buildings 'scape time's rust;
> But he whose name is graved in the white stone
> Shall last and shine when all of these are gone."[15]

Time is the great leveller. Naked we came into the world; naked we will leave it. Only those whose names are engraved in the book of life will "last and shine when all of these are gone." Christ is the Author of that eternal book of life and death, the narrator of the rolling years, the Alpha and Omega, the beginning and the end, who was, who is, and who is to come. He is the Ancient of Days who is before all time. The Scriptures assure us concerning the believer's eternal home, the dwelling place of our Lord Jesus Christ. In that place "there will be no more death or mourning or crying or pain, the old order of things has passed away" (Revelation 21:4 NIV) At the last, there will be no more misery, tragedy, or broken hearts for his people. We will no longer suffer remorse for a wasted past, nor plan for true happiness in an illusory future, but experience endless joy in the unbroken duration of his eternity.

Discussion questions

1. In what ways do you look forward to the passing of time?
2. In what ways do you dread the passing of time?
3. In what ways can *thinking about the nature of time* affect the way we think about God?
4. In what ways does the *way we spend our time* affect the way we think about God?
5. What do you notice about the way time is treated in our culture?
   (a) What does our culture's obsession with feeling and looking young tell you?
   (b) What does our treatment of our elderly tell you?
6. If we believed that time is a gift from God and is leading towards something greater, how would that change our attitude toward time in our own life?

7. If we believed that time is all there is and our own short life-spans are all the time we each have, how would that change our attitude toward time in our own life?
8. In what ways did this chapter help you to think more clearly about the nature of time?
9. What questions remain for you as you think about this topic?

Notes

1. Augustine, *Confessions*, translation by Albert C. Outler, revised and updated by Dr Tom Gill (Bridge-Logos, Gainsville, Florida, 2003), p. 322.
2. St Augustine, cited by Jaroslav Pelikan in, *The Mystery of Continuity: time and history, memory and eternity in the thought of Saint Augustine* (The University Press of Virginia, Virginia, 1986), p. 48.
3. Augustine, *Confessions*, translation by Albert C. Outler, revised and updated by Dr Tom Gill (Bridge-Logos, Gainsville, Florida, 2003), p. 328.
4. Albert Einstein, cited by Sharon M. Kaye and Paul Thomson, in *On Augustine* (Wadsworth, 2001), p. 52.
5. Augustine, *Confessions*, p. 322.
6. Augustine, *Confessions*, pp. 337–338.
7. Joe Boot, *Searching For Truth* (Crossway Books, 2002), pp. 53–54.
8. Sir Noel Coward, English dramatist, actor, composer (1899–1973), from *Blithe Spirit*, 1941.
9. Jaroslav Pelikan, *The Mystery of Continuity*, p. 50.
10. William Blake, "The Tyger," *Everyman's Poetry*, (J. M. Dent, London, 1996).
11. Blaise Pascal, "Pensées," in *Great Books of the Western World*, Volume 33, associate ed. Mortimer J. Adler (Encyclopedia Britannica, Inc., 1952), p. 203.
12. Sir Walter Raleigh, *The Times Book of Quotations* (HarperCollins, 2000), p. 703.
13. Isaac Watts, in *The Times Book of Quotations*, p. 704.
14. Augustine, *Sermons to the People*, translated by William Griffin (Image Books, 2002), pp. 72–73.
15. Anne Bradstreet (1612–72), *The Lion Christian Poetry Collection* (Lion Publishing, Oxford), p. 459.

CHAPTER 10

The Uniqueness of Christ

[First delivered at an apologetics seminar for the Oxford Centre of Christian Apologetics, Wycliffe Hall, Oxford.]

Without parallel

One could write volumes about almost any aspect of the unique character of Jesus Christ – His life and teaching, His historic impact, the titles ascribed to Him, His miracles, His resurrection, and His startling claims. Every aspect of His life, character and ministry cause Him to rise massive from the pages of history, dwarfing all others. Napoleon Bonaparte, Emperor of France, made a detailed study of the person of Christ during his extended exile and imprisonment. The following was his conclusion:

> "From first to last, Jesus is the same, always the same – majestic and simple, infinitely severe and infinitely gentle. Throughout a life passed under the public eye, He never gives occasion to find fault . . .
>
> I know men; and I tell you that Jesus is not a man. Everything in Him amazes me. His spirit outreaches mine, and His will confounds me. Comparison is impossible between Him and any other being in the world. He is truly a being by Himself. His ideas and His sentiments; the truth that He announces; His manner of convincing; are all beyond humanity and the natural order of things.
>
> His birth, and the story of His life; the profoundness of His doctrine, which overturns all difficulties, and is their most complete solution; His gospel; the singularity of His mysterious being; His appearance; His empire; His progress through all centuries and kingdoms; all this is to me a prodigy, an unfathomable mystery . . . I defy you to cite another life like that of Christ."[1]

Even Lord Byron, the profligate British poet affirmed, "If ever man was God or God was man, Jesus Christ was both."[2]

Though the person of Christ has overwhelmed the understanding of many people, even skeptics, this clearly does not always cause them to put their faith in Christ.

It is important to remember that the way in which people interpret the evidence presented will be largely governed by their overall perspective on reality. No matter how powerful evidence from prophecy or miracles may be, many people will seek a naturalistic or non-Christian accounting for the facts. The "faith" of many excludes from the outset any interpretation of the evidence that concludes that Jesus is the Son of God. For example, no matter how good the eyewitness testimony for the raising of Lazarus may be, the atheist who denies the supernatural as a tenet of their faith will naturally accept *any* explanation as more plausible than God bringing him back to life. This bias with respect to the evidence is governed by prior beliefs, governed by faith in something. It is not only the interpretation of isolated facts here and there (a miracle, say or a prophecy), that is at stake, but rather the very meaning of fact and history as a whole. The uniqueness of Christ confronts all human belief systems at this core level.

The plow, the telescope and cyber space

Because all that one hears about Christ will be interpreted in light of a prevailing perspective on fact and history, it is important to first understand what has shaped contemporary perspectives and paradigms in the modern world. How did we come to where we are today in the West? Why is a proclamation of the uniqueness of Christ so often difficult for Christians to communicate and so hard for today's biblical illiterate to accept?

In the ancient world, especially among the nations of the Levant and Mesopotamia, people's beliefs about reality were governed through **world-encounter**. It was a basic assumption that the world had a "givenness" about it that spoke of a supernatural order or architect. For the Hebrew nation, God was encountered in the world by His faithful providential activity in creation, unlike the pagans who encountered the world as a playground for various gods often personifying forces of nature. For the descendants of Abraham, God's Law and will were thought to supervene over all reality, His omnipotence clearly manifest in the creation. Seedtime and harvest, the regularity of the seasons, were means by which God's order was known and understood. The use of simple technologies in the ancient world like the plow illustrates well the human response to this confidence in God's governing activity. Human gratitude for this provision was shown often in terms of offerings from the harvest as produce granted under God's providence.

The modern era, in contrast to the ancient, has been one of *world-viewing*. Since Descartes, and perhaps as early as John Scotus Dunn, people began to see themselves as autonomous, not defined by the transcendent Law and providence of God but independent. God was no longer the ultimate point of reference for understanding reality, but human beings were. "Standing back" from reality, taking an "objective" stance, moderns began to *view* rather than encounter reality from this autonomous perspective. This mood can be illustrated well by the development of technologies like the telescope. This occurred accidentally in 1608 after the children of Dutch spectacle-maker Hans Lippershey were playing with their father's tools. It was developed and trained on the skies by the famous Christian astronomer from Italy, Galileo (1564–1642).[3] The microscope is the instrument that represents the rise of the modern, technophile era. Soon science (viewing and dissection) began to be practiced not in terms of the human encounter with God's activity (as it was for Galileo), but became driven by the desire for a human conquest of nature through the ideal of comprehensive knowledge. God was now being banished to the fringe of the universe – a "God of the gaps." The world post-Darwin is viewed not as a creation of God, but as a battle for survival.

Today's context is one of *world-making*. Whether we try to stand back in autonomous, rational objectivity in order to *view* reality, we remain part of created reality, with partial not comprehensive knowledge. Today, the mood of our time *makes* a new world in its own image. The world will be what the individual wants it to be. Truth will be what we want it to be. Reality will shape itself to service us, the cosmic consumer.

The mood is exemplified by the technological development of virtual reality, cyber space, and other digital fictions. Belief boils down to subjectivity; as long as it "works for you" it is good! Consequently, historical arguments about the uniqueness of Christ have a great deal to overcome in popular consciousness. Is Christ merely my private fiction, a God I have created after my own desires to suit my consumer needs?[4]

Nonetheless, it is equally true that there is no more powerful line of persuasion than a presentation of the person of Jesus, including the historical truth about Him. Were it not for Jesus I would not be a Christian, nor possibly even a theist. It is Jesus, the Word made flesh, who is the very centerpiece of all biblical apologetics. It is confronting the reality of who He is in the pages of Scripture that exposes all the fictions of this world.

The reliability of source material

The primary source of information about Jesus is, of course, the New Testament. I present here a number of reasons why historians regard the New Testament as a reliable and authentic account of Jesus' life and teaching.

The writers of the synoptic gospels, Matthew, Mark, and Luke, claimed they were eyewitnesses of the events of Jesus' life or that they had had direct contact with those that were. The Gospel According to St Matthew carries a very early date. The Library of Magdalen College, Oxford houses a papyrus fragment of part of Matthew's Gospel considered the oldest portion of the New Testament still in existence. This fragment, dated to around AD 70, or perhaps even earlier, establishes that Matthew's Gospel was in circulation while eyewitnesses to Jesus' life were still alive. In 1994, German scholar Dr Carsten Peter Thiede and British scholar Matthew D' Ancona published their book, *Eyewitness to Jesus*. Dr Thiede's opinion is that Matthew's Gospel was circulating as early as AD 30. In his book we read:

> "It now appears that the finished Gospel According to St Matthew was also circulating in Codex [book] form at that time (AD 30 to 60). It could conceivably have been read and handled by an eyewitness to the crucifixion."[5]

In an interview in 1996, Dr Thiede made the following statement:

> "What the papyrus fragments can prove is that the first records, the first complete gospels were copies and spread and multiplied during the first decades of the apostolic era in close vicinity to what actually happened among eyewitnesses. *So you could not invent the historical Jesus.* You might still dispute certain details if you like, but you could not dispute the basic fact of his existence and what he did."[6]

He believes that all three synoptic gospels were probably composed and in circulation between AD 30–60 when contemporary eyewitnesses would still have been alive to verify or refute the facts.

Many historians and critical scholars today believe that the Gospel according to St Mark was written as early as AD 50–54. Mark knew and traveled with Peter who is considered the main source for the sayings and miracles of Jesus in this Gospel. This is confirmed by a disciple of the apostle John, called Papias (AD 70–155), in his *Explanation of the Lord's Discourses*.

There is reason to believe that the Gospel according to St Luke was composed around AD 58–60 while he was living in Caesarea, during Paul's imprisonment for about two years. Like Mark, Luke had privileged access to all the key people. A Greek medical doctor, he was a painstaking historian, widely recognized as of the highest rank. For example, all of the fifty-three geographical locations that Luke mentions have been shown to be accurate. Complete copies of the Gospels dating back to within 200–300 years of writing are available for viewing at various museums in Europe and North America and we have fragments that date much earlier. If we did not have these documents, the New Testament could be reconstructed from quotations in books by the early Church fathers, all written within 150 years of the events.[7]

Some will still say that to have a possible interval of 30–40 years pass before a biography is committed to writing casts doubt on it. This may be true today, because of modern printing and the nature of transmission via reference works and the internet, but in the ancient world, oral transmission was the prime method of communication. Information was passed on in the form of the sayings of the teachers (the rabbis). Memorization by repetition meant that large bodies of material were learnt, so even the illiterate could develop an education. The Christian community would have continued this Jewish practice and memorized a relatively small corpus, the material later organized into the Gospels (the letters were obviously earlier and in written form from the outset). The eyewitnesses, i.e. the disciples who became the Apostles, either wrote or were the authority behind each of the Gospels would have heard and memorized the sayings of Christ verbatim. Since Jesus taught by using stories, questions, and pithy sayings, remembering His teaching would not have been difficult.

Compared to other religious traditions, the gospel accounts were written down staggeringly early. Historian Dr John Dixon writes:

> "(1) the earliest biography of the founder of Islam, Muhammad (AD 570–632) was composed around AD 760, 125 years after his death, and continued to be edited for another 50 years; (2) the first written records of the life and sermons of Siddhartha Gautama (the Buddha: 448–368 BC), appeared 350 years after his death; (3) the most famous of ancient Israel's rabbis was a great scholar named Hillel, who died early in the first century AD. His teachings and stories appear in writing for the first time in the Mishnah, composed about AD 200. Nevertheless, scholars still treat these writings as serious historical texts. The gospels were written within 40–60 years of Jesus death ... These establish beyond doubt that Jesus' teachings, death and resurrection, together with his status as Messiah-Christ, were being taught by missionaries and committed to memory by Christians in the early 30s AD."[8]

When we come to ask the critical question about Jesus' claims and self-understanding, we can be confident in the New Testament sources.

The claims of Jesus – how did He see Himself?

Perhaps the most important question to begin with when considering the person of Christ is to ask how He saw Himself. If Jesus did not consider Himself unique or singular in terms of His identity and mission, then we are simply imposing a theological understanding of his person, subsequent to Christ's own life and ministry – an invention of the disciples or Christians in the early centuries.

Leading Canadian New Testament scholar, Dr Craig Evans, argues powerfully that Jesus clearly accepted the major tenets of the Jewish faith and the authority of the Torah. He saw Himself as a prophet (Mark 12:1–11; Matthew 11:20–24; Luke 10:13–15) and assumed priestly functions by declaring people clean (Mark 1:41; Luke 7:22), forgiven (Mark 2:5; Luke 7:47ff.) as well as challenging temple policy and the ruling priests. Jesus referred to Himself as the "Son of Man" clearly alluding to Daniel 7; this was one of His favored self-designations, the clear meaning was that He would restore and establish the Kingdom of God.

Jesus claimed to be the Messiah and the disciples refer to Him as such (Mark 8:29–30). When John the Baptist asked if He was the "one to come," Jesus' response is filled with Messianic allusions to Isaiah 35:5–6; 61:1–2 (see Matthew 11:2–6; Luke 7:18–23). The blind Son of Timaeus also called to Jesus, "Son of David," a Messianic designation (Mark 10:47–48). Jesus rode a donkey into Jerusalem as Solomon the Son of David had done, an action the Messiah would need to do (Mark 11:1–7; 1 Kings 1:38–40). When the high priest asked Jesus if He was the Messiah, Jesus answered unequivocally, "I am" (Mark 14:61–62), and when Jesus was crucified, the sign above His head read "KING OF THE JEWS" (Mark 15:26, 32).

It is evident that Jesus understood Himself to be the Son of God. When asked if He was the Messiah the "Son of the blessed God," Jesus responds, *"I am, and you will see me, the Son of Man, sitting at God's right hand in the place of power and coming back on the clouds of heaven"* (Mark 14:61–62).[9] Jesus claims to have existed before Abraham (John 8:57–59), be one with the Father, be in the Father and have the Father in Him (John 10:37–38). He claims to be the way, truth and life (John 14:6), forgiving sin, accepting worship, performing miracles and challenging His accusers to find any sin in Him (John 8:46). All of this, for one who has a rudimentary grasp of the Jewish faith, context and culture, makes it very clear that Jesus claimed to be divine, God the Son, coming to fulfill the Law and the Prophets and to usher in the Kingdom of God. Though not immediately obvious to one who is biblically illiterate, if Jesus had made all these claims, but was not

God, He would have been committing blasphemy, a crime He was repeatedly accused of by those who opposed Him.

The real Jesus of history: separating myth from reality

Summing up the current state of New Testament scholarship and historical research, Ancient History expert Dr John Dixon writes:

> "... [I]n the ongoing study of Jesus, the texts at the centre of historical research are still the New Testament Gospels. They are the earliest, most plentiful and most reliable accounts of Jesus' life available to us."[10]

Dr Craig Evans affirms with equal confidence:

> "Ongoing archaeology and ongoing discovery and study of ancient documents will continue to shed light on this old story ... thus far, these discoveries have tended to confirm the reliability of the gospels and disprove novel theories. I suspect that ongoing honest, competent research will do more of the same."[11]

Given this solid and credible basis concerning the character and claims of Christ, and the authenticity of the documents, we must go on to ask, are there other witnesses both friendly and hostile that corroborate directly or indirectly the unique claims of Jesus? The answer is yes! There are sources that confirm the facts of Jesus' life and claims and the birth of the Christian faith in the first century.

From the earliest believers in the first century until now, Christians have acknowledged the divinity of Christ. Some people uninformed on the subject tend to think that these convictions were added later but we can prove that they were not. The Gospel of John is almost unanimously regarded as having been written somewhere between AD 80–90. He records very clear testimony concerning the identity of Christ. John the Baptist, who knew Jesus longer than any of the disciples, made Jesus' identity clear, "And I have seen and testified that this is the Son of God" (John 1:34 NKJV).

There are other important witnesses outside the New Testament.

Referred to as the Early Church Fathers, these men were leaders of the Church in the first three centuries. These were difficult times for Christians since they were often persecuted by the ruling Roman Empire. Polycarp (AD 69–155) was Bishop of Smyrna and a disciple of the apostle John. He wrote to fellow believers, "Now may the God and Father of our Lord Jesus Christ, and the High Priest himself, the [Son of] God Jesus Christ, build you up in faith"[12]

Ignatius, leader of the church in Antioch died as a martyr in the Colosseum in AD 110. He was a contemporary of Polycarp, Clement, and Barnabas. In his epistle to the Ephesians, he repeatedly refers to Jesus as "our God."[13]

Another early witness was Irenaeus (AD 125–200), a disciple of Polycarp. In his work *Against Heresies* (4:10) he speaks of the relationship between the Father and the Son, "For with Him were always present the Word and Wisdom, the Son and the Spirit, by whom and in whom, freely and spontaneously, He made all things, to whom also He speaks saying, 'Let us make man after our image and likeness.' "[14]

Justin Martyr (AD 110–166) one of the great early Christian apologists wrote, "Our Christ conversed with Moses under the appearance of fire from a bush." He refers to Christ as the "Angel and Apostle," "who is also God", yea "the God of Abraham, Isaac and Jacob", "the I AM that I AM."[15]

Finally, The Apostles' Creed, resting on the theological understanding of the first century likewise affirms, "I believe in God the Father Almighty, Maker of heaven and earth, and in Jesus Christ, his only Son, our Lord."

Hostile witnesses

There are also people hostile to the teaching of the early Church who may nonetheless be considered friendly witnesses to the historical Jesus because they recognize the historicity of His life. There are several important Jewish and pagan sources hostile to Jesus that confirm some of the important details found in the New Testament, thereby giving indirect support to the early claims about Jesus' unique ministry. Altogether, the correlation found in these hostile witnesses to the historical Jesus of the New Testament is remarkable.

Pagan historian Thallos (AD 55), in the third volume of his histories, mentions a "darkness" that he identifies as an eclipse of the sun coinciding with the crucifixion of Jesus. This is significant insofar as it shows that the report of this event was well known in pagan circles.[16]

Cornelius Tacitus (AD 56–120) was a public official and the greatest of Rome's historians. In an often quoted passage from his *Annals* 15:44, laced with anti-Christian venom, he touches on the death of Christ under the sentence of procurator Pontius Pilate and a deadly "superstition" most scholars consider a reference to the resurrection, which later broke out in Judea and then even in Rome.[17]

Josh McDowell's very useful and painstaking work in *New Evidence that Demands a Verdict* lists a number of further quotations from early sources hostile to Christianity. Suetonius was another Roman historian and court official under the Emperor Hadrian. In his *Life of Claudius* 25.4, he writes, "As the Jews were making constant disturbances at the instigation of Chrestus [another spelling for Christ], he [Claudius] expelled them from Rome."[18] This happened in AD 49, and St Luke refers to the same event in Acts 18:2. In *Lives of the Caesars* 26.2, Suetonius has occasion to comment on the fire that ravaged Rome in AD 64 during the infamous reign of Nero. He records, "Punishment by Nero was inflicted on the Christians, a class of men given to a new and mischievous superstition."[19]

Pliny the Younger (AD 61–113) is another important source who was a contemporary of Tacitus and a Roman administrator stationed in what is now Northern Turkey (Bithynia). In AD 110, he wrote to Emperor Trajan about the new sect called Christians. He asks whether he should continue executing them and reports the findings of his interviews with them:

> "The sum total of their guilt or error was no more than the following: They had met regularly before dawn on a determined day, and sung antiphonally [that is, alternately by two groups] a hymn to Christ as to a god. They also took an oath not for any crime, but to keep from theft, robbery and adultery, and not to break any promise."[20]

Here we have an independent pagan report that Jesus was regarded by His followers as God. The manuscript of these letters is stored in the Morgan Library East, 36th Street, New York.

And there is still more. Lucian of Samosata (AD 115–200) whose surviving Greek manuscripts are housed in the Vatican Library was a popular Greek satirist. In *The Death of Perigrinus* 11–13, he pokes fun at a fraudster called Perigrinus and describes in passing his travels among Christians in Palestine. Referring to the founder of Christianity, he writes:

> "... the one whom they still worship today, the man in Palestine who was crucified because he brought this new form of initiation into the world ... Moreover, that first lawgiver of them persuaded them that they are all brothers the moment they transgress and deny the Greek gods and begin worshiping that crucified sophist and living by his laws."[21]

Around the year AD 175, a Greek intellectual known to history only as Celsus wrote a book called *True Doctrine* in which he heaps ridicule on Christianity. He was ably rebutted by the response of early Christian apologist Origen in his work *Against Celsus* where he quotes Celsus in full. However, his work gives us an insight into how some of the Greek intelligentsia of the second century sought to attack the proclamation of the uniqueness of Christ. Writing off Jesus' birth as an illicit affair between Jesus' mother and a Roman soldier, he proceeds to describe the miracles of Christ as explicable in terms of the art of Egyptian sorcery,

> "... having tried his hand at certain magical powers, Jesus returned from there [Egypt], and on account of those powers gave himself the title of God."[22]

We also know something of the early Jewish view of Christ and the Christians outside of the New Testament. Flavius Josephus (AD 37–100) was a first-century historian, general and aristocrat. His massive *Antiquities* is an account of the entire history of the Jewish people. He covers uprisings and disturbances that occurred during the governorship of Pontius Pilate. He writes,

> "At this time there appeared Jesus, a wise man. For he was a doer of startling deeds, a teacher of the people who received the truth with pleasure. And he gained a following both among many Jews and among many of Greek origin.

> And when Pilate, because of an accusation made by the leading men among us, condemned him to the cross, those who had loved him previously did not cease to do so. And up until this very day the tribe of Christians, named after him, has not died out".[23]

This most famous passage from Josephus has probably been altered by copyists favorable to Jesus, but historians and other specialists have reconstructed it as they believe it would have read originally. This is not the only time Josephus mentions Jesus. In another passage that historians agree is free from any tampering, Josephus describes the high priest of Jerusalem, Ananus and touches on his treatment of James, the brother of Jesus around AD 62, about thirty years after the crucifixion; the incident described turns out to be the time of James' martyrdom. We know from Scripture that Jesus had several brothers and at least two sisters (see Mark 6:3) Josephus writes:

> "But this younger Ananus, who, as we have told you already, took the high priesthood, was a bold man in his temper, and very insolent . . . He assembled the Sanhedrin of judges, and brought before them the brother of Jesus the so-called Messiah-Christ, whose name was James and some others. When he had formed an accusation against them as breakers of the law, he delivered them over to be stoned to death".[24]

The final example I offer is from the ancient exposition of Jewish law called the Talmud in which we find two references to Jesus. In baraitha Sanhedrin 43a–b dated to between AD 100 to 200 we read a fascinating report of the case against Jesus that led to His trial and execution:

> "On the eve of Passover, Jesus was hanged (on a cross). For forty days before the execution took place, a herald went forth and cried, 'He is going forth to be stoned because he has practiced sorcery and enticed and led Israel astray. Anyone who can say anything in his favor, let him come forward and plead on his behalf.' But since nothing was brought forward in his favor, he was hanged on the eve of Passover."[25]

Historians are deeply skeptical about the claim that there was notice for Jesus' execution. It is surely an effort on the part of the authors to make

Jesus appear guilty since the passage affirms our knowledge from the New Testament that Jesus was executed on the Eve of Passover, sanctioned by the ruling Jewish council of Jerusalem known as the Sanhedrin.

From external sources, we can confirm these important historical facts about Christ. His name was Jesus or Christ. His public ministry in Judea was during the reign of Pontius Pilate. His mother's name was Mary. We know there was some doubt about the father of Jesus and the name of one of His brothers was James. Jesus was renowned as a teacher of notoriety as a miracle worker/sorcerer, appealing to the masses, both Jew and Greek. The title Messiah was applied to Him by many of His followers and He claimed kingly, even divine status. The time and manner of His execution are confirmed, on Passover Eve He was crucified with the involvement of both Jewish and Roman authorities. We even have confirmation that a period of darkness had been reported at the time of crucifixion. Following the death, a superstition about the resurrection spread among followers and there was rapid growth of a movement that worshiped Jesus in His own generation. Although these extra-biblical documents do not tell us much detail about the life of Christ, they serve to corroborate the most important facts about the historical Jesus and His unique status.

The claims of other religions

One of the most common objections to claims about the uniqueness of Christ is raised by comparison with other religions and philosophies. It is often suggested that all religions are superficially different but fundamentally the same. We hear people say how alike Jesus and Buddha are, or how much Islam and Christianity have in common; however, the reverse is actually true. Superficially, it may appear that there are many similarities, but when compared they are fundamentally different.

The idea of *revelation from God* is shared only by faiths with Jewish or Christian roots. There is a good reason for this – other faiths do not believe in a sovereign creator God who is interested in the lives of His creatures, who transcends time and can therefore intervene in history through prophecy. Buddhism, Hinduism, Confucianism and Taoism consist of striving for enlightenment. None of these faiths believes in a personal creator God who speaks and reveals Himself to human beings. They consist of philosophical reflections, ethical and political teachings, and mythological stories that can only be expounded by an expert, a guru. A Hindu's goal is the knowledge of an impersonal ineffable principle that underlies nature, or an escape into the impersonal One by escaping the cycle of reincarnation. No guru, teacher, or leader made claims even remotely comparable to Christ when the metaphysical understanding of the philosophy is understood. If you *are* god (as in classical Hinduism), you do not need revelation, but self-realization. On the other hand, consider these words of Jesus from the New Testament:

> "Truly, truly, I say to you, before Abraham was, I am." (John 8:58 NASB)

> " 'Are You the Christ, the Son of the Blessed One?' And Jesus said, 'I am; and you shall see the Son of Man sitting at the right hand of power and coming with the clouds of heaven.' " (Mark 14:61–62 NASB)

> "Jesus said to him, 'I am the way, and the truth, and the life; no one comes to the Father, but through me . . . He who has seen Me has seen the Father; how do you say, 'Show us the Father'? Do you not believe that I am in the Father and the Father is in Me?' " (John 14:6, 9–10 NASB)

We have seen that Jesus accepted worship, claimed to be sinless, forgave sin, healed the sick, and raised the dead and claimed equality with a personal God – the God of Abraham. What of the other founders of major religious traditions?

In *The Koran* we read what Muhammad is to understand about himself:

> "Say, I do not say to you, 'I possess the treasuries of God'; I know not the Unseen. And I say not to you, 'I am an angel'; I only follow what is revealed to me." (Surah 6:50)

> "Say, I am only a mortal the like of you; it is revealed to me that your God is one God." (Surah 18:110)

> "They do blaspheme who say, 'God is Christ, the Son of Mary.' But said Christ, 'O children of Israel! Worship God, my Lord and your Lord.' Whoever joins other gods with God – God will forbid him the garden, and the fire will be his abode." (Surah 5:75)[26]

Muhammad was not born of a virgin, was not raised to life, has only one miracle (of moving a mountain, outside of his military conquests) attributed to him; he never claimed to be sinless and appealed to the Old and New Testament for corroboration and support. He clearly never claimed to be anything other than an ordinary mortal who knew nothing of the unseen. Born in Mecca in AD 570, he was forty before he started having visions accompanied by violent convulsions, which he later claimed were revelations from Allah. Islam officially began after his rejection in Mecca when he fled to Medina. For the next ten years he was constantly at war to gain new converts and territory (he fought around sixty-six military campaigns) until he returned to conquer Mecca, establish his rule and die two years later, in 632. He offered no assurance of salvation, only guidelines for working one's way to possible favor with Allah. He was a polygamist who exceeded the number of wives prescribed by his own revelations (four). He also violated his own laws by plundering caravans on their way to Mecca.

The obvious conflict between *The Koran* and the Bible concerning the person of Christ is a major problem for Muslim scholars since Muhammad regarded Christ as a true prophet who was born of a virgin and performed miracles. Furthermore, he directs his readers to consult the Book (Christian Scriptures) and people of the Book who have this revelation. Muhammad never claimed that the Bible had been corrupted – this was a response developed long after Muhammad by Islamic apologists embarrassed by this glaring problem. We have seen from the textual evidence that this claim is baseless and without foundation. Christian scholars and apologists are still waiting for Islamic scholars to produce the "real" text of the New Testament, but no alternative text or proof of corruption has been forthcoming. Our texts date back to the second century, hundreds of years before Muhammad was born. Muhammad's claim to being a prophet is thus a world apart from the claims of Christ.

Consider the claims of Confucius. This oriental school of thought rests upon the writings commonly attributed to Confucius (551–479 BC). His teachings emphasized humaneness and gentlemanliness with ethical responsibilities being governed by one's social and family position. In *Analects* 7, we read:

> "The Master said, 'As to being a divine sage or even a Good Man, far be it from me to make any such claim. As for unwearying effort to learn and unflagging patience in teaching others, those are merits I do not hesitate to claim.'"

And again,

> "The Master said, 'Give me a few more years, so that I may have spent a whole fifty years in study, and I believe that after all I may be fairly free from error.'"

Or take the scriptures of Jainism. We read in *Acarangasutra* 9:

> "The Lord abstained from frequent speech. He uttered a few words, if and when necessary. If somebody asked, 'Who is there inside?' He would respond, 'It is I, a monk.'"

We see here again nothing like the life or claims of Christ. His claims are unique.

Today, the teaching of Siddhartha Gautama (the Buddha, meaning enlightened one, 563–483 BC) has gained currency in modified forms in the West. The Buddha sought to reform Hinduism, which he viewed as superstitious. The writings and sayings attributed to him were written about 400 years after his death (from food poisoning) about 480 BC. He rejected the rituals and occultism of Hinduism and developed an essentially atheistic religion that laid stress on desire as the source of suffering and enlightenment as the means of escape from desire. His four noble truths teach that the suffering caused by desire can be overcome by the eightfold path of religious education and moral principle. The goal is neither heaven nor God (as there is no God in his teaching). What is sought is Nirvana, escaping the cycle of reincarnation, where suffering and desire are eliminated by the enlightened realization that the self is an illusion.

Classical Theravada Buddhism denies any divine status to Buddha, though some sects began later to worship him and also ascribed divine status to him. Buddha is not a savior and made no such claim; his last words were, "Buddhas do but point the way; work out your salvation with diligence." In contrast, Jesus taught the continuance of identity in the afterlife – "today you will be with me in paradise"(Luke 23:43) – and He affirmed both this physical world and godly desire. For the Buddha, the world is an illusion and the self is eradicated when one reaches Nirvana, so you would not know you had reached it anyway. In the Buddhist Scriptures we read:

> "Monks, an inquiring monk, learning the range of another's mind, should make a study of the Tathagata, so as to distinguish whether he is a fully self-awakened one or not." (Majjhima Nikaya i.318)

Finally consider Hinduism. With a pantheon of over three hundred million gods, Hinduism consists of a varied group of religious traditions resting on the teachings of the Vedas (wisdom) and Upanishads (concluding portions – a synthesis of Vedic teaching), dominated by a monistic view of reality – though there are profound differences about the nature of personal identity. The general goal is understood to be liberation from an infinite cycle of reincarnation and the transmigration of the soul. Gurus are necessary to understand the sacred texts, so gurus are often considered holy and worshiped after their death.

The well-known concept of Karma, the accumulation of words and deeds in present and former lives, governs reincarnation. Liberation occurs when one expands consciousness to an infinite level to the realization that the self is the same as Brahman – the ultimate one from which all else proceeds. In other words, you must realize that you are God. This can be accomplished through various forms of yoga. Hindu rituals consist of demon worship, occultism, superstition, and retelling legendary stories. With no infinite personal and sovereign God, though some "Westernized" versions have adopted this kind of terminology, there is no identifiable authoritative *revelation* to human beings, no promise of salvation, only the vain hope of liberation from the onerous circle of reincarnation. Even death is no escape until one has been released from individuality.

Is there anything about other religious claimants that compares with that of Jesus Christ? Not one. He is singular. No one has ever lived a life like Him, spoken like He did, nor claimed with any credibility what He did. The New Testament is not a collection of fables or philosophical speculations, but the eyewitness accounts of the life, death, and teaching of the real person, Jesus. The Bible is a revelation from God that reveals to us our Savior, Jesus Christ, who has come from God and is the exact representation of His being.

Contemporary clowns and charlatans

Note something important about today's culture in the West. Jesus still stands out from other faiths and religious figures from history. There are many voices calling for allegiance and, given the startling difference between Him and all others, one possible way of dealing with the situation is to say, "If we cannot bring other faiths up to His level, we need to bring Him down to our level. So the Bible is just the same as every other writing, legend, speculation, fable and invention." Several bestsellers have been published recently attempting to do just that. If one could impeach the character of Christ and reduce Him to an ordinary man, Christ would no longer be unique. All that is required is a fertile imagination, a fragile grasp of history, a profoundly anti-Christian agenda, and you are ready to write a book about Jesus that could sell very well! Historian and New Testament scholar Dr Craig Evans is worth quoting in full here:

> "... this is what Michael Baigent, Richard Leigh and Henry Lincoln have done in their books ... They would have us believe that they have done careful, critical, research and have discovered the truth: Jesus and Mary Magdalene were lovers, had children, and these children, or their children, reached southern France and married into noble families, from which would eventually emerge the French Merovingians. The Knights Templar and the Priory of Sion, a secret society founded in 1099, knew all of this and did all in their power to keep it secret and thus protect the descendants of Jesus and Mary. Grand Masters of the Priory of Sion included Leonardo da Vinci, Sir Isaac Newton and Victor Hugo. How on earth did Baigent and company discover all this? They found some of the Priory's secret papers, hidden away in the Bibliotheque Nationale of France ... no credible historian believes any of it. And for good reason ... the whole thing is a hoax and the hoaxers have

> themselves admitted it. Baigent had been informed that it was a hoax sometime before publishing *The Holy Blood and the Holy Grail* . . . The hoaxers would eventually admit to what they had done . . . under oath in a French court of law. Plantard served time in prison for fraud. He died in 2000 . . . what Michael Baigent and Richard Leigh have given the public is pseudo-history. From rumors, legends and outright hoaxes they have fashioned a fairytale history about Jesus and Mary and much of the history of the church. Unfortunately these books have sold well and they have deceived many, among them Margaret Starbird and Dan Brown."[27]

Dr Evans' work *Fabricating Jesus* also exposed other authors who rely on stories that cannot be corroborated, and missing documents that cannot be seen by experts. Historian Dr John Dixon has identified one passage in Dan Brown's *Da Vinci Code* where his conspiracy theory about the Gospels and Church history is put into the mouth of fictional character Sir Leigh Teabing. Dixon writes,

> "There are no fewer than ten factual errors in these few paragraphs . . . These include false claims concerning Constantine, the Canon of Scripture, additional gospels, the Dead Sea Scrolls, the Nag Hammadi manuscripts, Jesus' marriage and the Vatican."[28]

Perhaps the most serious issue of misdirection in these books and others like them is the view propagated about the canon of Scripture especially the content of the New Testament. The word "canon" comes from the Greek term *kanon* meaning "reed." The reed was used as a measuring rod, a standard of measurement. When the Church councils met in AD 393 in Hippo and in AD 397 in Carthage, to consider which documents should be regarded as authoritative and inspired writing, they confirmed what was already accepted by the vast majority of the Church. The Jewish Bible was quoted extensively by Jesus Himself, so was recognized from the start of the Church. The decision reached for the books of the final canon was to use the version recognized by Jewish scholars at Jamnia in AD 90, excluding the Apocrypha. The bishops did not "choose" the canon, but reaffirmed the inspiration of the twenty-seven books of the New Testament in order to counter heretical teaching and distinguish these writings from spurious documents that had begun to circulate. By the end of the first century AD we find Bishop Clement of Rome writing to the church in Corinth quoting from Paul's earlier letter to them as though it carried the same authority as the Old Testament.

From the start, we find churches meeting together on a Sunday, to read from the Prophets and the writings of the Apostles. The development of the Canon of Scripture was a natural process and not the result of ecclesiastical regulation. Rather, ecclesiastical counsels ratified what was already accepted as carrying apostolic authority. The Early Church Fathers refer to the New Testament writings as Scripture. For example, Origen, who was born less than ninety years after the death of the apostle John, refers to the books of the New Testament in a way that exactly corresponds with our present list. Although there were some initial questions, disputes and discussions over authorship with some of the shorter letters in the New Testament (i.e. James, Jude, 2 Peter and 2 and 3 John), the vast majority of the Church already accepted what we today call the full canon. All disputes were handled openly and the evidence for a book's authenticity through manuscript evidence and tradition was considered in detail!

A few books, including the devotional *Shepherd of Hermas* and the *Epistle of Barnabas* proved more difficult to decide. They were eventually rejected on the grounds of insufficient inspiration and authority. It was important that a consensus was reached in order to prevent heresy. Several other documents, usually mystical writings often Gnostic in orientation, like the *Gospel of Peter*, *Dialogue of the Savior*, *The Gospel of Philip*, *The Gospel of Thomas*, *The Secret Gospel of Mark*, and *Secret Book of John* and a few others were never seriously considered by the universal Church as authentic, but as heretical distortions from non-eyewitnesses.

Thus commenting on the recent popular spate of pseudo-history resting on less than credible sources, Dr Craig Evans concludes,

> "Common to this hokum history and bogus findings are eccentric approaches that competent, trained historians find utterly implausible. Legends, rumors, forged documents, hoaxes and psychic intuition hardly constitute the stuff from which historical truth will be found"[29]

In reference to Dan Brown's *The Da Vinci Code*, Michael Baigent's *Jesus Papers*, and Tom Harpur's *Pagan Christ*, Craig urges readers to regard them for what they are, "They are not based on credible evidence; they do not follow recognized standards of critical investigation; and they do not offer anything approaching genuine history."[30]

The implications of the claims of Christ – what do they mean?

The consequences of embracing the Christ of history, the Jesus of the New Testament, the unique Son of God, are cosmic in their proportions. Critically, it means that truth – religious, moral or metaphysical – cannot be regarded as subjective, a matter of personal taste and preference, nor is truth relative to time, culture, and historical context. Rather, truth and meaning are found in Him. This world has a total meaning under God in terms of the story of the Bible. We might put it this way; acceptance of the *historical* Jesus as the unique Son of God means re-evaluating our entire view of history. If Christ is true history, history itself and everything in it has the meaning that He says it has. This is at the heart of understanding the implications of Christ's claims.

Many today are totally immersed in historical time, cut off from any meaning or reality that lies beyond it. If this is true, then history and even language itself, has no ultimate meaning, and Jesus' life must be explained away in purely naturalistic terms. Imagine for a moment that reality is in fact impersonal and that we exist because of blind chance and atomic necessity. All history would be devoid of the sacred and depersonalized. But if Christ is who He claims to be, the implications for history are monumental. Christ is both Creator and Redeemer and all things become the work of a sovereign, all-powerful and all-knowing God. The foundation for history becomes the eternity from which Christ came, not "the void." It was this claim to divinity, to being the great "I AM" that so offended many of Jesus' hearers.

Christ's unique claims have to be taken seriously. If they are true, then there is real transcendent and infallible truth revealed in His person and a personal, sovereign, creator God who has spoken to human beings. Without Christ, we are helpless creatures who cannot transcend ourselves (subjectivism), or our age (relativism), and so have no truth beyond the individual human mind (solipsism). If we deny the claims of Christ, we do not liberate but imprison ourselves in a meaningless history of endless cycles or impersonal chaos without hope and without God.

Jesus tells us that He existed before Abraham (John 8:58), and that He had glory together with the Father before the foundation of the world (John 17:5). In the book of Revelation, Christ tells us that He is "the Alpha and the Omega – the beginning and the end" (Revelation 1:8). This means that the future is *logically* but not *chronologically* first. The source and reservoir of historical time is eternity. Time is governed by God's sovereign plan (Hebrews 1:1ff.) and so moves from future to present to past – it unfolds as the future becomes present and past. The reverse is true for the humanist in our age. For evolutionary thought, the past is determinative. Time flows from an original chaos that by blind necessity has fully determined humanity to the present. As a product and slave of natural forces the disjunction between, man, beast, and plant is steadily eroded. Arising from irrational animals, we struggle for some kind of control, but having been reduced to subconscious animal drives conditioned by nature (hereditary and environment), we are deconstructed into a "void" to which we are not accountable. But the Bible's assurance is that our times are in God's hand (Psalm 31:15 KJV) and that God has "determined [people's] appointed times, and the boundaries of their habitation" (Acts 17:26 NASB). The claims of Christ do not simply affect a few isolated facts, they affect the meaning of all facts – of all reality! Rushdoony summarizes well the implications of a history into which God has spoken in His Son over against one in which He has not:

> "The best interpretation of reality which evolutionary philosophies of history can provide reduces history to sub-personal and sub-human forces. For the Darwinist, history is the product of impersonal biological forces; for the Marxist, the forces are economic; for the Freudian, psychological and unconscious. Not only is the meaning of history depersonalized, but man is depersonalized as well. Man begins by asserting the supremacy of his autonomous mind and reason and ends in total irrationalism. As Van Til has often stated, the fate of rationalism is total irrationalism and irrationalism rests on rationalism. 'When man makes himself and his reason, god over

> creation, he destroys all meaning in creation and leaves himself a chained and gibbering baboon, sitting in terror on a wired electric chair in the midst of a vast universe of nothingness.' "[31]

In contrast, hear the words concerning Christ from the canonical writer of Hebrews:

> "[God] in these last days has spoken to us in His Son, whom He appointed heir of all things, through whom also he made the world. And He is the radiance of His glory and the exact representation of His nature, and upholds all things by the word of His power . . . of the Son He [the Psalmist] says,
>
> 'Your throne, O God, is forever and ever,
> And the righteous scepter is the scepter of His kingdom.
> You have loved righteousness and hated lawlessness . . .
> You, Lord, in the beginning laid the foundation of the earth,
> And the heavens are the work of your hands;
> They will perish but You remain;
> And they all will become old like a garment,
> And like a mantle You will roll them up;
> Like a garment they will also be changed.
> But You are the same,
> And Your years will not come to an end.' "
>
> (Hebrews 1:2–3, 8–12 NASB).

These are the implications of, the meaning of, the claims of Christ. He is the door and there is only one way of salvation, through the Lord of all time and history. He is the gate for the sheep and the narrow path, the only name under heaven by which we must be saved (Acts 4:12). Grace and truth came through Jesus Christ.

The authenticity of His claims

There are a number of reasons to support the authenticity of Jesus' claims. One important task of Christian apologetics is to give reasons why we can have confidence in the claims of Christ. This will support our other apologetic task, which is to persuade others of Jesus' claim on their lives.

One line of evidence focuses on the miracles of Jesus, in particular the resurrection. Numerous excellent books from the popular to the scholarly have explored the vast body of evidence that supports the resurrection reports.[32] Another powerful form of support is the testimony of biblical prophecy. St Augustine and Blaise Pascal were deeply impacted by the compelling nature of biblical prophecy. There are some four hundred and fifty-six messianic passages in the Old Testament supported by around five hundred and fifty-eight references to ancient rabbinic writing. Of these, many are repeated, but biblical scholars identify one hundred and nine distinct prophecies that the Messiah had to fulfill. Jesus fulfilled them all. This is no mean feat. The probability of one person fulfilling just twenty of these prophecies, by chance, is less that one in one quadrillion, one hundred and twenty-five trillion!

Jesus truly was the Messiah. From the Pentateuch, Messiah would be like Moses, called out from Egypt, a great Lawgiver and being preceded by a forerunner (fulfilled by John the Baptist), and would be a descendant of King David. The prophetic writings give us predictions of the virgin birth happening in Bethlehem. Messiah's ministry would fulfill the prophecy of Isaiah 53 and 61. These include being cut off for the sins of the people, His betrayal for thirty pieces of silver, His silence before His accusers, being spat on and struck, pierced, scorned and forsaken, soldiers gambling for His clothes, none of His bones being broken. All of these prophecies were fulfilled in Christ as witnessed by the authentic accounts of the New Testament. Jesus' side was pierced, He was buried with the rich and He rose again. All this is foretold in the Old Testament prophets.[33] These could not be post-event predictions – forged prophecies written down after the events of Jesus' life – because at the very latest, the books of the Old Testament were completed at least two hundred, more probably four hundred years before Jesus' birth. This is beyond dispute because we know that the Septuagint, the Greek translation of the Hebrew Bible, was written around 200 BC. Most scholars agree that the Hebrew original existed as a complete text at least a hundred, and more like a hundred and fifty years before the Greek translation was begun. This means all 109 prophecies were committed to writing at least 250–400 years before Christ was born. The book of Isaiah alone contains over fifty Messianic prophecies and a complete scroll of Isaiah was found in the Qumran cave discoveries, the Dead Sea Scrolls, dated to the time of Jesus, proving that the text has not altered from that time until now.

Another form of support that deeply impressed Christian apologist Blaise Pascal was the explanatory power of the biblical plotline. In particular, the Fall and original sin of our first parents, for him, clearly accounted for the complexities and contradictions inherent in the human condition. His unique work, *Pensées*, wonderfully develops the themes of the explanatory power of Scripture to account for both the glory and wretchedness of our condition.

Furthermore, we have external corroboration that comes in the forms we have looked at already such as historical textual support and archaeological findings. For example, ossuaries (stone boxes for storage of bones used in a short period of years during the Roman Empire) have been found dating as early as AD 50 with inscriptions referring to Jesus and the hope of the resurrection. The pool of Bethesda reported in the Gospel of John, chapter 5, long thought a fiction by skeptics, was unearthed in 1888. More recently, the famous "Pilate Inscription" was found by an Italian archaeologist in 1961. Despite non-Christian historical support, Pontius Pilate had been thought by many skeptics to be an invention of the New Testament. But on the steps to the Caesarea theater an inscription was unearthed referring to Pontius Pilate as the prefect of Judea. This silenced the doubters!

Not only is there ample of evidence, but philosophically, the Christian worldview alone has the resources to adequately make sense of the basic assumptions and practices of human experience. Only Christianity enables the world to be what it appears to be, revealing the unintelligibility of contrary views.[34]

The priority of Jesus

Ultimately, people who are Christians are so because of the person of Jesus; there is no one like Him. I have been involved in many open forums and public debates at universities over the years and I have found that no matter how clever (or foolish) my arguments, the reason people come to belief is the person of Jesus Christ. Alongside the explanatory power of the Christian worldview that is lacking in the nonbelievers' system, Pascal maintained that the best evidence for the Christian faith is the life and miracles of Jesus, the historic witness of Moses and the prophets to Christ and their fulfillment in His life. The holiness of Christ and His teaching, the uncanny assent it gains in the conscience of people, the witness of a Christian life and the continuity of the Church all corroborate the power of the Christian message. Pascal, being a scientist, recognized that the ordering of the world was important evidence for the existence of God, but he was skeptical about its impact on the blinded unbeliever. Pascal famously remarked:

> "Jesus Christ is the only proof of the living God. We only know God through Jesus Christ. Without His mediation, there is no communication with God. But through Jesus Christ, we know God. All who have claimed to know God and to prove His existence without Jesus Christ have done so ineffectively ... In Him and through Him, we know God. Apart from Him, and without Scripture, without original sin, without the necessary mediator who was promised and who came, it is impossible to prove absolutely that God exists, or to teach sound doctrine and sound morality. Jesus Christ therefore is the true God of men."[35]

In saying these things, Pascal was following Augustine. For Augustine, belief in the authority of the incarnate Christ led to understanding. To him, there was no true wisdom and understanding available to men and women without faith in Christ.

In his apologetic work, *The Advantage of Believing*, Augustine gives seekers a helpful pointer. What B. B. Warfield[36] has referred to as Augustine's "golden chain" is found in the following quotation:

> "So he who brought the remedy that would heal corrupted morals established authority with miracles, won belief with authority, held the masses with belief, endured through the masses and made religion strong by enduring.[37]

The order is God's **activity through miracles** (the life and work of Christ), **authority established** by Christ through His Apostles who witnessed His words and works recorded in Scripture; **faith in Christ's authority**, **growth in numbers** through belief, and **enduring witness to the present day**; strengthening faith through the continuity of His Church. Notice the centrality of Christ and His Body, the Church, from first to last in this chain of reasoning.

We are introduced to faith by the authority of Christ, and having received it by faith are made able to grow in understanding as reason reflects on revelation. Augustine has summarized the uniqueness of Christ well for us:

> "Take Aristotle, put him near to the rock of Christ and he fades away into nothingness. Who is Aristotle? When he hears the words, 'Christ said', then he shakes in hell. 'Pythagoras said this', 'Plato said that'. Put them near the rock and compare these arrogant people with him who was crucified."[38]

Discussion questions

1. What do you think is the most compelling reason to accept the claims of Christ?
2. Discuss some of the ways in which Jesus is unique in comparison with other great historical or religious figures.
3. Which of the historical evidences discussed here do you find most convincing?
4. How would you address a person who claims to believe what is written about Jesus in *The DaVinci Code* or one of the non-canonical gospels?
5. Why do you think these writings have had such a wide impact despite their dubious historical value?
6. Do you think most people reject the claims of Christ because of ignorance of the evidence or for some other reason? Why do you think this?
7. In what ways can this chapter assist you in conversation with someone who does not accept the uniqueness of Christ?
8. Why do you think focusing on Christ is crucial in apologetics?

Notes

1. Tim LaHaye, *Jesus, Who Is He?: The amazing truth about Jesus Christ* (Marshall Pickering, Basingstoke, 1997), pp. 50–51.
2. LaHaye, *Jesus, Who Is He?*, p. 49.
3. Reader's Digest *Book of Facts*, ed. Magnus Magnusson (The Readers Digest, London, 1985), p. 394.
4. I owe an intellectual debt to my friend Dr Phil Meadows for his illustrations of technology that exemplify the three phases of thought, "world encounter," "world viewing" and "world-making" identified above.
5. Dr Carsten Peter Theide and Matthew D' Ancona, *Eyewitnesses to Jesus* (Doubleday, New York, 1996), p. 163.
6. Gregory A. Boyd, *Cynic, Sage or Son of God* (Victor Books, Wheaton, 1995), p. 239.
7. For a comprehensive collation of sources, scholarly dating of New Testament and discussion of the textual evidence see, John McDowell, *The New Evidence that Demands a Verdict* (Nashville: Thomas Nelson, 1999), pp. 33–68.
8. John Dixon, *The Christ Files: How historians know what they know about Jesus* (Blue Bottle Books, Sydney, 2006), pp. 57–58.
9. Craig A. Evans, *Fabricating Jesus: How modern scholars distort the Gospels* (IVP, Downers Grove, Illinois, 2006), pp. 223–229.
10. *The Christ Files*, p. 68.
11. *Fabricating Jesus*, p. 235.
12. Citations from J. B. Lightfoot and the Apostolic Fathers in, *Jesus, Who Is He?, pp.52 — —54.*
13. *Jesus, Who Is He?*, pp. 52–54.
14. *Jesus, Who Is He?*, pp. 52–54.
15. *Jesus, Who Is He?*, pp. 52–54.
16. *The Christ Files*, pp. 17–18.
17. *The Christ Files*, p. 20.
18. Suetonius, cited in, Josh D. McDowell, *The New Evidence that Demands a Verdict* (Thomas Nelson, Nashville, 1999), p. 121.
19. Suetonius, in *New Evidence*, p. 121.
20. Suetonius, in *New Evidence*, p. 21.
21. Suetonius, in *New Evidence*, p. 22.
22. McDowell, *New Evidence*, p. 23.
23. McDowell, *New Evidence*, p. 27.
24. McDowell, *New Evidence*, p. 29.
25. McDowell, *New Evidence*, p. 30.
26. All citations from sacred texts of other faiths are taken from, *World Scripture: a comparative anthology of sacred texts*, ed. Andrew Wilson (Paragon House Publishing, Minnesota, 1995), pp.468–470.
27. Craig Evans, *Fabricating Jesus*, pp. 208–209.
28. *The Christ Files*, pp. 91–92.
29. *Fabricating Jesus*, p. 221.

30. *Fabricating Jesus*, p. 221.
31. Rousas John Rushdoony, *The Biblical Philosophy of History* (Vallecito: Ross House Books, 1997), p. 11.
32. Josh McDowell references much of this work in his comprehensive work, *The New Evidence that Demands a Verdict* (Thomas Nelson, Nashville, 1999).
33. For a detailed analysis of the Messianic Prophecies and their fulfillment see *The New Evidence*, pp. 164ff.
34. Joe Boot, *Why I Still Believe* (Baker Books, 2005).
35. Blaise Pascal, *The Mind on Fire: From the works of Blaise Pascal*, ed. James M. Houston (Bethany House Publishing, Minneapolis, 1997), p. 147.
36. See the brilliant study of Augustine's theory of Knowledge by Benjamin Breckinridge Warfield, *Studies in Tertullian and Augustine* (Greenwood Press, Connecticut, 1970).
37. St Augustine, *On the Advantage of Believing, On Christian Belief– the works of St Augustine Part 1*, Volume 8 (New City Press, Hyde Park, New York, 2005), p. 143.
38. St Augustine, cited by Malcolm Muggeridge, *A Third Testament* (Little, Brown and Co., Boston, Toronto, 1976), p. 51.

CHAPTER 11

Reasoning About Faith!

[First delivered to a group of skeptics at an event hosted in a bookshop cafeteria in Calgary, Canada.]

> "Your approval or disapproval means nothing to me, because I know you don't have God's love within you. For I have come to you representing my Father, and you refuse to welcome me, even though you readily accept others who represent only themselves. No wonder you can't believe! For you gladly honor each other, but you don't care about the honor that comes from God alone." (John 5:41–44)

Ignorance is bliss

A school teacher once asked his class, "What is the difference between ignorance and indifference"? A student down at the front muttered, "I don't know and I don't care." Humorous as this reply is, it is not an uncommon attitude when it comes to the ultimate questions that we all must face. This irresponsible attitude has led, in my generation, to a widespread apathy – an apathy generated by the philosophy of our times. But, as I never tire of reminding skeptics, it is crucial that we each take the time to stop and think about what we believe and why. Equally, we must consider the practical implications of our beliefs for unless we consider what behavior our beliefs should produce, we are bound to live inconsistently with our avowed doctrines, or fall unwittingly into a potentially tragic consistency, which can be terrifying if your beliefs are misguided. For one frightening example of a godless consistency, one need only examine the life of the Marquis de Sade, from whose name we derive the term sadism. On the other hand, for a truly inspiring consistency, we might consider the life and faith of a man like William Wilberforce, the great English reformer who worked for the abolition of slavery. What is absolutely certain is that indifference and apathy in these ultimate matters is our greatest enemy, for indifference itself expresses a very specific approach to life and faith with significant and serious consequences.

Charlatan or sage

So what is it that you and I believe about ourselves, God and this world, and why? On what basis do we reach conclusions and form beliefs? What authorizes our use of reason in search of valid conclusions and on what criterion do we weigh and assess evidence? You may have heard of the sixteenth-century French seer Nostradamus, who was to be found in the Renaissance court of King Henry II of France. He was known as a practitioner of astrology and other magical arts. Most of his predictions were not specific and open to a variety of interpretations. Practicing initially as a physician, he gained a reputation as something of a miracle worker. His keen interest was the mystical arts. His passion for astrology and magic led him to convert his attic into a primitive observatory. From there he gazed at the heavens where he claimed to receive the secrets of the future from what he called the "internal light, the voice." He had published nearly 2,000 cryptic prophecies by 1557, using what he called a secretive way of expression, employing French, but also a smattering of Italian, Greek, Spanish, Hebrew and Latin phrases. He admitted he used an almost *unfathomable style* that protected him from persecution by those offended by his prophecies. Those more skeptical might suggest that the evident vagueness of his writing was studied and deliberate in order to allow for any number of interpretations. Indeed, around 400 varying interpretations of his work *Centuries* have been produced, each claiming to reveal the secrets of the age. It was certainly convenient for Nostradamus to claim, "My writings will be better understood by those who come after my death." It is claimed in one popular story that Nostradamus summoned an angel, asking him to reveal the future fate of

Queen Catherine's children in a magic mirror. This strange astrologer obsessed with horoscopes has been regarded variously as a prophet or clever charlatan.[1]

What do you think when you hear such stories? How do you assess them? How do you react? Have you ever asked yourself why you react in the way that you do? The truth is, we assess these stories, these "prophecies" using a set of assumptions and presuppositions about the world. The credibility and plausibility of the stories concerning Nostradamus are almost unconsciously weighed, as we consider them in the light of our controlling perspective or worldview. All of us have a worldview that is grounded in some faith or another. That I use the word "faith" may surprise you in this context. It is a fact that as limited creatures, finite and fallible, we do not and cannot know everything. We are not everywhere at all times in this universe. As such, we accept the witness of others and have to assume certain things; we have to put faith in certain universals. We all do this. Our understanding and interpretation is always based on certain assumptions, presuppositions, about reality.

Pure presumption

My grandmother was a wonderful cook. She was especially good at baking and baked the most delicious cakes. She seemed to know exactly what ingredients were required and how to combine them, as well as the perfect cooking time to produce exquisite culinary delights. Yet she quite unconsciously made certain philosophical assumptions she never gave a second thought. Most important was the assumption that the present would be like the past. In scientific terms, she assumed the uniformity of nature – by repeating the same procedure in the same way each time, she could get the same delicious result. And she did! This belief is the very foundation of all scientific inquiry. Yet this principle is not proven by science, it is assumed on faith. Before the event, the laws of motion implied the possibility of rocket propelled probes being fired into deep space. NASA scientists assumed that the laws at work here on Earth could be applied to a craft to be landed on the moon, taking into account predictable differences in gravitational forces due to the moon's mass and that of other planetary bodies. Someone might say, "But we see this uniformity everyday." However, the fact that we observe uniformity in our experience does not prove that this uniformity is universally true, nor can it guarantee that this consistency will hold true for tomorrow. Indeed any arguments to prove the principle of induction (the move from general observation of particular instances to a wider conclusion) are inductive arguments themselves. For a hypothesis to advance to the status of a possible theory, experiments designed to test the theory have to give consistent results. Yet this principle is applied by faith, being presupposed by all scientists in order to make the scientific enterprise intelligible. Consider the words of Scottish empiricist philosopher David Hume, as he reflects on causality and our ignorance of the ultimate causes that sustain this apparent uniformity of causes and general principles, we observe.

> "...we may discover the reason why no philosopher who is rational and modest has ever pretended to assign the ultimate cause of any natural operation or to show distinctly the action of that power, which produces any single effect in the universe ... *The most perfect philosophy of the natural kind only staves off our ignorance a little longer ... Thus the observation of human blindness and weakness is the result of all philosophy, and meets us at every turn, in spite of our endeavors to elude or avoid it.*"[2] (emphasis added)

Conditional faith

So we may theorize about general principles, but the ultimate cause of these regular principles are "totally shut up from human inquiry." We simply believe these principles will be sustained. Of course, faith assumptions are not just made by scientists; they are made by us all. It is impossible for us to say anything about reality from which we can draw conclusions without presupposing certain preconditions. As an example, if I were to point out to you, "There is a beautiful blue sky outside," I am assuming a number of things necessary for you to understand me. I am assuming that there is a correlation between what I see and think and what you see and think. I am assuming that my mind is giving me valid information about the world, and I am assuming that my senses are not deceiving me. There are numerous assumptions about the external world, my senses, language, grammar and logic that constitute the essential preconditions of my statement about the sky having any intelligible meaning for you. Yet we take all of these preconditions for granted.[3] It is worth our time then to ask about the basis of our beliefs so easily assumed as valid without rational reflection.

Starting points

People often have divergent assumptions that govern how we understand our world. Some people, like myself, believe in a personal God who has revealed Himself in the Bible. Others maintain a faith that denies the God of Scripture, perhaps assuming that there is no deity at all. For some, any deity that may or may not exist must be finite, a product of nature, thrown out of the nothingness like all other objects in the cosmos. Still others nurture the religious belief that rational thought, reason, and logic can account for themselves without requiring a God. For many, the universe is nothing more than matter in motion, while others, influenced by eastern, or idealist thought, maintain that the universe itself is an illusion, existing in the mind alone.

These belief systems naturally sporn ethical and political theories. For example, atheism combining with evolutionism inspired both Nazi fascism and Marxist ideologies – the latter seeing economics as the driving force behind history, reflected in the class struggle between the ruling class and the proletariat and the former seeing the evolutionary struggle for existence with the emergence of the Aryan race "man-god's" (Nietzsche's Over-man) as the key to politics and ethics. Hinduism, with its belief in reincarnation and karmic law gives us the caste system as a social order. In the Western world, the rejection of God came to stark expression in the existentialist philosophy, the epitome of the mood of our time. Individuals having "being" but no "essence" (no pattern that defines them), find that the world of objective meaning outside of themselves has completely collapsed – each person must define themselves with no referent beyond themselves. They are left with the loneliness of choice and "freedom" in a void – choice is all that matters.

We are, they say, "forlorn" as we face an absurd existence. Jean Paul Sartre, the twentieth-century French atheist philosopher cryptically wrote of human identity and existence, "For we are a choice, and for us, to be is to choose ourselves."[4] These few examples are sufficient to illustrate that we each hold to certain presuppositions on a given authority (even if only our own), that work themselves out practically in our moral decisions and commitments. The way we see the world, our worldview, constitutes a perspective on life that is the frame of reference by which we live and interpret everything around us.

Piece by piece

When I was a child, I used to do jigsaw puzzles. These puzzles varied in size from 100 to 3,000 pieces. Sometimes we would work on puzzles for days. The first thing I do when beginning a jigsaw puzzle is to find the corner pieces and all the straight edges to establish a frame. This frame enables me to fill in the rest of the picture quickest. A worldview works in a similar way to the outside edge of the jigsaw puzzle; it forms the frame of reference inside which the interconnected pieces of our belief system come together.[5] Each of us has a *synoptic view* no matter how ill-conceived or undeveloped it may be. It is this synoptic view of reality that philosophers call metaphysics.

Some people believe they construct this view by themselves, on their own authority; they think they rely entirely upon their own opinions. This is an illusion, since nobody has an opinion that is completely original to them – we are all dependent upon others and all that we have learned is directly or indirectly influenced by those around us who shape our understanding. The question then becomes, who should we look to in order to piece together the puzzle of life?

Once we cut ourselves loose from the idea of revelation from God (that God has communicated with His creatures), we are of necessity only left with the opinions of finite people. Typically, the views most often valued and applied to society tend to be those of philosophers, intellectuals, and academics, in other words, the beliefs of the cultural elite. These views become dominant in the classroom, and their ideas are eventually assumed to be true by the general public. This has led to the progressive moral disintegration of our culture. A consistent subjectivism was found in the work of influential German thinker Friedrich Nietzsche and applied to moral thought. If moral categories were also subjective, then moral values are only an "appearance," so how can one person's "appearance" (personal view) be a basis for condemning another person's "appearance"? This approach is a common species of ethical thought on university campuses today. For example, Nietzsche writes:

> "It is of cardinal importance that the real world should be suppressed . . . war against war the hypotheses upon which a real world has been imagined. The notion that moral values are the highest values belongs to this hypothesis. The superiority of the moral valuation would be refuted, if it could be shown to be the result of an immoral valuation – a specific case of real immorality: it would thus reduce itself to an appearance, and as an appearance it would cease from having any right to condemn appearance."[6]

The rot sets in

How did we arrive at where we are today? Modern philosophy is often said to have begun with Descartes (1596–1650). He decided, when asking the important question "What is truth?" to begin with himself as a doubting subject as the ultimate criterion for truth. This set up a new precedent in modern philosophy – echoing ancient Greek skepticism and setting aside the Christian era – that knowledge must be established on humans, not God and revelation. Perhaps you recall Descartes' now famous dictum "I think, therefore I am." He believed that valid knowledge could be acquired by methodological doubt (doubting everything), until finally finding a starting point that could not be rationally doubted, and from there proceed to build a valid knowledge from "clear and distinct ideas" that follow. However, other rationalists, who wholeheartedly agreed with Descartes' project and method, came to differing conclusions about which "clear and distinct ideas" are self-evident and what conclusions should follow from this autonomous starting point.

Bishop George Berkeley (1685–1753), one of a famous trio of British empiricists that included Locke and Hume, thought that all we can be certain of (when taking this Cartesian starting point of human autonomy) is "mental events" and properties. Given that in human experience, knowledge comes from sensory impressions processed by the human mind, how can we know that there really is a material world outside the mind? Berkeley suggested the notion that sensory impressions come directly from God with no material world mediating the impressions in between – only minds exist, matter does not. Ironically, he developed this line of thought in an attempt to refute materialistic atheism. It was only an obvious next step to the thought of Scottish philosopher David Hume (1711–1776) who thought that we cannot possibly know that there really is a God, although he never sought to deny the existence of God, "out there" sending us these sense impressions at all. We only know that we exist and we cannot even prove that deductively! If we are merely a "bundle of sensations" (Hume was skeptical about the very idea of a self), how can we know that we have any real knowledge at all?

Damage control

Critically then, within a climate of mounting doubt and in an attempt to rescue science and knowledge from the radical and inexorably logical skepticism of Hume, German philosopher Immanuel Kant (1724–1804) thought he might find a way out of this vicious circle by offering a new method – a synthesis of rationalism and empiricism. He conceded that we cannot know "things in themselves" (the noumenal), because our minds intuitively impose ideas of causality, extension, space, and so forth upon the world of our senses. However, what we *can* know is the world as it appears to us (the phenomenal) as an aspect of our experience and so rescue science. He writes:

> "It has hitherto been assumed that our cognition must conform to the objects; but all attempts to ascertain anything about these objects *a priori*, by means of conceptions, and thus to extend the range of our knowledge, have been rendered abortive by this assumption. Let us then make the experiment whether we may not be more successful in metaphysics, if we assume that

> the objects must conform to our cognition . . . *If the intuition must conform to the nature of objects, I do not see how we can know anything of them a priori. If, on the other hand, the object conforms to the nature of our faculty of intuition, I can then easily conceive the possibility of such an* a priori *knowledge.*"[7]
>
> (emphasis added)

The language is a little tortuous, but Kant's "Copernican revolution" is highly significant for understanding modern thought. Thus far, he says, we have sought to conform and shape our thinking to reality "out there," but if we have no intuitive conception of objects, material things, prior to our experience of them, then we are stuck with Hume's skepticism; we are receiving a bombardment of sensory impressions about which we cannot have any real knowledge. Kant turns the table and suggests that objects of knowledge conform to our minds. Consequently, he does not fall into the empiricist trap of being bombarded with raw data to which we must conform our thinking, leaving us, in fact, without knowledge or any justification for the "customs" of thought about which Hume speaks.

The new gods

Kant's philosophy, which is so influential today, implicitly elevates human beings to the status of creators of heaven and earth because these realities are in fact structured by my mind. In this sense, the world may be seen as a construct of our individual imaginations. This idea leads to the conclusion that humans have literally become God.

Kant assumes then that our thought structure does not give us access to reality as it is in itself, but how can he know this without insight into the things themselves? Because the human mind shapes reality, any god there may be cannot be known and certainly cannot speak to human beings by revelation, since any such revelation would itself be structured by the human mind. Thus the human mind becomes an alternative for God.

However, because human reason is severely limited by Kant, he leaves room for faith. Indeed, a God concept is necessary for one can hardly make sense of the ideas of moral duty, human freedom and immortality, without some notion of God. One could argue that Kant unwittingly brought us to the skepticism so prevalent today where "science" must describe the human mind more than it does the real world. Kant's view leaves us asking whether there are other minds in the world, can we know if there is indeed anyone out there, and if there is, do their conceptions bear any relation to our own? We must face the lonely choices of our new found deity, forlorn, alone and isolated. We are "gods" face to face with the abyss.

Resurrecting the alternative

On the other hand, I have put my confidence and faith in the resurrected Christ and His revelation, the Scriptures. I begin with faith, not in myself or any other human being who is as limited, weak, and morally wretched as I am. My ultimate criterion for judging what is true is located in the Word of God revealed in the Bible. I do not begin with faith in the authority and sufficiency of unaided human reasoning, which endlessly contradicts the reasoning of others, but rather with faith in the triune God revealed in Scripture. Because we have differing paradigms, it may well be that our worldviews are in collision. I believe in the authority of Jesus Christ. Perhaps you do not. I interpret all of life from the biblical perspective. I believe that God has spoken with authority and I accept the testimony of Scripture as the revelation of an infinite God who knows all, created all, and sustains all. I know that I am not the creator. I am not God and refuse to delude myself into believing that I am. Your faith assumptions may differ widely from mine, and as a result, there is no neutral area of knowledge in our discussion that is unaffected by our respective faith-based presuppositions. As Christian Philosopher, Cornelius Van Til, has written:

> "Now it is of course true that many of the sciences do not, like theology proper, concern themselves directly with the question of religion. Granting this it remains a matter of great significance that ultimately all the facts of the universe are either what they are because of their relation to the system of truth set forth in Scripture or they are not. In every discussion about every

> fact, therefore, it is the two principles, that of the believer in Scripture, and that of the non Christian, that stand over against one another. Both principles are totalitarian. Both claim all the facts. And it is in the light of this point that the relation of the Bible as the infallible Word of God and the 'facts' of science and history must be finally understood."[8]

All "facts" are interpreted through our worldview; they are understood in the light of our ultimate authority and criterion for truth. It appears that in the end it comes down to the question of authority. Who speaks the truth? What is truth?

Profane age

Canada today, like most of the Western world, is a largely secular society. This holds true with respect to education, government, and social philosophy. Often, the misused principle of the separation of Church and state is touted to exclude Christian belief from the public forum in order to keep the Scriptures from influencing public life and, crucially, the public purse. We are told that the opposition of secularism to Christianity is in the interest of our multicultural reality and pluralistic fairness. Secularism requires civil liberty to be maintained, except the liberty of the Christian believer! What is it that underlies such a naive view? It is the assumption drummed into us through state education that all religious views (except that of secular humanism) are *beyond the scope of empirical investigation and rational proof.* The notion of the God of Scripture is regarded as mythology and superstition of primitive peoples of the past, an idea invented by people, which no longer has currency in the twenty-first century. This is the logical conclusion of the philosophical frameworks discussed earlier. Ideas have consequences.

The handmaiden of modern secularism is the ethical doctrine of relativism, which holds that no absolute truth exists or at least can be known by us. Incidentally, that statement reveals the absolute nature of relativism. It assumes that it is objectively true that nothing can be objectively true. All beliefs should be treated with equal respect (apart from those we especially don't like such as the doctrines of Adolf Hitler or

Osama Bin Laden). Although postmodern thinkers might deem this an oversimplification and deny that they are true relativists, they cannot supply an alternative that transcends subjective opinions. Without a referent beyond, above, and outside the human mind, relativism is all that is left to us regardless of our protestations to the contrary.

One root of our current crisis lies in a misunderstanding about the relationship between faith and reason. Most of us accept the popular myth that faith is something required in the absence of scientific support or rational warrant. Some would go as far as to say that faith is something we hold in the absence of, or even contrary to, the plain evidence. On occasion, students have said to me, "I wish I could believe what you believe, but I just don't have enough faith." Often, what they really mean is that although they find the ideas attractive, they cannot accept the teaching of Christ because as rational people they cannot be that naïve or stupid. But this view is mistaken. As we have seen, every worldview is a faith system – a synoptic view of reality – because presuppositions are faith commitments that are not proven directly by logic. Reason, then, cannot be separated from faith or opposed to faith, but rather, *reason is based upon some faith.* Faith, in an important sense, precedes reason, because we all whether consciously or not, believe certain things when we use and apply our reasoning faculty. Faith is not a leap, but a foundation. The basic assumptions that we each hold on faith must therefore be identified and admitted, then must be justified.

Know it all?

At this point, let us ask ourselves how we know what we know and what is the source of that knowledge? We should all face this question with integrity. Imagine for a moment that you have never eaten anything. Try to imagine that you have never seen a peach, never mind eaten one. In fact, you have never tasted food before in your life. A friend comes by one day eating a peach and tries to describe the taste of that fruit to you. How can your friend even begin to describe the taste of a peach when you have never tasted anything? It would be impossible for your friend to convey the taste of the peach; they will need to give you a bite. If then, later on, you run into another friend eating a candy and they tell you that the candy is peach flavor you now have a point of reference to make sense of what they are saying. This illustration shows us that you must first know something in order to know something. We can only reason from knowledge to knowledge. What is it then that you know and by what authority do you know it? Our conclusions on any subject in the pursuit of knowledge can only be sound if they rest on some previously established knowledge; what is the source of that pre-established knowledge and is it adequately grounded?

As another example, for any science fiction fans, the Star Trek Next Generation episode *When Silence Has Lease*, puts the Star Trek crew in an interesting predicament. Their ship the *Enterprise* is enveloped in a rip, a hole in space that reads as nothing on their instruments. It has no horizon and inside appears to be without dimensions – no depth, length, width or height. They reverse course at high speed but encounter no stars, no referent whatsoever, only black silence. They are utterly bemused and without any explanation. They then drop a signal buoy as a referent, from which to measure the distance traveled and engage their engines, plotting a course in one direction but find they simply come back to their marker buoy. Again the illustration shows that without a referent for knowledge, in a dimensionless nothing we can have no knowledge, we need a fixed referent for knowledge – a source of knowledge, for from knowledge comes knowledge.

Immaterial laws or human conventions?

The critical question then becomes, how do we justify what we think we know? All of our reasoning assumes the validity of certain logical principles – most of us call it common sense. For example, if I said to you that of my family of six, including four sons, my mother is the shortest member of our family, it would obviously be faulty reasoning to conclude that my brothers are shorter than my mother! For meaningful communication, we must assume that these logical laws are not subject to change and that they are binding for all thought and language. If they were not, the simplest tasks in the course of our day from shopping, to tasks at home and work, even ordering a coffee would become practically impossible. The important philosophical question to ask ourselves then, is what must be true about reality for our belief and confidence in the use of logic to be justifiable? In other words, what gives us rational warrant or authorizes us to employ logic in the world of our experience? To put it philosophically, what are the preconditions for an intelligible use of logic? If naturalism is true and all our rational capacities are the result of natural processes, what warrant do I have for trusting the conclusions of my mind? The use of logic is just one example among many possible aspects of thought that requires certain preconditions to be intelligible to us.

We assume a great deal that we cannot prove if we try to communicate our knowledge to others. We assume the existence of other minds, other consciousnesses, which cannot be proved to exist either. We also noted that we all live by the assumption of the uniformity of nature; we believe that the present and the future will be like the past. But this is not an empirical observation. We can only see what happens, not what will happen. It is not descriptive, but rather, it is a faith commitment about the predictability of unobserved future events. In fact, even in the present we only see succession, we do not *see* causation. Nonetheless, we believe in the principle of causation to make life work. The question is *what must be true of reality for the principle of uniformity in nature to be valid?*[9]

Avoiding the issue with unintelligent designs

Undaunted by this huge challenge, the secular humanist faith (philosophical naturalism and materialism) holds sway in the public arena and dominates the thinking of most ordinary people today. It would seem that the goal of many educators in the West is to protect this cherished religion by preventing debate about their naturalistic, evolutionary hypothesis. We are routinely told that religious views should not be muddled with science and so challenges to universal Darwinism are dismissed as dogmatic, religious creationism. Yet many Darwinists and neo-Darwinians hold to beliefs that cannot be justified using their own system of thought, so can equally be classified as religious belief. It is therefore impossible to keep faith out of the classroom for all thinking rests upon one belief or another. The relevant question is which faith is to be propagated? Novelist and skeptic Ian McEwan, considered one of today's leading humanistic thinkers said,

> "What I believe but cannot prove is that no part of my consciousness will survive my death. I exclude the fact that I will linger, fadingly, in the thoughts of others, or that aspects of my consciousness will survive in writing, or in the positioning of a planted tree or a dent in my old car. I suspect that many . . . will take this as a given: true but not significant. However, it divides the world crucially, and much damage has been done to thought as well as to persons by those who are certain that there is a life – a better, more important life – elsewhere. That this span is brief, that consciousness is an accidental gift of blind processes, makes our existence all the more precious and our responsibilities for it all the more profound."[10]

We should analyze this, for if this is what the world's leading thinkers believe, then we are indeed in trouble. Consider, the list of evolutionary atheists, fascists and Marxists include human butchers like Hitler, Stalin, Mao Zedong, Pol Pot and Mussolini. These and other hatchet men of the most violent period in all human history, who have killed more people than died in all the so called "religious wars" of previous times put together, were not known for their God-fearing belief in a judgment and afterlife! Have they not done considerable damage to the secular humanist thought? But as any student of logic should know, just because I do not like their ideology or its results, it does not follow that their belief system is false.

To use the phrase, "damage has been done to thought" implies a criterion to judge right from wrong, good from bad thoughts – otherwise there could be no "damage." In reference to epistemology, the study of how we gain knowledge, we might ask Mr McEwan how "blind processes" provide a criterion for valid or invalid rational and ethical judgments, or how we can arrive at a "precious" existence or profound "responsibility" from an accidental consciousness, courtesy of evolution, that is blind to good and evil, truth and falsehood, where no objective value judgments are even possible. Only "pitiless indifference" (Richard Dawkins) is left. The heartless actors named above on the stage of the twentieth century's theaters of war and its aftermath were at least logically consistent with the philosophy McEwan professes to believe. For, in light of his worldview, how can there be "persons" to "damage" when all reality, including human beings, are nothing more that matter in flux, the offspring of blind necessity – people are reduced to *raw material* and by these ideologies have been treated as such. So from where do we get this "precious profundity"? McEwan is indeed right that this is what he "believes" but cannot prove. Religion is unavoidable in life, no less in the school classroom. McEwan has an ardent faith to rival many a Christian.

The evolution of belief

For naturalistic thinkers, this universe is time, plus matter, plus chance. This world is ultimately the unintended product of chance (chaos), as is the mind of humans – there is no design plan. All knowledge therefore has a random source. By some process of alchemy, knowledge has come from total ignorance – the ignorance of unthinking, blind matter! Rationality has emerged from total irrationality. Yet, *materialist* evolutionists still want to believe in the validity of empirical science and its use of *logic* and *reason – immaterial, abstract, universals*! They also believe in the reliability of memory and mind, despite the fact that there *is* no *mind* in the naturalistic universe, only brain. They believe uncreated energy interacted in an undirected, unsupervised, chance process out of which emerged law and order – the rational from the irrational. Inorganic chemical disorder eventually became organic biota by powers and means inexplicable, as life sprang from non-life. These information rich, highly complex, coded systems just self-assembled.

In an earlier chapter we noted that the semiotics (the meaning and information content of words) on a page cannot be explained purely in terms of the physics and chemistry of the ink and paper. Yet this is essentially what we are to believe about the meaning of the genetic *code*; that it is explicable on the basis of physics and chemistry alone. Finally, this grand hypothesis that particles became people is neither verifiable nor falsifiable because it either happened too fast (in evolutionary terms), in too restricted geographical locations to leave material evidence (of basic types transitioning to other basic types), or it is happening too slowly to be substantiated in the present. However, we are asked to believe that this is the ultimate truth about reality.

Much of secular culture subscribes to a kind of faith in the improvable hypothesis that no supernatural being has ever revealed knowledge to humanity in the past. Indeed, they assume such a thing is impossible. But, claims about origins made by many working in the sciences are actually faith convictions. This is affirmed by Nobel Laureate Leon Lederman who acknowledges . . . "To believe something while knowing it cannot be proved is the essence of physics".[11]

Faith commitments, then, are at the heart of every worldview. The conflict between the Christian and the unbeliever is a conflict between alternative worldviews – a set of presuppositions that will determine how we interpret the evidence and use the tool of reason. It has not been a dispute about the nature of the few, isolated facts. We are wearing completely different spectacles to see reality. The only question to be asked is "Which view makes our human experience intelligible in the real world?"

Protagoras or the logos

When offering proof for anything, the evidence should correspond to the nature of the thing we are seeking to prove. As a consequence, I do not look for God who created the material universe and the space-time continuum in a test tube or in outer space, as though He were living behind the planet Jupiter. To justify belief in the God of the Bible, it is not to empirical investigation that we must turn (though there are many important empirical evidences that support belief), nor to supposed self-evident "clear and distinct ideas" (as in rationalism), nor even to pragmatic considerations (positing that whatever works in achieving a goal justifies belief), because this presupposes we know what the goal of life should be. In speaking of what is useful in life, we assume a pre-established goal or pattern.

There are obviously different criteria that I apply when deciding whether or not my daughter is in the house than when I am seeking to determine whether my wife still loves me! One is a material question and the other is not. Similarly, knowing if God is real is not the same kind of question as knowing whether there is milk in the fridge – their status is different. Materialism can never encounter God, who is Spirit and distinct from the material world of sense experience. Equally, to depend entirely upon human reason in order to decide what is real excludes the possibility that anything exists which is beyond our comprehension.

In today's culture, we see the old maxim of Protagoras again: "Man is the measure of all things." As already noted, the history of philosophy reflects human attempts to explain the great questions of life by starting with purely human authority, making humans the final point of reference in deciding what is true. The person without supernatural revelation is like a man who is made of sand, trying to build a sand castle to view the dunes in the desert. What a hopeless picture that is! By making ourselves the final point of reference, people are confronted with and are part of, a vast sea of undifferentiated, chaotic particulars (desert sands). In this universe, all reality is reduced to isolated bits of unconnected raw data. Matter in motion, like the swirling sands of the desert, is pure chaos. All the particular grains, representing all the particulars of our experience, have no ultimate meaning to interpret them. All facts are brute facts, unrelated by plan, design or purpose. And so in trying to gain knowledge, the man made of sand living in the desert sands in the castle made of sand, as his own source of truth and reference point, cannot even distinguish himself from his surroundings – knowledge is totally impossible.

The problem is that we are not big enough to do the measuring. We simply cannot be the final referent and criterion for knowledge. Descartes' well-intentioned project, the long-term results of which he neither wanted nor predicted, was doomed from the beginning. Our philosophies have shown themselves to be arbitrary, incoherent and blind. The reason for this is given to us in Scripture. We are not the Creator; we are the creatures. Because of this, we cannot find the true interpretation of reality by ourselves, for we neither created, control, nor sustain ourselves or our environment. Think back. If we begin like Descartes, with ourselves acting as the source of truth, we have nothing to which we can point with proper confidence. In such a case, we would need to know everything before we could know anything with certainty – a situation which is impossible for finite human beings. We need a transcendent point of reference, an omniscient referent outside of ourselves; we need, after all, revelation. We need the God of the saints of old.

The claim of Scripture is that truth has come down from God to us. Consider the implication if this is true. The Gospel of John opens in the following manner:

> "In the beginning the Word already existed. He was with God and he was God. He was in the beginning with God. He created everything there is. Nothing exists that he didn't make. Life itself was in him, and this life gives light to everyone. The light shines through the darkness, and the darkness can never extinguish it. God sent John the Baptist to tell everyone about the light so that everyone might believe because of his testimony. John himself was not the light; he was only a witness to the light. The one who is the true light, who gives light to everyone, was going to come into the world but although the world was made through him, the world didn't recognize him when he came. Even in his own land and among his own people he was not accepted. But to all who believed him and accepted him, he gave the right to become children of God. They are reborn! This is not a physical birth, resulting from human passion or plan, this rebirth comes from God. So the Word became human and lived here on earth among us. He was full of unfailing love and faithfulness. And we have seen his glory, the glory of the only Son of the Father." (John 1:1–14)

Here, God speaks for Himself as the infinite Creator to His creatures. He presents the truth on His own authority as One who knows all, because He made and governs all. He has a plan and has established a pattern. I believe as a Christian that God has spoken truthfully, though not exhaustively in Scripture. It is on this basis that we, as subjects, can know an absolute, objective truth with as much certainty as our human weakness is capable, without having to know truth absolutely or exhaustively with perfect objectivity. Exhaustive, absolute knowledge is for God alone and so the humanistic dream of grounding truth independent of God is futile.

Though we receive it through the use of our minds and senses, revealed truth as our authority is not finally *grounded* on our IQ, logical acumen, or sense experience – it rests upon an absolute God who shares His knowledge with us. Here, the Christian doctrine of revelation is seen as necessary in order for us to know anything as it truly is, in its proper context or within its true light. He gives the universe and human mind its rationality – we must conform our thought to His thought. Reason and logic themselves point us back to the Creator who made us to think in this way as rational creatures and so to be able to arrive at true knowledge about this rationally-ordered world. God is our ultimate point of reference and the light that enlightens everyone. God alone is able to grant us the foundational knowledge necessary for us to gain true knowledge in all the fields of human endeavor. In His light, we see light.

The light of the mind

The Christian argument in its essence is that reason and logic, math and science, morality, dignity, language and learning only have an adequate ground and foundation, when we acknowledge that God has communicated with us in creation, in our rational nature, and in the Scriptures. Scripture teaches us that we have all been made in God's image and that, deep down, we know we are creatures of God. Because of this, we cannot help living by, and believing in, the validity of our reasoning, logic, language, science and moral truth. This is in spite of the fact that what unbelievers profess to believe about reality would destroy the possibility of human reasoning altogether. We live in the rational world of a rational Creator God and as such can succeed in our use of logic and science only because God has so constituted this world and us in it. We employ and take for granted these principles and use them to make life work. Were unbelievers truly consistent with what they profess to believe, the non-Christian worldview would destroy the basis upon which we think and live. Nonbelievers defeat themselves on their own ground. If this world is not created by a sovereign God, then the facts are destroyed before we ever get to them – they are devoid of all meaning and we cannot interpret them.

As a Christian, I believe that the story of human history and philosophy is the result of a rejection of God since the Fall. Christ calls us to be converted from our intellectual folly by renouncing pride and self-sufficiency and believing the Word of God in Christ. The Creator and Redeemer of the world comes in His Father's name and gives believers the gift of the Holy Spirit so that we might be transformed in our thinking to see the truth (John 5:43–44). The Scriptures give historic testimony to His life, death and resurrection – the Word became human. In the words of Scripture we can encounter Christ, the Word of truth, and by His Spirit know direct testimony of his eternal reality.

"Nothing but" religion

What must be true for my human experience to be what it appears to be and not to be rendered total nonsense? What must be true about reality in order for laws of logic, science, and every other meaningful aspect of my experience to exist in the first place? What can make sense of life and love, good and evil, justice and injustice? I have sought to show that the personal, triune God, His being, light, life and illuminating presence in the human heart and mind is the very precondition of intelligible experience. Without Him, whether we acknowledge Him or not, we could have no knowledge. All of reality belongs to God. All wisdom and knowledge, Scripture tells us, is found in Jesus Christ who claims to be "... the way the truth and the life" (John 14:6). Magnus Verbrugge sums up the situation succinctly for us:

> "The proposition that God is the origin who created the universe cannot be subjected to scientific tests. It is a religious proposition. Its alternative is the religious negation of the creator. And since its adherents cannot escape their own idionomy, they too must keep searching for the origin. They too come up with a religious proposition. They end up with the proposition, 'Everything is nothing but ... ' i.e. something in creation ... It is the nothingness of a man who tried to go beyond his limits. He got lost and never found the meaning he was looking for. So now man has arrived at the station he finds at the end of the road away from God. It is 'nothing but' a black hole of questions with no answers."[12]

What light do you have in your life to illuminate all of the facts? To interpret rightly any aspect of our experience, the revelation of God in Christ must be taken by faith and it will be justified in the light of its own evidence. The Christian view is seen to be true in the light of the self-destructive nature of all other worldviews on their own criteria. It is Christ alone who provides a sound basis for knowing. Only the Bible provides the foundational premises necessary for rational thought and discourse, because it gives us the transcendent, sovereign, Creator God who communicates with His creatures. One may deny this view, but I contend that in doing so you must borrow from it! In order to justify knowledge, the absolute, Creator God of Scripture, must be invoked. He is properly basic. We may continue to work to suppress our knowledge of God by a deliberate act of rebellion. But I have chosen to agree with the great father of the Western Church, St Augustine, who said, "I believe in order that I may understand." Christ is the Light of the World, the Sun from which all other light derives its energy and in whose rays things can be seen for what they are. God is calling you and me, even in the use of our minds, our reason, in the day-to-day activities of our lives, to come to Him that we might have life. The question remains, on whose authority will you build? Will you trust the One who said he comes in His Father's authority, bringing light into our darkness, or will you trust yourself or some other human personage who will lead us down a blind alley into a black hole of questions with no answers?

Discussion questions

1. Do you agree with the claim that everyone accepts authority of some kind for their ultimate beliefs?
2. What do you think are the most common authorities accepted by people in our culture today?
3. Rate the order in which the following serve as authorities for popular thought:
   (a) academic philosophers
   (b) scientists
   (c) God
   (d) talk-show hosts

(e) school teachers/university professors
(f) historians
(g) authors
(h) celebrities
(i) religious figures/church authority
(j) religious texts
(k) individual autonomy
(l) peers
(m) rational arguments

4. Rate the authorities listed above in terms of how likely each is to bring one towards true belief.
5. In which principles does one need to have faith in order to reason or to do effective science?
6. Why, as this chapter insists, do we need God in order to ground those principles?
7. In what ways do you think Christian apologetics would suffer if it rests on reason instead of revelation?
8. How do you think Christians can most sensitively communicate the implications of denying God for life and thought?

Notes

1. "Great Mysteries of the Past," *Reader's Digest*, 1991, p. 174.
2. David Hume, *Concerning Human Understanding, Great Books of the Western World Vol. 35, Encyclopedia Britannica*, 1952, p. 460.
3. This transcendental line of thought can be formulated into an indirect proof for theism. The argument is that knowledge and communication are possible only if the world exhibits a coherent, relational structure and human minds share a common conceptual schema, which properly reflects that structure. Only this precondition would allow for correspondence between the way the world is and the way we think it is – else we are applying arbitrary laws in the mind to irrational particulars all around. The argument might be formulated like this:
   (1) Knowledge and communication are only possible if the world manifests a coherent relational structure and our minds possess a common conceptual scheme reflecting that structure allowing a correspondence between the way the world is and the way we think it is.
   (2) If theism is not the case, then there are no grounds for believing premise (1).
   (3) Therefore, if theism is not the case, then there are no grounds for believing that human knowledge and communication are possible.

(4) There are grounds for believing knowledge and communication are possible.
(5) Therefore, theism is the case.

4. Sartre, Jean Paul, *The Wisdom of Jean Paul Sartre* (Philosophical Library, New York, 1956), p. 40.
5. The religious doctrine of evolutionism as an explanation for all reality and existence is a prime example of this.
6. Friedrich Nietzsche, cited by R. J. Rushdoony, *To Be As God* (Ross House Books, 2003), p. 174.
7. Immanuel Kant, *The Critique of Pure Reason: Preface to the second edition, 1787, Great Books of the Western World, Volume 42, Encyclopedia Britannica*, 1952, p. 5.
8. Cornelius Van Til, *Christian Theory of Knowledge* (P & R Publishing, 1969), p. 37.
9. This classic epistemological argument posited by Cornelius Van Til can function as an indirect proof for theism. The premises and conclusion might be arranged in the following manner when more formally stated:
   (1) If theism is not the case, then one cannot account for the uniformity of nature presupposed by inductive reasoning.
   (2) If one cannot account for the uniformity of nature presupposed by inductive reasoning, then beliefs based on inductive reasoning are not warranted.
   (3) Beliefs based on inductive reasoning are warranted.
   (4) Therefore, theism is the case.
10. Ian McEwan, *What We Believe but Cannot Prove*, edited by John Brockman (Harper Perennial, 2006), p. 36.
11. Leon Lederman, cited by Ian McEwan, *What We Believe but Cannot Prove*, p. xvi.
12. Magnus Verbrugge, *Alive – An enquiry into the origin and meaning of life* (Ross House Books, 1984), p. 141.

CHAPTER 12

A Beautiful Life

The wonder of Christmas

[*First delivered at a Christmas event for seekers called "Capture the Wonder of Christmas," at Knox Presbyterian Church, downtown Toronto, Canada.*]

> "Mercy and truth have met together;
> Righteousness and peace have kissed.
> Truth shall spring out of the earth,
> And justice will look down from heaven . . .
> Righteousness will go before Him,
> And shall make His footsteps our pathway." (Psalm 85:10–11, 13 NKJV)

> "At dawn, the sun shines on the mountains. As the day progresses the sun lights up the lowest places on the earth. When Christ came, he first enlightened the Apostles, the mountains. They, in turn, illumined other persons, the sheltered valleys on the earth. If you want help, the great preachers, the mountains, will assist you. But they give only what they received from Christ, the sun. Therefore, we must put all our hope in Christ alone." (St Augustine on Psalm 35:9)[1]

The calendar and the culture

In its widest sense, "culture" is best understood as the *public manifestation of the faith of a people*. In much of the Western world today, we live in an ideologically multi-cultural society. The old Latin word *religo*, related to our term "religion" literally means "to tie back, or bind" and referred to the art of vine dressing where grape vines are tied to a frame and thus trained to grow in the same direction without becoming tangled up – this makes them healthy and fruitful. The ultimate concerns constitute the religion of a people, be it secular, humanistic, Islamic, Hindu or Christian faith. A society is only unified to the degree to which people accept the values and principles of the prominent faith perspective.

When a society as a whole embraces a certain religious perspective, the values of that religion are reflected in the behavior, laws, practices, and art that form the culture of that group. For example, the Islamic faith produces nations and cultures like Pakistan and Saudi Arabia; Hinduism gives us India; Buddhism gives us Tibet; Communism, Taoism and Confucianism give us China; Christianity birthed medieval and modern Europe and the dominant culture in the North American continent, although our nations today increasingly reflect paganism and humanism. Often different cultures produce their own cultural calendars that reflect significant cycles of life and punctuate the year with religious significance. All calendars are products of a religion; a source of ultimate meaning and significance. The events and stories we celebrate and commemorate in the movement of the passing years invest life with its meaning and define its significance.

Historically, Christ is at the center of the Christian calendar in the West (as Christianity replaced pagan themes) because of His unique status and claim to be the Son of God – "the way the truth and the life" (John 14:6). Sadly for many Christians who care about the calendar as defining the identity of a people, today, Anno Domini (the year of our Lord), has been replaced by the "Common Era" in history texts and in our institutions of learning. Easter bunnies have replaced the significance of the resurrected Christ. "Santa Claus" and the word "holidays" increasingly replace the word "Christmas." Today's average Canadian (or westerner in general) could be forgiven for totally missing the actual meaning of these festivals. Why is Christmas called Christmas? Because the meaning of the word itself, comes from the words *Christes masse* ("Christ's mass"), because a special Eucharist (mass or communion), was celebrated on that day. But even the word "holiday" has a Christian origin – it literally means "holy day."

During the earliest period of the Christian Church, different parts of the world celebrated Christmas on different dates throughout the year because the exact time of year of Jesus' birth was not known. By the beginning of the fifth century, initiated by Pope Julius I, East and West had coordinated their practice holding 25th December as the anniversary of Jesus' birth – that is why we give gifts and celebrate on the 25th. The later division between Eastern Orthodox and West arose only in the eighteenth century. The East retained the old calendar, the Western church adopted the Gregorian calendar with an adjustment of twelve days. But other dates in the Christian calendar also, like Advent (advent calendars!), Epiphany, Easter, Pentecost, Ascension and All Saints Day, were there to remind us of our Christian identity. Admittedly today, the faith of the Fathers is now a forgotten story; we are like children who cannot remember the name of their great grandfather.

Fact not fiction

Like it or not, our Western calendar and primary festivals are dated from the birth year of Jesus Christ, the man who cleaved history in two. Although there are a few who deny it, the fact that Jesus Christ was born over 2,000 years ago cannot be disputed with any scholarly credibility. However, the most important claims about Him remain the subject of considerable controversy. People disagree about the meaning of Jesus' *arrival* as a baby and therefore they are divided in their opinion of His *identity*.

The extract quoted above from Psalm 85 is understood by theologians to be a prophecy about the coming of Christ, the Messiah, which was written over 1,000 years before it happened. There are many good reasons to believe that Christ really was born into the world, lived a remarkable life being known for extraordinary deeds, died by Roman execution and that His early followers really believed they had seen Him raised to life – there is good reason why our calendar is dated from Christ.[2]

As we all know, since the first proclamation of Christ's resurrection in Jerusalem Christianity has progressively extended into every corner of the globe, constituting the largest religious faith in the history of the world. Christian leader and pastor, Dietrich Bonhoeffer, speaking in Nazi Germany during a time of great political turmoil and personal suffering, in his Christmas address of 1940 tries to put into words the historical significance of the person of Christ. Bonhoeffer not only believed the outline of historical detail affirmed in secular history, but also accepted the testimony about Christ in the New Testament. He writes of the Christmas event,

> "This is about the birth of a child, not of the astonishing work of a strong man, not of the bold discovery of a wise man, not of the pious work of a saint. It really is beyond all understanding: the birth of a child shall bring about great change, shall bring to all mankind salvation and deliverance. What kings and statesmen, philosophers and artists, religious leaders and moral teachers have labored for in vain is now brought about by a new born child. Here a child born into the midst of world history, has put to shame the wisdom and efforts of the strong. A child born of a human mother, a Son given by God, that is the secret of the salvation of the world. All the past and all the future is here encompassed."[3]

The core of the New Testament is the eyewitness testimony to the life and teaching of Jesus. There is supporting data about the unusual character and far-reaching significance of a real, historical, man called Jesus Christ in extra-biblical sources that affirm many critical aspects of the New Testament account. This is only to be expected since we can have legitimate confidence in what the New Testament tells us about Him. This is especially so in light of the Old Testament prophecies, written hundreds of years earlier, concerning Christ, since both testaments support and confirm each other. When you carefully examine His life, it becomes clear why Jesus is history's most celebrated Child.

The beauty of Christ – signals of transcendence

Have you ever noticed the extravagance of beauty in creation? On a recent morning when reading in my study, I heard the beautiful sound of a robin singing. Did you know that robins have as many as fifty-seven different songs in their repertoire? This would not result simply from a need for successful reproduction since many other successful species have only a few songs. This, to me, reflects the extravagance of the Creator.

In the beautiful "green and pleasant land" of England where I grew up, the iconic, red-breasted robin has become a symbol of the beautiful Christmas season – for he does not migrate for winter. In Canada where I now reside, Christmas is an equally beautiful celebration. Blankets of crisp snow cover the ground. White lights adorn houses and lampposts, trees are dressed with ornate decorations, and tinsel brightens the home. At Christmas, scented candles burn and "real logs" spit on the fire. We dress in our best clothes, and leave our behind Kraft Dinners and microwave meals. Instead, we fill our table with slow-cooked turkey, stuffing, roast potatoes and good wine. For me there is no more beautiful time of year. Why are these beautiful things important for many Christians during this season? It is because we have recognized and participate in the wonder of Jesus' *beautiful life*, which the Christmas season is meant to celebrate. Christ's birth punctuates the year with unparalleled significance. It is a rip in the rolling ages, a tear on eternity and a breaking into the world of a new and singular beauty.

Most of us, regardless of our opinion about Christ, will appreciate something of the festivities because they are aesthetically pleasing. Yet the purpose of these beautiful things is to point us to a beauty beyond these simple things to the One who is the *measure and standard of all beauty*. In the Bible, Jesus is presented not only as a Jewish man, an historical figure, but as the unchanging, transcendent Creator God who has come to us as one of us. The beauty of Jesus is the beauty of the eternal Word made flesh (John 1:14). When we look at Jesus, we are looking at God. Such is the beauty of God to those who know Him that the Psalmist wrote, "One thing I have asked of the LORD, that I shall seek ... to behold the beauty of the LORD ..." (Psalm 27:4 NASB). One cannot judge anything as beautiful without a referent to give us a standard and measure of beauty.

Christmas celebrates the coming of the most beautiful life. Read the Gospels and see His life, His character, His words and His work. Just as listening to the most beautiful symphony or looking at a breath-taking landscape captures our imagination and stirs our hearts, so recognizing Christ for who He is transports the soul. The winter landscape, candles and lights, decorations, gifts and best clothes, foods and fine wine remind us of the joyous reality of His presence, the scent of His fragrance, the sound of His words, the sight of His works, and the taste of His love. In other words, from these physical things of beauty that delight our senses we move upward towards Christ who is Beauty itself. Here we can dine at the table of true beauty and capture the wonder of our Creator.

Are our minds and hearts able to recognize the Christ child for who He is? I have sometimes wondered about whether the animals in the stable recognized that the infant child lying in the manger was their Maker. Sheep recognize their shepherd and our pets recognize us by our scent and voice. The prophet Isaiah wrote, "The ox knows its owner and the donkey its master's crib; but Israel does not know, my people do not consider" (Isaiah 1:3 NKJV). Perhaps the animals, that first Christmas, recognized their Maker, yet many of us today, like Israel of old, do not perceive the beauty of Christ; we do not recognize His identity.

Beauty always communicates something to us; we feel appreciation, insight, wonder, amazement, joy, hope, or peace whenever we encounter it. Why is it then that the eternal unchanging beauty became a human being? According to Scripture, it was to communicate something to us, to bring us a message of peace, hope, joy, gladness, contentment, forgiveness, and new life. Early Church apologist, St Augustine, wrote:

> "In order to speak to others, the thought in our minds changes into a sound, called speech which, through the ears of the listener, enters the latter's mind. In this transition our thought is not changed but remains entire in itself as it passes into speech in order to penetrate the listener's ears. The thought does not deteriorate in the process. In like manner, the Word of God was not changed as it assumed flesh in order that He might be with us."[4]

When Augustine finally became a Christian after a youth of religious skepticism and immorality, he wrote of his discovery of Jesus Christ, "late have I loved thee, O beauty ever ancient, ever new. Late have I loved thee."[5]

Truth has sprung from the earth

From ancient times, philosophers have discussed the True, the Good and the Beautiful. The Christ child born into the manger 2,000 years ago claimed to embody and personify all three. The Psalmist foretells, "... truth shall spring out of the earth" (Psalm 85:11 NKJV). What does this mean? To understand it, one must understand something of the imagery of the biblical story. In John 14:6 Jesus makes a startling claim about Himself: "I am the way, the truth, and the life. No one comes to the Father except through me." Unlike other prophets, sages, and philosophers, Jesus did not say that He had discovered some truth or could point us towards truth; He claimed that He *was* the truth. At His trial he says to the procurator Pontius Pilate, "Everyone who is of the truth hears My voice" (John 18:37 NKJV). Christ is described repeatedly as *the Word* of God:

> "In the beginning was the Word, and the Word was with God, and the Word was God, He was in the beginning with God. All things were made through Him and without Him nothing was made that was made. In Him was life, and the life was the light of men." (John 1:1–4 NKJV)

In John 17:17, we read, "Your word is truth." This is referring to Christ. Jesus Christ *is* the "truth that has sprung from the earth." The Truth that overflowed heaven's banks has burst forth from the earth to lie in the arms of a human mother. This phrase in Psalm 85 means that the Truth has become a human being and been born of a woman. He has taken both an earthly human body and soul. "Earth" is another word for "flesh." In Genesis 2:7, we are taught that God fashioned human beings from the "dust of the ground." The chemical constituents of the human body can all be found in the ground. When human beings sinned and turned from God, God's judgment was pronounced: "In the sweat of your face you shall eat bread till you return to the ground, for out of the dust you were taken; For dust you are, and to dust you shall return" (Genesis 3:19 NKJV).

Thus, the eternal truth sprang from the dust of the earth, becoming a human being for our redemption. Though He was before earth ever was, He emptied himself, "taking the nature of a servant" as Philippians chapter

2 describes Him. He was conceived and carried in the womb of a woman so that the "seed of the woman" might "bruise the serpent's head" (Genesis 3:15). Yes, "the Lord Himself will give you a sign," says the prophet Isaiah, "Behold, the virgin shall conceive and bear a Son, and shall call His name Immanuel" (Isaiah 7:14 NKJV). This name, *Immanuel*, means "God is with us." As the Virgin Mary lays that baby in a manger, we sing in the words of the carol: "Veiled in flesh the Godhead see, hail the incarnate deity!" Augustine tries to find the words for this wonderful mystery:

> "He the creator of humans, he the ruler of the Heavens, became human so he might become a baby at the breast, so that he the divine bread might be hungry, so that he the fountain of life might be thirsty, so that he the Eternal Light might fall asleep, so that the Way might be weary from a journey. God became a human being so that the Truth might be accused by false witness and the judge of the living and the dead be judged by a mortal judge. He became human so that strength might be shown as weak, that the author of life might die."[6]

Squandering the gift

The Bible declares that we were created in God's image, made from dust, and then brought to ruin by our sin. Because of sin, we have traded life for death, hope for despair, joy for gloom, truth for error, and fullness for emptiness. This is true of every individual, people group and nation, regardless of social status.

As R. L. Stephenson put it in one of his Christmas sermons,

> "The sands run out, and the hours are 'numbered and imputed' and the days go by; and when the last of these finds us, we have been *a long time dying and what else?* ... To look back upon the past year, and see how little we have striven and to what small purpose ... friendships fall through, health fails, weariness assails; year after year, we must thumb the hardly varying record of our own weakness and folly."[7]

Year on year we make rather lame efforts to keep New Year's resolutions hoping to correct our follies, but repeatedly find ourselves powerless to transform ourselves.

Justice looks down – a Christmas rescue!

How is recovery from our fallen and ruined state possible? Well, the Psalmist quickly adds that, "Righteousness [justice] shall look down from heaven" (Psalm 85:11 NKJV). Psalm 85:10 reads, "Mercy and truth have met together, righteousness [justice] and peace have kissed." Christ, the only truly just man, has had mercy on us, the unjust. He was born into the world to justify us before God. *Truth sprang from earth so that we could be justified by divine mercy and grace.* Truth and mercy, justice and peace, have kissed in the person of Christ – they have come together and been revealed for all time.

For the Christian, Christ is the brightness of God's glory and the "express image of His person" (Hebrews 1:3 NKJV). In His humanity, He revealed the likeness of God that you and I were made to reflect. Like coins that start to lose the royal image when rubbed with sandy earth long enough, human beings are constantly worn down by pride, sin and shame so that their royal image is obscured. But Christ came to stamp us again with His likeness, so that, as the Psalmist puts it, "righteousness will go before Him and shall make His footsteps *our pathway*" (Psalm 85:13 NKJV, emphasis added). For, although Christ "sprang from the earth" through an earthly mother, *He was also the heavenly man without a human father.* As our sinless Creator, He could become our redeemer. But in order to rescue us, He would have to come to die.

I recently read a story that occurred Christmas 2001. A brave young man called Ian Duffey woke up early Christmas morning to find a fire raging through his grandmother's house in Toronto. He woke his eighteen-year-old sister and told her to climb out of the window and get help. Running to his grandmother's bedroom, he woke her and helped her out of the second-storey window. His younger sister of fourteen was still in the house and Ian went back inside to get her. Choking amidst the dense smoke on a bitter Christmas morning, he struggled to her bedroom in a heroic attempt to rescue her. Tragically, he was overcome by the poisonous fumes and both he and his sister perished in the fire. His courage and self-sacrifice won him a posthumous Medal of Bravery.[8]

Our condition is no less serious. Every one of us needs to be rescued by the sacrifice that Christ offered for us. We were dying in the fumes of our own selfishness and were oblivious to our condition when Jesus came to rescue us from the poison of sin and allowed Himself to be overcome by it instead. Jesus, who is fully God and fully human is the only one who could rescue us. Unless He had become a mortal human, He could not have died, since He was also the immortal God. And He could not have rescued us if He were only a human, because only God could give us His immortality. Thus Paul writes:

> "The first man was of the earth, made of dust; the second Man is the Lord from heaven. As was the man of dust, so also are those who are made of dust; and as is the heavenly Man, so also are those who are heavenly. And as we have borne the image of the man of dust, we shall also bear the image of the heavenly Man." (1 Corinthians 15:46–49 NKJV)

This is what Christmas is all about. This is what the Psalmist is foretelling in Psalm 85. It is because truth has sprung from the earth, because Christ is born, that justice has looked down from heaven. And because in Christ righteousness and peace have kissed, we can be rescued from our hopelessness and bondage to sin and death. Jesus Christ "took flesh." He was born into this world to die for our sin. That was His purpose. His gift to us is Himself, and to receive Him is to receive life itself. As the apostle John said, "he who has the Son has life" (1 John 5:12 NKJV).

The gift of peace

At Christmas time, we hear a great deal about peace and we know that the angels sang "peace on earth" and "goodwill to men," or as the best version of the Greek text has it, "to men of goodwill,"[9] to the shepherds in the fields on that amazing night. This often seems like an unrealistic hope since many are trampled on by people who do not care. There is so much unrest in the world, how can peace be realized?

Yet Jesus is called the "Prince of Peace" by the prophet Isaiah. St Paul tells us we "have peace with God through our Lord Jesus Christ."

"Blessed are the peacemakers" (Matthew 5:9), Jesus tells us, because people like that are children of God. The untold possibility for the reign of righteousness and peace in this world is found in this, that as Christ brings us to peace with God He enables us to make peace with others, giving us the grace and strength to do so!

The incredible potential of that peace flowing from the crib of Christ is well illustrated for us by the true account of the most famous of all military truces. On 24th December 1994, a fully researched article from the associated press, dateline London appeared in numerous newspapers.[10] Over ninety years ago on the first Christmas Day of World War I, British and German troops put down their guns and celebrated peacefully together in "No Man's Land" between the trenches. For a short time, the Great War came to a standstill. Both sides prompted the brief armistice when, in one incident, British troops lit fires and let off rockets and in another German soldiers lit candles on Christmas trees on top of the parapets so that British centuries could see them in the distance. Private Oswald Tilley of the London Rifle Brigade wrote to his parents:

> "Just while you were eating your turkey ... I was out talking and shaking hands with the very men I had been trying to kill a few hours before!! It was astounding."

Although that terrible war claimed around ten million lives, for a brief moment, the power of the Prince of Peace was manifest by the *shared memory of the manger* halting the great war of the world. That Christmas Day, as they sang carols, exchanged gifts, visited opposing trenches, played soccer between the shell holes and traded names and addresses, soldiers on both sides, having met other men much like them, were forced to ask why they were trying to kill each other. Diaries of the high command at the time reflected anxiety that the Christmas festivity would sap the soldiers' will to fight.[11] Where Christ is present, peace can begin to rule in hearts and minds; that is the power of the cradle.

Wrapping up the story

The vast majority of people say they want peace in their own lives, in their families, their nation, and the world. However, few people speak of wanting righteousness or justice. But the Bible tells us that this is the secret of peace: "Righteousness and peace have kissed." In other words, love righteousness and you will have peace. For these two are friends who have kissed. If you do not love righteousness and justice, then peace will not come to you. A paraphrase of this psalm might read, "Coming along the road from different directions, justice and peace saw each other at a distance and ran to each other with open arms."

The angels sang the day the Prince of Peace was born as a human being, because they heralded a radical peace that is beyond our understanding, a peace this disordered world cannot give us. He is our peace, and He offers this peace freely to all who will believe. If we will turn in love to Christ, we can have peace. Peace within, peace with God, and His indwelling power to make peace with others. Peace on earth to people of goodwill.

The message of Christmas is profoundly challenging. Sometimes we do not understand truth, while at other times we understand it all too well, but do not want to face it. The truth that the virgin birth communicates to us at Christmas is sometimes too much for our eyes and too difficult for our hearts to bear. There is only one thing we can do in such a condition; we need to respond as the shepherds did and kneel at His cradle to weep and worship, so that our eyes may *see salvation*. Before such a God, in the light of such humility, who comes to become one of us – in what other way could we respond? There is no other appropriate reaction to the message of the manger. Dietrich Bonhoeffer offers us this challenge:

> "How shall we deal with such a child? Have our hands, soiled with daily toil, become too hard and too proud to fold in prayer at the sight of this child? Has our head become too full of serious thoughts to be thought through and problems to be solved, that we cannot bow our head in humility before the wonder of this child? Can we not forget all our stress and struggles, our sense of importance, and for once worship the child, as did the shepherds and the wise men from the East, bowing before the divine child in the manger like children? Can we not be like the aged Simeon, who took the child in his arms and saw the fulfillment of all his waiting, and in this moment recognize the fulfillment of our whole life"?[12]

This Christmas, let us come to God like children, rubbing the sleep from our eyes, asking God to reveal the mystery and majesty of *the beautiful life* to us. Let us place all our hope in Christ, the Son of the morning, shining down upon the mountains.

Discussion questions

1. In what way do you think the loss of Christian symbols from public life has affected our culture?
2. In what ways would Christmas look different today if it reflected the values of Christ rather than secularism?
3. From the Gospels, what ways would you describe Jesus' life as especially beautiful compared to any other life?
4. What do you think is the best way to communicate the beauty and uniqueness of Jesus to someone who in not well-versed in the Bible?
5. How can we use both of these styles of communication to complement each other in our apologetics?
6. Does being sensitive to different worldviews and experiences of questioners affect how we approach this topic? In what ways?

Notes

1. St Augustine, *Sermons: Works of St Augustine*, translated by Edmund Hill, O. P. (New City Press, New York, 1993), p. 42.
2. See chapter 10 – "The Uniqueness of Christ."
3. Dietrich Bonhoeffer, *Dietrich Bonhoeffer's Christmas Sermons*, edited and translated by Edwin Robertson (Zondervan, Grand Rapids, 2005), pp. 150–151.
4. Augustine in *Christian Doctrine* 1, 13.
5. *Confessions*, 10:27.
6. St Augustine, Sermon 191:1, *Christmas Day*, AD411 or 412.
7. *A Christmas Sermon and other Essays*, pp. 9, 19–20 (emphasis added).
8. Cheryl MacDonald, *Christmas in Ontario* (Altitude Publishing, Alberta, 2004), pp. 108–109.
9. The modern eclectic, or "critical" text of the Greek New Testament, published in the twenty-sixth edition of the Nestle / Aland *Greek New Testament* and in the third edition of the United Bible Societies' *Greek New Testament*. In The Holy Bible, The New King James Version (Thomas Nelson Publishers, Nashville, Camden, New York, 1983).
10. "Enemies Kept Christmas Truce in Trenches 80 Years Ago," in the *Elizabethton Star*, 25th December 1994, p. 3A.
11. Malcolm Brown, and Shirley Seaton, *Christmas Truce*, 1984.
12. Bonhoeffer, *Christmas Sermons*, pp. 151–152.

CHAPTER 13

War and Peace

[*First delivered at a Remembrance Day guest service near Toronto.*]

> "Therefore, since we have been made right in God's sight by faith, we have peace with God because of what Jesus Christ our Lord has done for us. Because of our faith, Christ has brought us into this place of highest privilege where we now stand, and we confidently and joyfully look forward to sharing God's glory. We can rejoice, too, when we run onto problems and trials, for we know that they are good for us – they help us learn to endure. And endurance develops strength of character in us, and character strengthens our confident expectation of salvation. And this expectation will not disappoint us. For we know how dearly God loves us, because he has given us the Holy Spirit to fill our hearts with his love." (Romans 5:1–5)

> "Jesus on the cross asked His Heavenly Father to forgive those who crucified Him because they did not know what they were doing. Therefore, we should forgive our enemies in order to imitate Christ's forgiveness of His persecutors." (St Augustine)[1]

Lest we forget

In our time, we seldom devote ourselves to the reflective task of *remembering*. In fact, many Western nations have lost their cultural memory. I regard this as a great tragedy because who we *are*, is inextricably tied to who we *were*. Thus, on this Remembrance Day, which is set aside for the special purpose of recollecting past sacrifice, it is good for us to stop and think about our forebears who laid down their lives to give us the freedoms and privileges that we so often take for granted. Remembering the heroic sacrifices of the past is a much needed remedy for the increasing shallowness, indifference, ignorance, and ingratitude on display in our culture. It is meaningful for me to remember my grandfather who served during World War II in the French Foreign Legion and later in the Dutch Navy. Having been dropped into battle during the Narvik campaign in some of the early action of the conflict and badly injured by shell fire, he was later reassigned to duty on a mine sweeper in the Navy. After the War, he suffered severely from post-traumatic stress. Not only he, but thousands of others like him, put their lives on the line for God and country. They sacrificed themselves so that we might enjoy peace and prosperity. The nineteenth-century poet, Christina Rossetti, writes of the "blessed dead":

> "They lie at rest, our blessed dead;
> The dew drop cool above their head,
> They knew not when sweet summer fled.
>
> Together all, yet each alone;
> Each laid at rest beneath his own
> Smooth turf or white allotted stone.
>
> When shall our slumber sink so deep,
> And eyes that wept and eyes that weep
> Weep not in the sufficient sleep?
>
> God be with you our great and small,
> Our loves, our best beloved of all,
> Our own beyond the salt sea-wall."[2]

When remembering wars and our fallen brothers and sisters, we are not only to remember the fact that people died, but we should also reflect on the great tragedy of war and its causes. As horrible and destructive as war is, wars are often fought for freedom from other terrible realities, such as aggressive and unprovoked attacks, tyranny, oppression, ideological hate, fascism, and genocide. On 18th June, 1940, Winston Churchill made a characteristically stirring speech on Waterloo Day as the French government moved toward an armistice that would leave Britain politically isolated:

> "What General Weygand called the Battle for France is over. I expect that the Battle of Britain is about to begin . . . Upon this battle depends the survival of Christian civilization. Upon it, depends our own British life and the long continuity of our institutions and our Empire. The whole fury and might of the enemy must very soon be turned on us. Hitler knows that he will have to break us in this island or lose the war. If we can stand up to him, all Europe may be free, and the life of the world may move forward into broad sunlit uplands; but if we fail, then the whole world, including the United States, and all that we have known and cared for, will sink into the abyss of a new dark age made more sinister, and perhaps more protracted, by the light of a perverted science . . . Let us therefore brace ourselves to our duty, and so bear ourselves that, if the British Commonwealth and its Empire last for a thousand years, men will still say, 'This was their finest hour.' "[3]

The Second World War was a battle for what Churchill called the "survival of Christian civilization." Considering the horror of what Europe and the world would have endured under Hitler's Third Reich, there is certainly much truth to Churchill's statement. Although we should respect the freedom of pacifists to follow their own conscience, what Augustine termed "just wars" are sometimes necessary to protect among much else, even the treasured freedom to be a conscientious objector. Although not always easy to understand, under His mysterious providence, war has been sanctioned by God at times and many of His servants in Scripture were great warriors: Samson, Gideon, Joshua and David. God has permitted war in His sovereignty. Wars do not spring up unprovoked; people make war! In a fallen world, so that sin and wickedness is not allowed to run unchecked through history, sometimes wars have been a *necessary* evil. This is not true of all conflicts; sometimes war could have been avoided, but war mongering or imperial ambitions have tragically prevailed.

The notion of the "just war" is not an apologetic for war, but rather an attempt to limit armed conflict. Romans 13 explains that the state is ordained by God in order to protect its citizens. A "just war" is not a manifesto for imperialism. But at certain times, the most unloving, unjust, and immoral thing to do in the face of the suffering of others would be a failure to declare war. Tragically, people have been plotting against each other since the time when Cain slew his brother Abel in cold blood. Thus, on days like Remembrance Day, there is cause to remember the horrors of war and to consider the reasons for war in order that we might act to further peace and justice rather than oppression and injustice.

According to the Christian world-view, all wars are ultimately the result of sin. War in human society is a concrete, historical manifestation of the long war waged against God in the human heart. People make war against God and His Law, so they proceed to make war against one another. They do not love God and neither do they love their neighbor as themselves. They act without the right order of love. Instead, they act out of lust for power, dominion motivated by greed, hate, and selfishness. God in His sovereignty resists such arrogance and has raised up people and nations in history to fight such aggressors and stem the advance of wickedness. Not only Britain but Canada and many other nations also played a highly significant role in both world wars of the twentieth century. We should pause to remember previous generations of Britons, Canadians and others who gave their lives for freedom from tyranny, and who recognized the supremacy of God, the foundation of that freedom. This is especially important since in our careless forgetfulness we are now attacking many of the values our forebears fought for in those great conflagrations of the last century – the very survival of Christian civilization.

Different kinds of war

The Bible speaks of various kinds of war. These wars will continue until the Prince of Peace comes to reign in righteousness and justice. First, there is a war between God and Satan, darkness and light, the Kingdom of God and the kingdom of this world. This spiritual war began in Genesis chapter 3 and continues to the end of time, when our adversary the devil will finally be destroyed.

Secondly, because of sin and the Fall, recorded in the early chapters of Genesis, there is also war between the sinful hearts of people and their creator God. God has offered armistice and peace in His Son, but we still propagate a long war against God. The only way to escape this is to throw down our arms and abandon this illegitimate insurrection against our Creator and Redeemer (Romans 8:6–8).

Thirdly, manifesting this spiritual war against God, physical wars between fellow members of the human race have broken out, like those wars we remember on this special day of remembrance. As we have seen, in Scripture, resisting evil by means of war is seen, at times, as a necessary evil in a fallen world – an extension of the jurisdiction of the state's duty under God to punish evildoers and bear the sword (Romans 13:4).

Fourthly, in Romans chapter 7, Paul highlights an internal, subtle and personal war, a conflict experienced by the Christian as the old sinful nature wars with the new nature being renewed by the Spirit. Paul writes, "But I see a different law in the parts of my body, waging war against the law of my mind and taking me prisoner to the law of sin in the parts of my body" (Romans 7:23 HCSB).

Lastly, the Church is also in conflict with the spiritual powers of darkness – the kingdom of Satan – hence the Bible's metaphor that Christians are soldiers and need the whole armor of God (Ephesians 6:10–17). The strongholds and fortresses we face are not pill boxes and battlements, armored vehicles or anti-aircraft batteries, but speculations, false knowledge and lying ideologies that set themselves up against the knowledge of God (2 Corinthians 10:3–5).

All these different types of war will continue until the Prince of Peace comes again. Until then we are to be *peacemakers*, not merely *peacekeepers*. This can only be accomplished through the preaching of the gospel of peace manifest in Christ (Romans 10).

The battle for the mind

Paul tells us in Romans 12:2, "Do not be conformed to this age, but be transformed by the renewing of your mind, that you may discern what is the good, pleasing and perfect will of God" (HCSB). The greatest battle of all in our day, as indicated in 2 Corinthians 10, is the battle for the mind and heart. Paul uses a military image when he instructs us to take thoughts captive and make them in obedience to Christ. We are pulling down arguments and all high ideas or speculations that oppose the lordship of Jesus Christ.

Jesus tells us "blessed are the peacemakers," not "blessed are the peacekeepers" (Matthew 5:9). There is a difference. God condemned the false prophets in Jeremiah for saying "peace, peace" when there was no peace (Jeremiah 6:14; 8:11). To compromise the truth or to negotiate with falsehood may temporarily keep an artificial and superficial truce but will not make for peace. By way of illustration, if Britain had surrendered to some of Hitler's demands regarding the Balkans and Western Europe, it may have briefly kept the peace for the British Isles, but it would not have made peace; it would have led to tyranny and, eventually, to war anyway. British Prime Minister Neville Chamberlain's great error prior to the Second World War was famously engraved on the memories of the English on his return from a meeting with the Führer in Munich:

> "My good friends, this is the second time in our history that there has come back from Germany to Downing Street peace with honor. I believe it is peace for our time. We thank you from the bottom of our hearts. And now I recommend you to go home and sleep quietly in your beds."
>
> (1st October 1938)[4]

In the light of what followed, that statement is enough to send a cold shiver down the spine for, while Chamberlain was delivering his eerily deluded message in Britain "go home and sleep peacefully," Hitler was remarking to his aides:

> "If ever that silly old man comes interfering here again with his umbrella, I'll kick him downstairs and jump on his stomach in front of the photographers."[5]

With goodwill, Chamberlain believed the lies of a dictator in the face of mountains of evidence to the contrary, so desperate was he to preserve an empty peace. In part, this was because Europe was still reeling from the terrible effects of World War I. A very different spirit was needed in Britain during Europe's *hour of danger*. This came in the form of the great statesman, Winston Churchill, a man who rose from relative political obscurity (at that time), in the twilight of his career and the evening of his days, to become first Lord of the Admiralty and then Prime Minister. A man who led the British Commonwealth to victory in a battle against a vile dictator with a disregard for life, a genocidal hated of the Jews and without any respect for the law of Christ. Possibly Churchill's most famous speech showed the power of oratory used for a righteous end:

> "We shall not flag or fail. We shall go on to the end. We shall fight in France, we shall fight on the seas and oceans, we shall fight with growing confidence and growing strength in the air, we shall defend our Island, whatever the cost may be. We shall fight on the beaches, we shall fight on the landing grounds, we shall fight in the fields and in the streets, we shall fight in the hills; we shall never surrender." (4th June 1940)[6]

Canada's historic function has been peacemaking, but today there is a strong emphasis on peacekeeping, using the model of the global citizen. But this image is an illusion. This mentality has affected every aspect of domestic concern. We try to enforce by law toleration of all faiths except Christianity in an increasingly anti-biblical, politically correct, egalitarian society in which the only sin left is condemning anything as wrong. We end up persecuting the righteous and robbing our freedom of speech in the process. For example, it is becoming unacceptable to be "for Christ" or "for Christmas or Easter," for life at conception, for sexual abstinence until marriage between one man and one woman. In Canada, our provincial and federal governments are desperate to "keep the peace" by silencing dissenting opinions through the courts, but are not concerned with getting to the root of the problem, those things which disrupt peace – the reality of sin, our relationships with God and each other. But God essentially declared war on Satan in Scripture, in order to make peace between God and humanity. We must declare war on sin, evil, injustice and selfishness, even in ourselves, if we are to know life in all its fullness.

Why is the battle for the mind so critical and how does this relate to reflecting on the causes of war? In our current culture, we are living in a time of war over people's minds, especially the minds of the young. That battle is only an expression of the battle between God and Satan that occurs as God's truth in home, school, and church life is challenged by the empty speculations and ideas that Satan and his unwitting spokespersons peddle to the minds of people. Ideas have consequences, and the false knowledge and ideologies inspired by Satan have an impact in our world and in people's lives. Satan craves war, destruction, chaos, immorality, death, and the triumph of evil. In our time, there is a risk that we too may say "peace, peace" failing to recognize that there is a conflict, a war for the minds of the young, even in our own families. Physical wars do not begin with the rhetoric of politicians but in the home and classroom, which is why a transformation of our thinking is so important.

In a 1943 article entitled *Who are the War Criminals?*, George Orwell writes of the previous decade:

> "When one thinks of the lies and betrayal of those years, the cynical abandonment of one ally after another, the imbecile optimism of the Tory press, the flat refusal to believe that the dictators meant war, even when they shouted it from the housetops, the inability of the moneyed class to see anything wrong whatever in concentration camps, ghettos, massacres and undeclared wars, one is driven to feel that moral decadence played its part as well as mere stupidity."[7]

These strong statements about the pre-war thirties tell a great deal about the blindness of many cultural influencers of the time to the looming realities of impending war – despite the open articulation of ideologies of hatred – in part due to complacency and moral decadence. In Germany and Britain, segments of the Church were complicit in some of this blindness and decadence. The Nazi dictator was not hiding his intentions. In a pre-war address to his generals in August 1939, Adolf Hitler said,

> "Genghis Khan had millions of women and men killed by his own will and with a gay heart. History sees him only as a great state builder . . . I have sent my death's head units to the East with the order to kill without mercy men, women and children of the Polish race or language. Only in such a way will we win the Lebensraum that we need. Who after all speaks today of the annihilation of the Armenians?"[8]

Regarding the treatment of the handicapped, he stated in a new authorization regarding euthanasia,

> "Reichsleiter Bouhler and Dr. Brandt are entrusted with the responsibility of extending the rights of specially designated physicians, such that patients who are judged incurable after the most thorough review of their condition which is possible, can be granted mercy killing."[9]

These doctors had their powers greatly expanded until they were little more than murderers in white coats. Where do such ideas come from and how do they gain ascendancy in a supposedly civilized culture? It is done through the marginalization and elimination of biblical Christianity among the young in school. Part of Hitler's success in Germany was the Nazi Youth organization and his propaganda machine in schools indoctrinating children. Silencing the Church by state control was also critical; one need only study the life of Deitrich Bonhoeffer to understand this. Hitler understood well that to govern and influence the minds of the young is to govern the course of the future!

Nurseries of humanism and the battle for children

The increasingly flagrant anti-Christian indoctrination of children by those that frame the curriculum in Canada, the United Kingdom and the United States is driven by humanistic philosophies that are hostile to Christ and His lordship. Many Christian symbols have been excluded from public schools and the public sphere altogether, while pagan symbols are permitted. Carols and nativity scenes are avoided because of the possible offense they might cause, while Halloween, a pagan, druidic festival is welcomed. The Ten Commandments are seen as offensive and not for public display, whereas same-sex marriages, families, and gay adoption are taught as completely normal. Christian opposition to these practices is largely viewed as offensive or sometimes even as "hate crime."

Is it possible that we have lost our soul, our identity and our will to fight for truth and justice because we no longer know what it is? Is what our nations are becoming the countries our forebears envisaged for the future when they boldly went to war against ruthless foes in the two great wars? To seize control and govern Germany, Hitler needed to control the minds of the young and this is what he did, through propaganda in the schools and the Nazi youth organization. It is crucial now for people to pay careful attention to who is teaching and captivating our children's minds and hearts – for what they become will shape the course of the future. What they are taught and what we teach our own children is a blueprint for the future.

Guiding the ship to shore

The essence of the gospel is that the long war with God can be over. The war against our fellow human beings can be over. The war and restlessness in our own conscience can be over. By faith, we can have peace with God through Jesus Christ. Christ waged war on Satan, died and rose again in victory! It is the victor, Christ, who tells us to take the bread and wine together "in remembrance of me." In the mystery of communion, we proclaim His glorious death until He comes to conquer and put all His enemies under His feet.

Christians are called to battle as soldiers of Christ, not against flesh and blood, but against our spiritual foe and the ideologies he has created. Remembering fallen soldiers whose graves are marked with the cross, the symbol of our faith, reminds us also of Christ's death for our freedom so that we might have true and lasting peace with our God. Scripture tells us in Colossians that He was making peace by His blood:

> "For God in all his fullness was pleased to live in Christ, and by him God reconciled everything to himself. He made peace with everything in heaven and on earth by means of his blood on the cross. This includes you who were once so far away from God. You were his enemies, separated from him by your evil thoughts and actions, yet now he has brought you back as his friends."
> (Colossians 1:19–22)

One day we will all hear the last post calling us back from our duty to the final barracks of His dwelling where death will be no more (Revelation

21:4). On that day, when the trumpet sounds, the land and sea will give up their dead to resurrection life and the judgment. There the Prince of Peace will bring His just verdict and wars will be made to cease as swords are beaten into plowshares. In the perils of this life, its wars and tumults, storms and raging seas, only He whom even the wind and the waves obeyed can deliver us from the devastations wrecked by the long war against God. As a lighthouse amidst a rock-strewn shoreline, He alone can guide us to our final harbor safely. In the perilous voyage of life, He alone can grant us clear horizons. So in the memorable words of President Franklin D. Roosevelt's favorite hymn, so often sung aboard naval vessels, we pray,

> Eternal Father, strong to save
> Whose arm hath bound the restless wave
> Who bid'st the mighty ocean deep
> Its own appointed limits keep,
> O hear us when we cry to thee
> For those in peril on the sea.
>
> O Christ, whose voice the waters heard
> And hushed their raging at thy word
> Who walkest on the foaming deep,
> And calm amidst the storm didst sleep;
> O hear us when we cry to Thee
> For those in peril on the sea. (William Whiting, 1825–1878)

Discussion questions

1. Do you have a family member or a friend who has fought in or lived in a war context? If so, how does this affect your view of war and peace?
2. How do recent or current violent conflicts affect your view of war and peace?
3. If you believe in the concept of a "just war," what would a war need to look like in order to be just?
4. What do you think it means to be a peacemaker?
   (a) How do you think we can best promote peace in our own lives?
   (b) How do you think we can best promote peace in a global context?

5. Do you think our culture at large views most Christians as peacemakers? Why or why not?
6. Comment on how you think each of the following has affected public opinion about war:
   (a) News media coverage
   (b) War movies/novels
   (c) Personal experience
   (d) The Bible
   (e) Other religious texts
   (f) Current events
   (g) Anti-war activism/writings
7. How does this chapter change how you would approach the issue of war in an apologetic context?

Notes

1. Augustine, *On Psalm 70*, p. 3.
2. Christina Rossetti, quoted in *The Lion Christian Poetry Collection*, compiled by Mary Batchelor (Lion Publishing, Oxford, 1995), p. 479.
3. Winston Churchill, speech extract from 18th June 1940, cited in *History in Quotations*, compiled and arranged by M. J. Cohen and John Major (Cassell, 2004), p. 846.
4. *History in Quotations*, p. 825.
5. *History in Quotations*, p. 825.
6. *History in Quotations*, p. 845.
7. *History in Quotations*, p. 829.
8. *History in Quotations*, p. 828.
9. *History in Quotations*, p. 831.